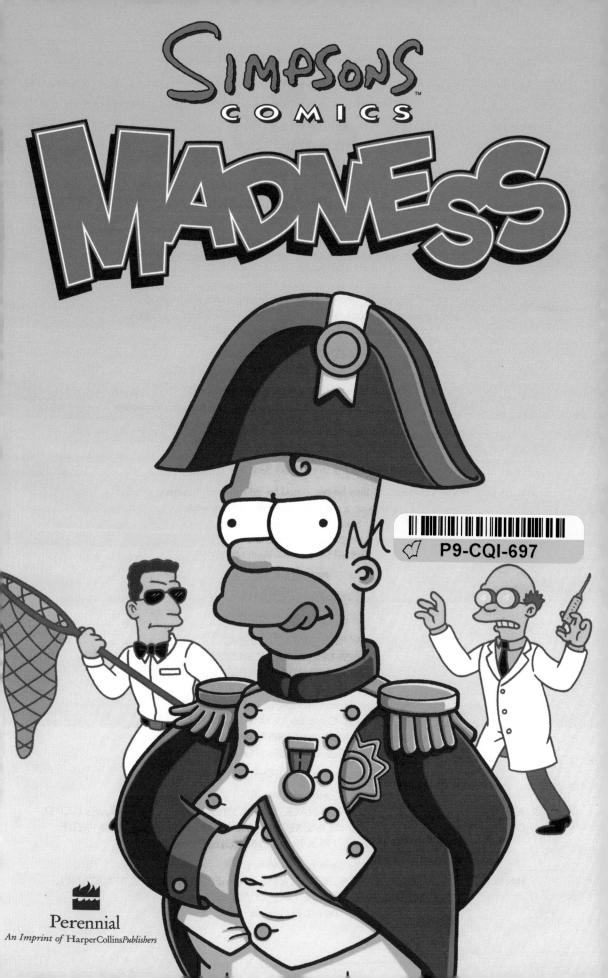

SIMPSONS
COMICS
MADNESS

P9-CQI-697

Perennial
An Imprint of HarperCollins*Publishers*

Dedicated to Snowball I:

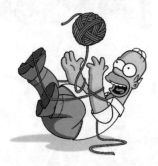

You may be gone, but the extra yarn from
Mom's sewing basket never goes to waste.

SIMPSONS COMICS MADNESS

Copyright © 2000, 2001 & 2002 by
Bongo Entertainment, Inc. All rights reserved.

FIRST EDITION

ISBN 0-06-053061-8

05 06 QWM 10 9 8 7

Publisher: MATT GROENING
Creative Director: BILL MORRISON
Managing Editor: TERRY DELEGEANE
Director of Operations: ROBERT ZAUGH
Art Director Special Projects: SERBAN CRISTESCU
Art Director Comic Books: NATHAN KANE
Production Manager: CHRISTOPHER UNGAR
Legal Guardian: SUSAN GRODE

Trade Paperback Concepts and Design: SERBAN CRISTESCU

Contributing Artists:
KAREN BATES, TIM BAVINGTON, JEANNINE BLACK, TIM HARKINS, NATHAN KANE, JAMES LLOYD,
OSCAR GONZÁLEZ LOYO, DAN NAKROSIS, KEVIN M. NEWMAN, PHIL ORTIZ, JULIUS PREITE,
STEVE STEERE, JR., ERICK TRAN, CHRISTOPHER UNGAR

Contributing Writers:
IAN BOOTHBY, TERRY DELEGEANE, ROBERT L. GRAFF, MICHAEL LISBE, JESSE LEON McCANN,
NATHAN REGER, ERIC ROGERS, SCOTT SHAW!

PRINTED IN CANADA

TABLE OF CONTENTS

BONGO COMICS GROUP
SIMPSONS COMICS
#43
US $2.50
CAN $3.50
APPROVED BY THE COMICS CODE AUTHORITY
©1999 BONGO ENTERTAINMENT, INC. THE SIMPSONS ©&TM TWENTIETH CENTURY FOX FILM CORPORATION. ALL RIGHTS RESERVED.
SQUISH-ZILLA
64 OZ
GROENING

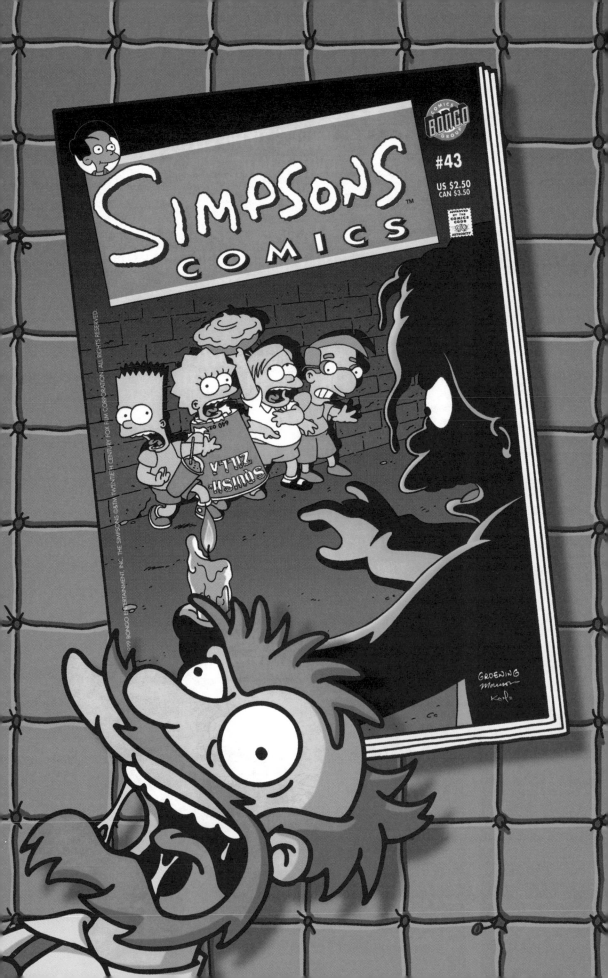

BOY, I CAN'T WAIT TO HEAR HOW *THIS* HAPPENED!
I'M SURE MY SON IS THE CAUSE OF IT ALL!

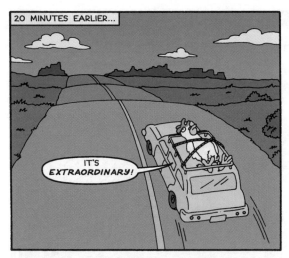

20 MINUTES EARLIER...

IT'S *EXTRAORDINARY!*

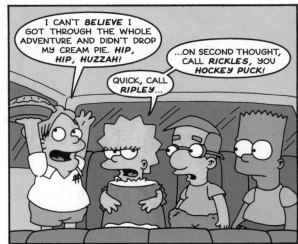

I CAN'T *BELIEVE* I GOT THROUGH THE WHOLE ADVENTURE AND DIDN'T DROP MY CREAM PIE. *HIP, HIP, HUZZAH!*

...ON SECOND THOUGHT, CALL *RICKLES,* YOU *HOCKEY PUCK!*

QUICK, CALL *RIPLEY...*

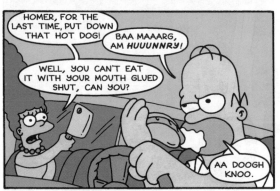

HOMER, FOR THE LAST TIME, PUT DOWN THAT HOT DOG!

BAA MAAARG, AM *HUUUNNRY!*

WELL, YOU CAN'T EAT IT WITH YOUR MOUTH GLUED SHUT, CAN YOU?

AA DOOGH KNOO.

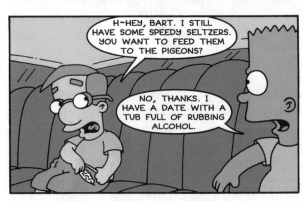

H-HEY, BART. I STILL HAVE SOME SPEEDY SELTZERS. YOU WANT TO FEED THEM TO THE PIGEONS?

NO, THANKS. I HAVE A DATE WITH A TUB FULL OF RUBBING ALCOHOL.

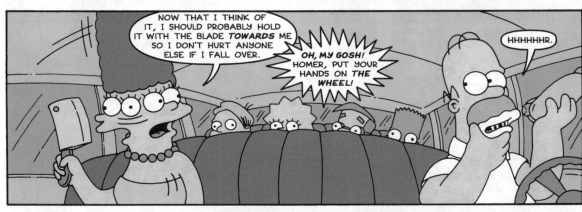

NOW THAT I THINK OF IT, I SHOULD PROBABLY HOLD IT WITH THE BLADE *TOWARDS* ME SO I DON'T HURT ANYONE ELSE IF I FALL OVER.

OH, MY GOSH! HOMER, PUT YOUR HANDS ON *THE WHEEL!*

HHHHHHR.

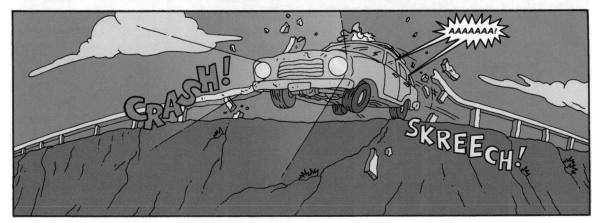

AAAAAAA!

CRASH!

SKREECH!

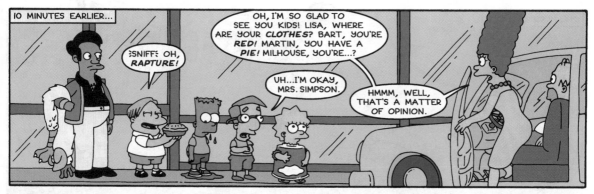

10 MINUTES EARLIER...

OH, I'M SO GLAD TO SEE YOU KIDS! LISA, WHERE ARE YOUR *CLOTHES*? BART, YOU'RE *RED*! MARTIN, YOU HAVE A *PIE*! MILHOUSE, YOU'RE...?

:SNIFF: OH, *RAPTURE*!

UH...I'M OKAY, MRS. SIMPSON.

HMMM, WELL, THAT'S A MATTER OF OPINION.

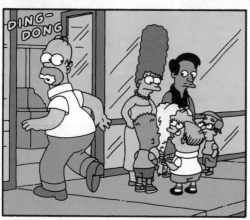

DING-DONG

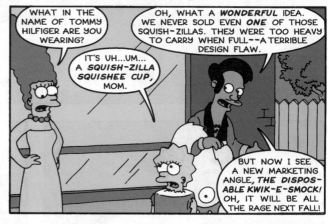

WHAT IN THE NAME OF TOMMY HILFIGER ARE YOU WEARING?

IT'S UH...UM... A *SQUISH-ZILLA SQUISHEE CUP*, MOM.

OH, WHAT A *WONDERFUL* IDEA. WE NEVER SOLD EVEN *ONE* OF THOSE SQUISH-ZILLAS. THEY WERE TOO HEAVY TO CARRY WHEN FULL--A TERRIBLE DESIGN FLAW.

BUT NOW I SEE A NEW MARKETING ANGLE, *THE DISPOSABLE KWIK-E-SMOCK!* OH, IT WILL BE ALL THE RAGE NEXT FALL!

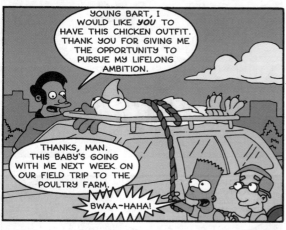

YOUNG BART, I WOULD LIKE *YOU* TO HAVE THIS CHICKEN OUTFIT. THANK YOU FOR GIVING ME THE OPPORTUNITY TO PURSUE MY LIFELONG AMBITION.

THANKS, MAN. THIS BABY'S GOING WITH ME NEXT WEEK ON OUR FIELD TRIP TO THE POULTRY FARM.

BWAA-HAHA!

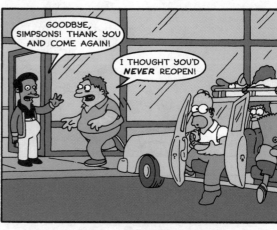

GOODBYE, SIMPSONS! THANK YOU AND COME AGAIN!

I THOUGHT YOU'D *NEVER* REOPEN!

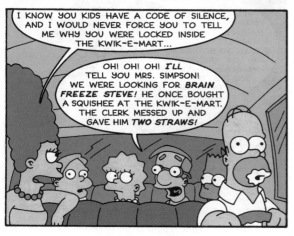

I KNOW YOU KIDS HAVE A CODE OF SILENCE, AND I WOULD NEVER FORCE YOU TO TELL ME WHY YOU WERE LOCKED INSIDE THE KWIK-E-MART...

OH! OH! OH! *I'LL* TELL YOU MRS. SIMPSON! WE WERE LOOKING FOR *BRAIN FREEZE STEVE!* HE ONCE BOUGHT A SQUISHEE AT THE KWIK-E-MART. THE CLERK MESSED UP AND GAVE HIM *TWO STRAWS!*

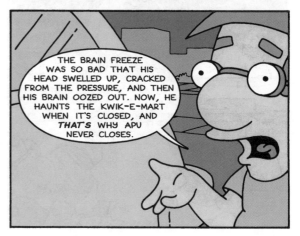

THE BRAIN FREEZE WAS SO BAD THAT HIS HEAD SWELLED UP, CRACKED FROM THE PRESSURE, AND THEN HIS BRAIN OOZED OUT. NOW, HE HAUNTS THE KWIK-E-MART WHEN IT'S CLOSED, AND *THAT'S* WHY APU NEVER CLOSES.

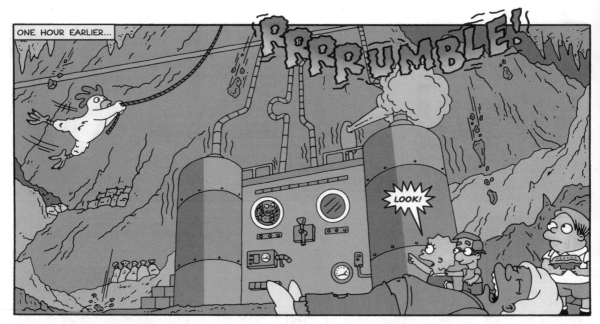

ONE HOUR EARLIER...

RRRRUMBLE!

LOOK!

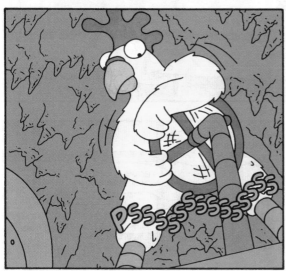

PSSSSSSSSSSSS

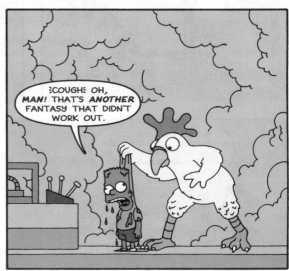

≋COUGH≋ OH, *MAN!* THAT'S *ANOTHER* FANTASY THAT DIDN'T WORK OUT.

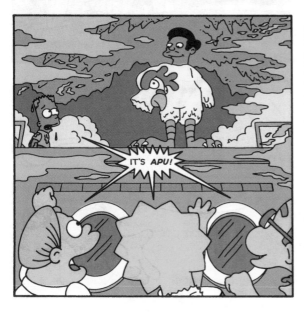

IT'S *APU!*

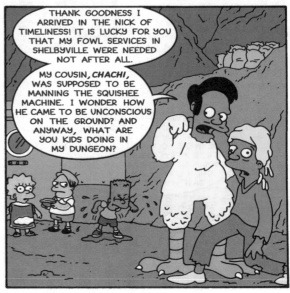

THANK GOODNESS I ARRIVED IN THE NICK OF TIMELINESS! IT IS LUCKY FOR YOU THAT MY FOWL SERVICES IN SHELBYVILLE WERE NEEDED NOT AFTER ALL.

MY COUSIN, *CHACHI,* WAS SUPPOSED TO BE MANNING THE SQUISHEE MACHINE. I WONDER HOW HE CAME TO BE UNCONSCIOUS ON THE GROUND? AND ANYWAY, WHAT ARE YOU KIDS DOING IN MY DUNGEON?

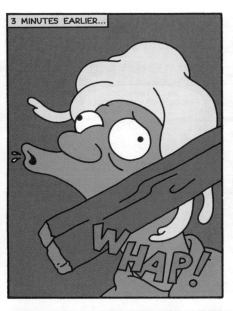

3 MINUTES EARLIER...

WHAP!

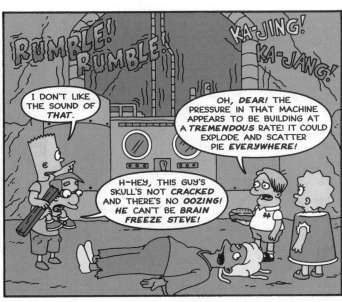

RUMBLE! RUMBLE!

KA-JING! KA-JANG!

I DON'T LIKE THE SOUND OF *THAT*.

OH, *DEAR!* THE PRESSURE IN THAT MACHINE APPEARS TO BE BUILDING AT A *TREMENDOUS* RATE! IT COULD EXPLODE AND SCATTER PIE *EVERYWHERE!*

H-HEY, THIS GUY'S SKULL'S NOT *CRACKED* AND THERE'S NO *OOZING!* HE CAN'T BE *BRAIN FREEZE STEVE!*

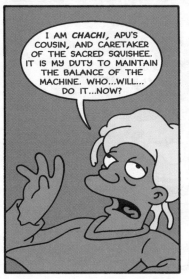

I AM *CHACHI*, APU'S COUSIN, AND CARETAKER OF THE SACRED SQUISHEE. IT IS MY DUTY TO MAINTAIN THE BALANCE OF THE MACHINE. WHO...WILL... DO IT...NOW?

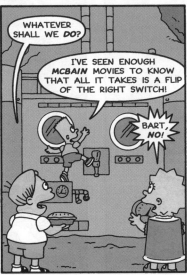

WHATEVER SHALL WE *DO?*

I'VE SEEN ENOUGH *MCBAIN* MOVIES TO KNOW THAT ALL IT TAKES IS A FLIP OF THE RIGHT SWITCH!

BART, NO!

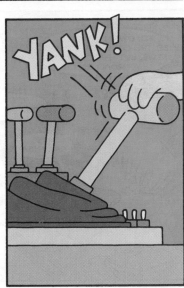

YANK!

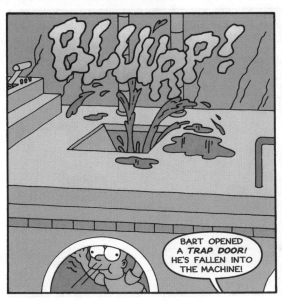

BLUURP!

BART OPENED A *TRAP DOOR!* HE'S FALLEN INTO THE MACHINE!

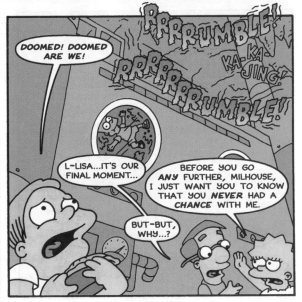

RRRUMBLE! KA-KA-JING! PRRRRUMBLE!

DOOMED! DOOMED ARE WE!

L-LISA...IT'S OUR FINAL MOMENT...

BEFORE YOU GO *ANY* FURTHER, MILHOUSE, I JUST WANT YOU TO KNOW THAT YOU *NEVER* HAD A *CHANCE* WITH ME.

BUT-BUT, WHY...?

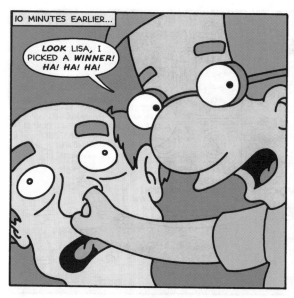

LOOK LISA, I PICKED A *WINNER!* HA! HA! HA!

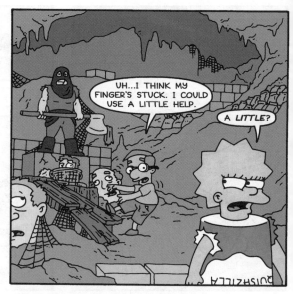

UH...I THINK MY FINGER'S STUCK. I COULD USE A LITTLE HELP.

A *LITTLE?*

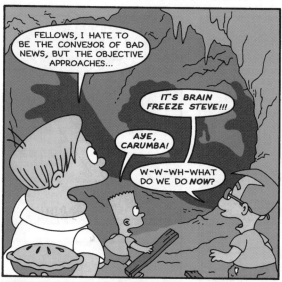

FELLOWS, I HATE TO BE THE CONVEYOR OF BAD NEWS, BUT THE OBJECTIVE APPROACHES...

IT'S BRAIN FREEZE STEVE!!!

AYE, CARUMBA!

W-W-WH-WHAT DO WE DO *NOW?*

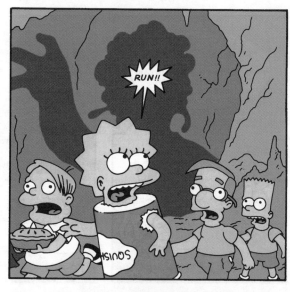

RUN!!

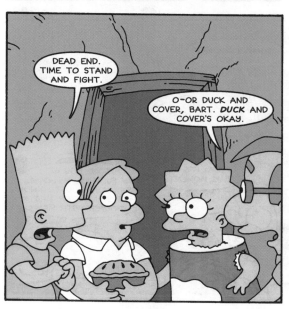

DEAD END. TIME TO STAND AND FIGHT.

O-OR DUCK AND COVER, BART. *DUCK* AND COVER'S OKAY.

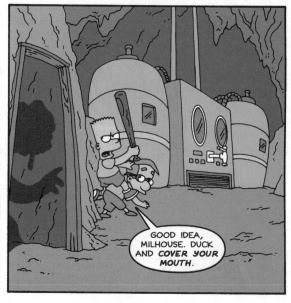

GOOD IDEA, MILHOUSE. DUCK AND *COVER YOUR MOUTH.*

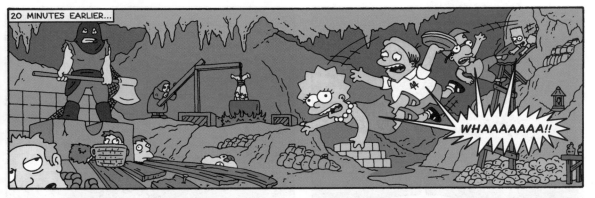

20 MINUTES EARLIER...

WHAAAAAAAA!!

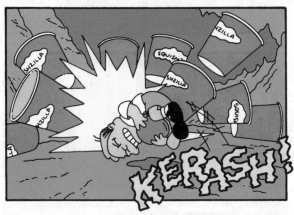

KERASH!

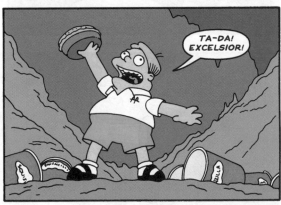

TA-DA! EXCELSIOR!

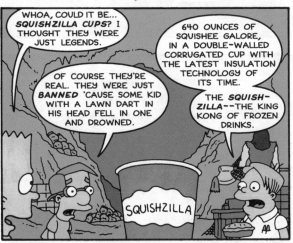

WHOA, COULD IT BE... *SQUISHZILLA CUPS?* I THOUGHT THEY WERE JUST LEGENDS.

OF COURSE THEY'RE REAL. THEY WERE JUST *BANNED* 'CAUSE SOME KID WITH A LAWN DART IN HIS HEAD FELL IN ONE AND DROWNED.

640 OUNCES OF SQUISHEE GALORE, IN A DOUBLE-WALLED CORRUGATED CUP WITH THE LATEST INSULATION TECHNOLOGY OF ITS TIME.

THE *SQUISH-ZILLA*--THE KING KONG OF FROZEN DRINKS.

SQUISHZILLA

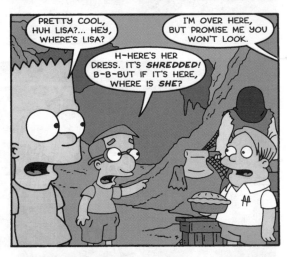

PRETTY COOL, HUH LISA?... HEY, WHERE'S LISA?

I'M OVER HERE, BUT PROMISE ME YOU WON'T LOOK.

H-HERE'S HER DRESS. IT'S *SHREDDED!* B-B-BUT IF IT'S HERE, WHERE IS *SHE?*

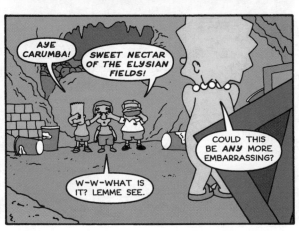

AYE CARUMBA!

SWEET NECTAR OF THE ELYSIAN FIELDS!

W-W-WHAT IS IT? LEMME SEE.

COULD THIS BE *ANY* MORE EMBARRASSING?

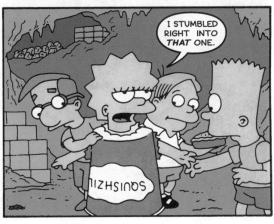

I STUMBLED RIGHT INTO *THAT* ONE.

SQUISHZILLA

15 MINUTES EARLIER...
WHAT IS IT?
NO, ME FIRST! ME FIRST!
STOP PUSHING. WE'RE GONNA FA...
HEY, LOOK! THAT WAX DUMMY IS MAKING JERKY TREATS!
N-NO WONDER THE JERKY ENDS ARE SHEARED SO CLEAN. JUST THE WAY I LIKE 'EM.
YAAAAAH!
KA-BOOM!
AND LOOK! THAT'S HOW APU MAKES HIS FAMOUS SWISS TOFU!
SLICE!
POP!
POP!
CRACK!
HOW INGENIOUS! APU HAS CONVERTED THIS OLD WAX MUSEUM INTO AN AUTOMATED FACTORY. THIS IS WHERE HE MAKES THE KWIK-E-MART'S EXCLUSIVE LINE OF HOME-COOKED ITEMS.

10 MINUTES EARLIER...
WAKE UP, CHOSEN ONE. THE MOMENT OF YOUR DESTINY HAS ARRIVED.
THIS WILL BE YOUR NEW HOME.
NO, YOU FOOL. YOU ARE APPLYING TOO MUCH PRESSURE TO THE NOZZLE! THINK OF THE LEVER AS AN EXTENSION OF YOUR BODY!
WHACK!
CLUMSY BUFFOON! YOU WILL KEEP DOING IT UNTIL YOU GET IT RIGHT!
...GET IT RIGHT!
GET IT RIGHT!
UNTIL YOU GET IT RIGHT!
MUST... GET... IT...RIGHT...
CLONNG!
OOOWWWRRRRR!!!

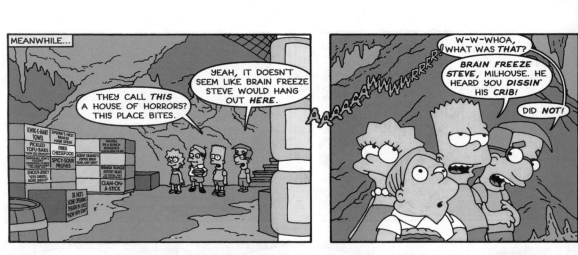

MEANWHILE...

THEY CALL *THIS* A HOUSE OF HORRORS? THIS PLACE BITES.

YEAH, IT DOESN'T SEEM LIKE BRAIN FREEZE STEVE WOULD HANG OUT *HERE*.

KWIK-E-MART TOWEL

SPIDER'S NEST BRAND HAIR SPRAY

PANTIES IN A BUNCH BOUQUETS

PICKLED TOFU-BARS

FRIED CHEESEFOOD

SMILEDOG-JOW FASHION CHIPS

SPICY-SOUR PRUNES

AGENT ORANGE'S PEPPER SPRAY 'BURN, BABY, BURN'

BERMUDA TRIANGLE MYSTERY MEATS

SNOUT-JERKY 'LESS GRISTLE, MORE SNOUT'

CLAM-ON-A-STICK

DR. NICK'S HOME OPENING TISSUE IN A JUICE 'NOW WITH KNIFE'

AAAAAAIIIIIIRRRRRRR!

W-W-WHOA, WHAT WAS *THAT*?

BRAIN FREEZE STEVE, MILHOUSE. HE HEARD YOU *DISSIN'* HIS *CRIB*!

DID *NOT*!

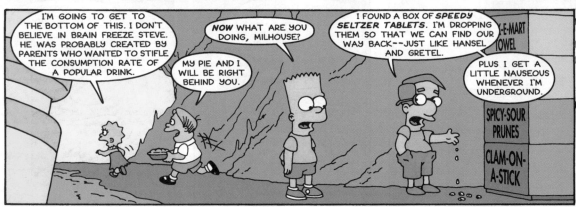

I'M GOING TO GET TO THE BOTTOM OF THIS. I DON'T BELIEVE IN BRAIN FREEZE STEVE. HE WAS PROBABLY CREATED BY PARENTS WHO WANTED TO STIFLE THE CONSUMPTION RATE OF A POPULAR DRINK.

MY PIE AND I WILL BE RIGHT BEHIND YOU.

NOW WHAT ARE YOU DOING, MILHOUSE?

I FOUND A BOX OF *SPEEDY SELTZER TABLETS*. I'M DROPPING THEM SO THAT WE CAN FIND OUR WAY BACK--JUST LIKE HANSEL AND GRETEL.

PLUS I GET A LITTLE NAUSEOUS WHENEVER I'M UNDERGROUND.

-E-MART TOWEL

SPICY-SOUR PRUNES

CLAM-ON-A-STICK

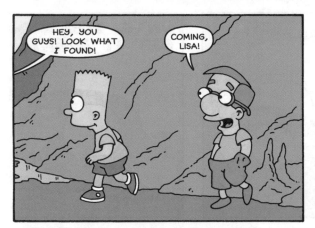

HEY, YOU GUYS! LOOK WHAT *I* FOUND!

COMING, LISA!

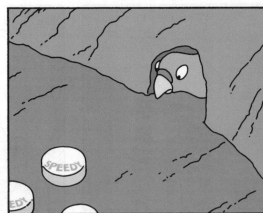

SPEEDY

EDY

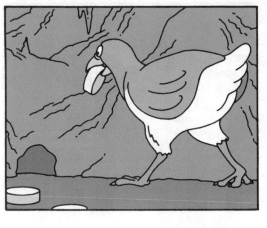

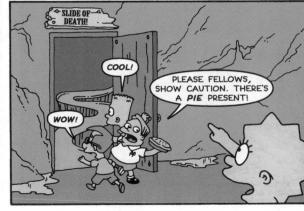

SLIDE OF DEATH!

COOL!

WOW!

PLEASE FELLOWS, SHOW CAUTION. THERE'S A *PIE* PRESENT!

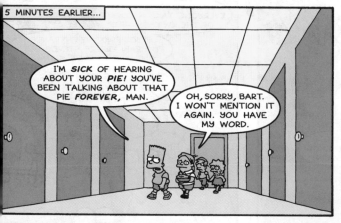

5 MINUTES EARLIER...

I'M *SICK* OF HEARING ABOUT YOUR *PIE!* YOU'VE BEEN TALKING ABOUT THAT PIE *FOREVER,* MAN.

OH, SORRY, BART. I WON'T MENTION IT AGAIN. YOU HAVE MY WORD.

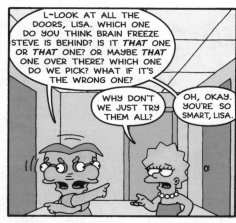

L-LOOK AT ALL THE DOORS, LISA. WHICH ONE DO YOU THINK BRAIN FREEZE STEVE IS BEHIND? IS IT *THAT* ONE OR *THAT* ONE? OR MAYBE *THAT* ONE OVER THERE? WHICH ONE DO WE PICK? WHAT IF IT'S THE WRONG ONE?

WHY DON'T WE JUST TRY THEM ALL?

OH, OKAY. YOU'RE SO SMART, LISA.

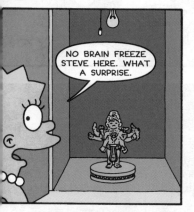

NO BRAIN FREEZE STEVE HERE. WHAT A SURPRISE.

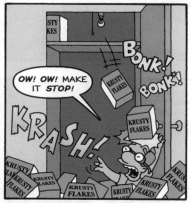

OW! OW! MAKE IT *STOP!*

BONK!

BONK!

KRASH!

KRUSTY FLAKES

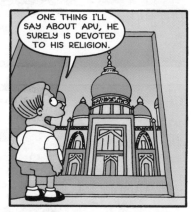

ONE THING I'LL SAY ABOUT APU, HE SURELY IS DEVOTED TO HIS RELIGION.

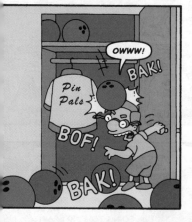

OWWW!

BAK!

Pin Pals

BOF!

BAK!

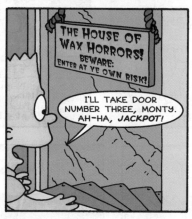

THE HOUSE OF WAX HORRORS! BEWARE: ENTER AT YE OWN RISK!

I'LL TAKE DOOR NUMBER THREE, MONTY. AH-HA, *JACKPOT!*

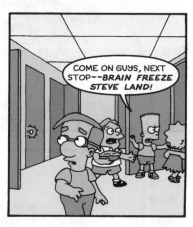

COME ON GUYS, NEXT STOP--BRAIN FREEZE STEVE LAND!

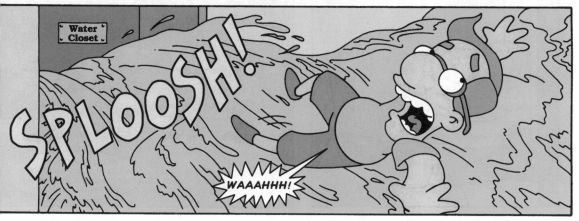

Water Closet

SPLOOSH!

WAAAHHH!

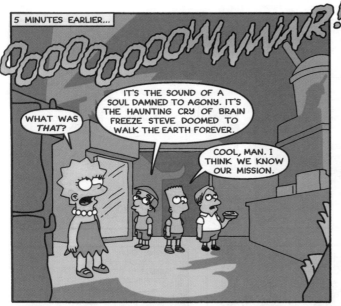

OOOOOOOOOOOWWWNR!

WHAT WAS *THAT*?

IT'S THE SOUND OF A SOUL DAMNED TO AGONY. IT'S THE HAUNTING CRY OF BRAIN FREEZE STEVE DOOMED TO WALK THE EARTH FOREVER.

COOL, MAN. I THINK WE KNOW OUR MISSION.

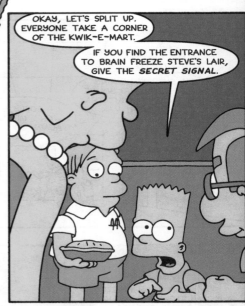

OKAY, LET'S SPLIT UP. EVERYONE TAKE A CORNER OF THE KWIK-E-MART. IF YOU FIND THE ENTRANCE TO BRAIN FREEZE STEVE'S LAIR, GIVE THE *SECRET SIGNAL*.

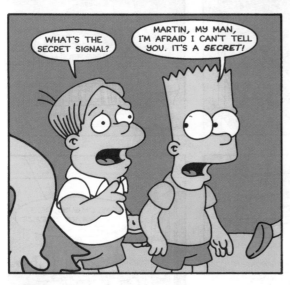

WHAT'S THE SECRET SIGNAL?

MARTIN, MY MAN, I'M AFRAID I CAN'T TELL YOU. IT'S A *SECRET!*

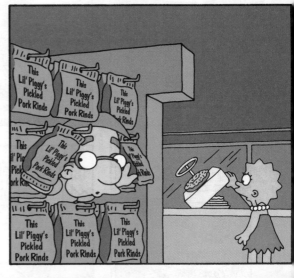

This Lil' Piggy's Pickled Pork Rinds

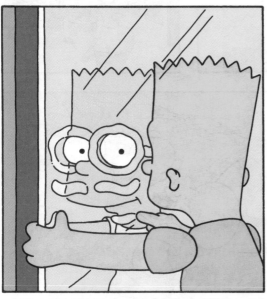

NOTHING, BART.

ME NEITHER.

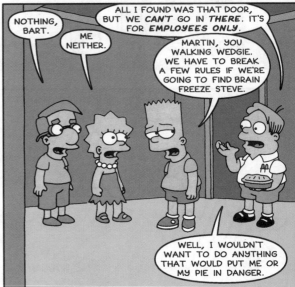

ALL I FOUND WAS THAT DOOR, BUT WE *CAN'T* GO IN *THERE*. IT'S FOR *EMPLOYEES ONLY*.

MARTIN, YOU WALKING WEDGIE. WE HAVE TO BREAK A FEW RULES IF WE'RE GOING TO FIND BRAIN FREEZE STEVE.

WELL, I WOULDN'T WANT TO DO ANYTHING THAT WOULD PUT ME OR MY PIE IN DANGER.

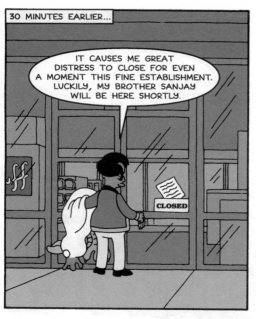

30 MINUTES EARLIER...

IT CAUSES ME GREAT DISTRESS TO CLOSE FOR EVEN A MOMENT THIS FINE ESTABLISHMENT. LUCKILY, MY BROTHER SANJAY WILL BE HERE SHORTLY.

CLOSED

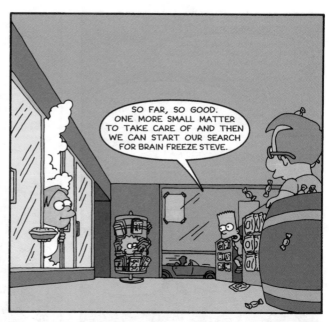

SO FAR, SO GOOD. ONE MORE SMALL MATTER TO TAKE CARE OF AND THEN WE CAN START OUR SEARCH FOR BRAIN FREEZE STEVE.

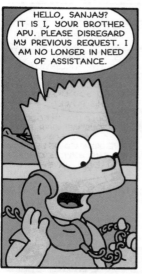

HELLO, SANJAY? IT IS I, YOUR BROTHER APU. PLEASE DISREGARD MY PREVIOUS REQUEST. I AM NO LONGER IN NEED OF ASSISTANCE.

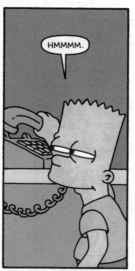

HMMMM.

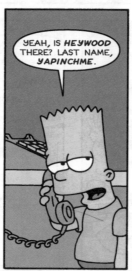

YEAH, IS *HEYWOOD* THERE? LAST NAME, *YAPINCHME*.

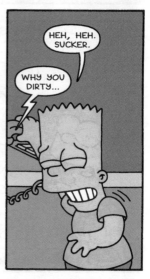

HEH, HEH. SUCKER.

WHY YOU DIRTY...

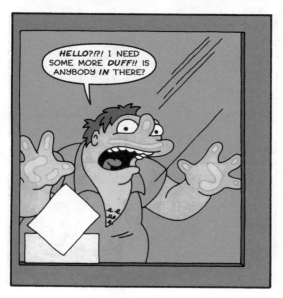

HELLO?!?! I NEED SOME MORE *DUFF!!* IS ANYBODY *IN* THERE?

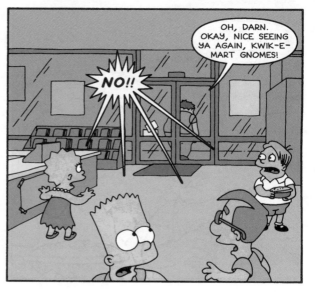

NO!!

OH, DARN. OKAY, NICE SEEING YA AGAIN, KWIK-E-MART GNOMES!

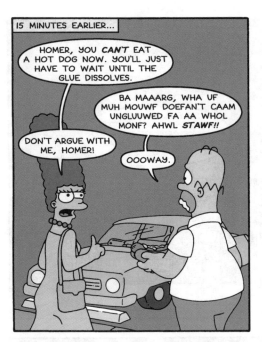

15 MINUTES EARLIER...

HOMER, YOU *CAN'T* EAT A HOT DOG NOW. YOU'LL JUST HAVE TO WAIT UNTIL THE GLUE DISSOLVES.

BA MAAARG, WHA UF MUH MOUWF DOEFAN'T CAAM UNGLUUWED FA AA WHOL MONF? AHWL *STAWF!!*

DON'T ARGUE WITH ME, HOMER!

OOOWAY.

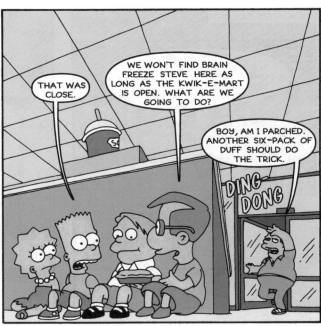

THAT WAS CLOSE.

WE WON'T FIND BRAIN FREEZE STEVE HERE AS LONG AS THE KWIK-E-MART IS OPEN. WHAT ARE WE GOING TO DO?

BOY, AM I PARCHED. ANOTHER SIX-PACK OF DUFF SHOULD DO THE TRICK.

DING-DONG

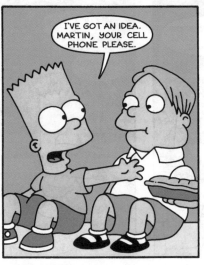

I'VE GOT AN IDEA. MARTIN, YOUR CELL PHONE PLEASE.

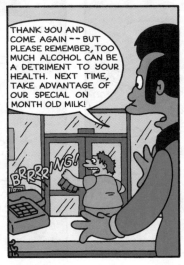

THANK YOU AND COME AGAIN -- BUT PLEASE REMEMBER, TOO MUCH ALCOHOL CAN BE A DETRIMENT TO YOUR HEALTH. NEXT TIME, TAKE ADVANTAGE OF OUR SPECIAL ON MONTH OLD MILK!

BRRRRING!

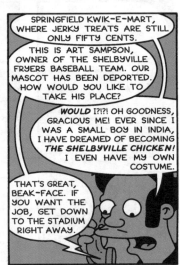

SPRINGFIELD KWIK-E-MART, WHERE JERKY TREATS ARE STILL ONLY FIFTY CENTS.

THIS IS ART SAMPSON, OWNER OF THE SHELBYVILLE FRYERS BASEBALL TEAM. OUR MASCOT HAS BEEN DEPORTED. HOW WOULD YOU LIKE TO TAKE HIS PLACE?

WOULD I?!?! OH GOODNESS, GRACIOUS ME! EVER SINCE I WAS A SMALL BOY IN INDIA, I HAVE DREAMED OF BECOMING *THE SHELBYVILLE CHICKEN!* I EVEN HAVE MY OWN COSTUME.

THAT'S GREAT, BEAK-FACE. IF YOU WANT THE JOB, GET DOWN TO THE STADIUM RIGHT AWAY.

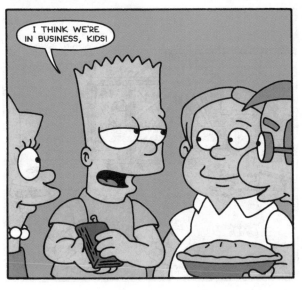

I THINK WE'RE IN BUSINESS, KIDS!

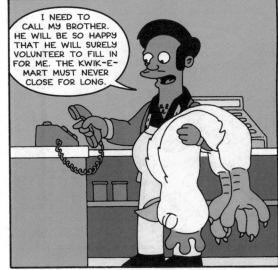

I NEED TO CALL MY BROTHER. HE WILL BE SO HAPPY THAT HE WILL SURELY VOLUNTEER TO FILL IN FOR ME. THE KWIK-E-MART MUST NEVER CLOSE FOR LONG.

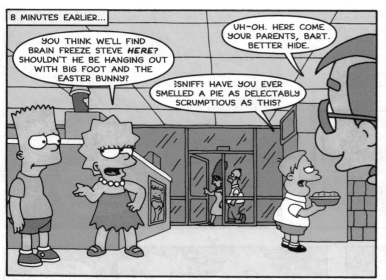

8 MINUTES EARLIER...

YOU THINK WE'LL FIND BRAIN FREEZE STEVE *HERE*? SHOULDN'T HE BE HANGING OUT WITH BIG FOOT AND THE EASTER BUNNY?

UH-OH. HERE COME YOUR PARENTS, BART. BETTER HIDE.

¡SNIFF¡ HAVE YOU EVER SMELLED A PIE AS DELECTABLY SCRUMPTIOUS AS THIS?

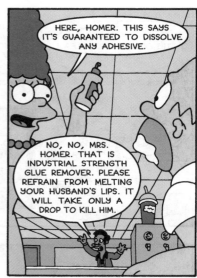

HERE, HOMER. THIS SAYS IT'S GUARANTEED TO DISSOLVE ANY ADHESIVE.

NO, NO, MRS. HOMER. THAT IS INDUSTRIAL STRENGTH GLUE REMOVER. PLEASE REFRAIN FROM MELTING YOUR HUSBAND'S LIPS. IT WILL TAKE ONLY A DROP TO KILL HIM.

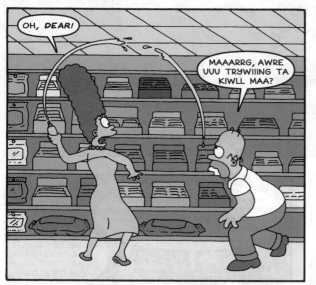

OH, *DEAR*!

MAAARRG, AWRE UUU TRYWIIING TA KIWLL MAA?

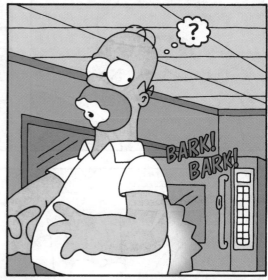

BARK! BARK!

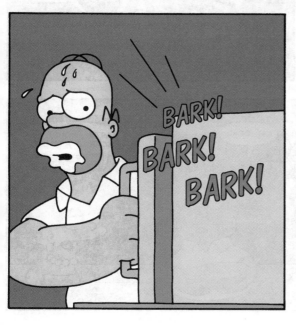

BARK! BARK! BARK!

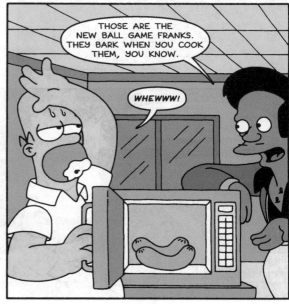

THOSE ARE THE NEW BALL GAME FRANKS. THEY BARK WHEN YOU COOK THEM, YOU KNOW.

WHEWWW!

8 MINUTES EARLIER...
I WISH TO PURCHASE THIS EXQUISITE PIE, PLEASE. $4.38 IS A VALUE THAT I CANNOT PASS UP!
YES, YES, WHATEVER. YOU WILL PLUMP WHEN YOU EAT IT.
KWIK-E-DOG
ARE YOU GOING TO EAT THAT WHOLE PIE BY YOURSELF, MARTIN?
OH, NO, NO, NO. THIS CONFECTIONERY TREAT IS FOR MY MOTHER. WON'T SHE BE PLEASED?
ONLY A GEEK WOULD BUY A PRESENT FOR HIS MOM WHEN HE COULD'VE BOUGHT A SQUISHEE LIKE ME.
THANK GOODNESS, THEY'RE STILL OPEN. TIME FOR MORE DUFF!
NO, BART!
WHAT THE HAY?!
SMACK!
SPLATT!!
WHAT'D YOU DO THAT FOR?!?!? YOU RUINED A PERFECTLY GOOD SQUISHEE! MY SQUISHEE TO BE MORE PRECISE!
A-A-ACK!
YOU ALMOST DRANK A SQUISHEE WITH TWO STRAWS! HAVEN'T YOU EVER HEARD OF BRAIN FREEZE STEVE?!? HE ONCE DRANK A SQUISHEE WITH TWO STRAWS AND HIS HEAD CRACKED OPEN.
YEAH, YEAH, I KNOW. HE HAUNTS THE KWIK-E-MART, COMING OUT ONLY WHEN IT'S CLOSED.
HEY, GUYS, I'VE GOT AN IDEA! LET'S GO EXPLORING FOR BRAIN FREEZE STEVE.
YEAH, WE CAN BE JUST LIKE THE GOONIES!
OH, DEAR.
MARTIN, YOU'RE NOT SCARED ARE YOU?

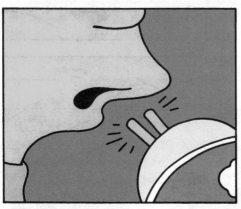

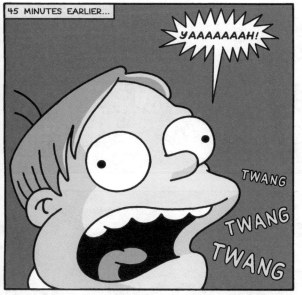

YAAAAAAAH!

TWANG

TWANG

TWANG

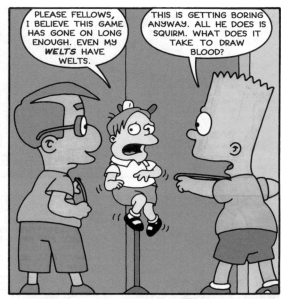

PLEASE FELLOWS, I BELIEVE THIS GAME HAS GONE ON LONG ENOUGH. EVEN MY *WELTS* HAVE WELTS.

THIS IS GETTING BORING ANYWAY. ALL HE DOES IS SQUIRM. WHAT DOES IT TAKE TO DRAW BLOOD?

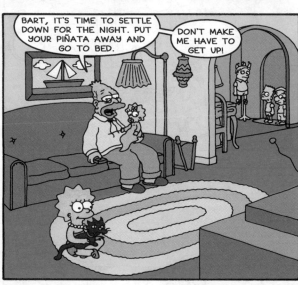

BART, IT'S TIME TO SETTLE DOWN FOR THE NIGHT. PUT YOUR PIÑATA AWAY AND GO TO BED.

DON'T MAKE ME HAVE TO GET UP!

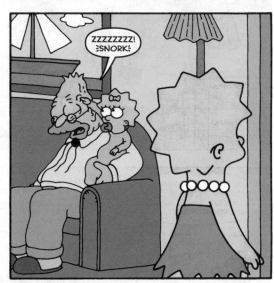

ZZZZZZZZ! ¡SNORK!

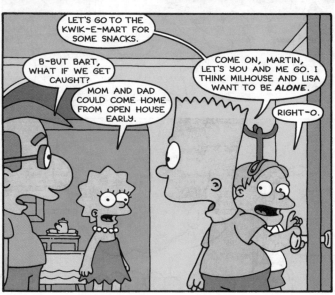

LET'S GO TO THE KWIK-E-MART FOR SOME SNACKS.

B-BUT BART, WHAT IF WE GET CAUGHT?

MOM AND DAD COULD COME HOME FROM OPEN HOUSE EARLY.

COME ON, MARTIN, LET'S YOU AND ME GO. I THINK MILHOUSE AND LISA WANT TO BE *ALONE*.

RIGHT-O.

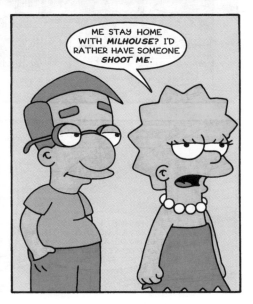

ME STAY HOME WITH *MILHOUSE*? I'D RATHER HAVE SOMEONE *SHOOT ME*.

10 MINUTES EARLIER...
KLACKITY-KLACK-KLACK-KLACK!
KLACKITY-KLACK-
KLACK-KLACK!
THIS CONCLUDES OUR DEMONSTRATION. COOKIES AND JUICE ARE AVAILABLE IN THE HALL...FOR THOSE OF YOU WHO DIDN'T GLUE YOUR MOUTHS SHUT EATING PASTE.
PARENT-TEACHER NIGHT!
R'OH!
SO WILLIE'S A WALL-HANGING NOW, IS THAT IT? YA KOOL-AID SUCKING GREASE-COMBERS, YA!
OH, I ALMOST FORGOT-- THE WINNER OF TONIGHT'S DOOR PRIZE IS MARGE SIMPSON!
OH, MY!
IT'S A BEAUTIFUL, NEW, STAINLESS STEEL, MEAT CLEAVER.
HMMMM. I SUPPOSE I SHOULD HOLD IT WITH THE BLADE AWAY FROM ME, SO I DON'T HURT MYSELF IF I FALL OVER.

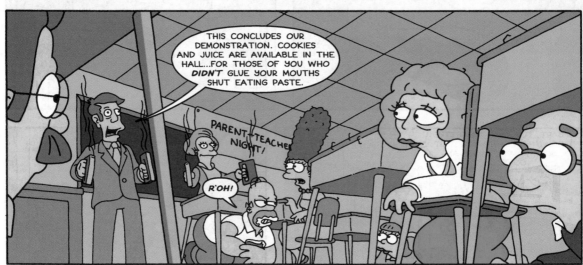

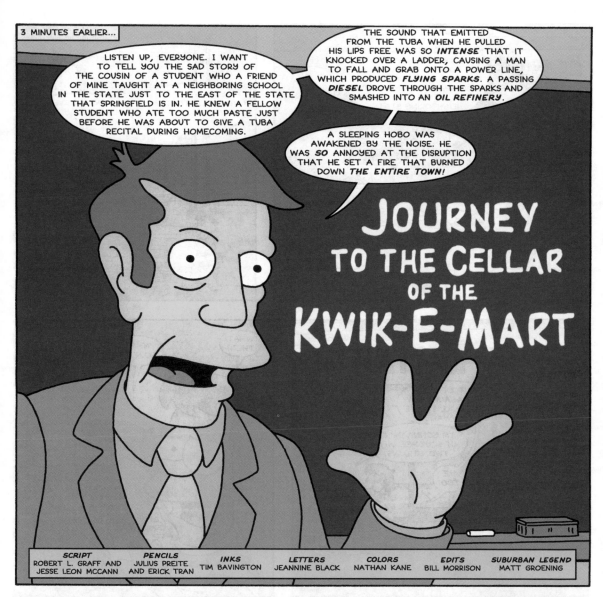

3 MINUTES EARLIER...

LISTEN UP, EVERYONE. I WANT TO TELL YOU THE SAD STORY OF THE COUSIN OF A STUDENT WHO A FRIEND OF MINE TAUGHT AT A NEIGHBORING SCHOOL IN THE STATE JUST TO THE EAST OF THE STATE THAT SPRINGFIELD IS IN. HE KNEW A FELLOW STUDENT WHO ATE TOO MUCH PASTE JUST BEFORE HE WAS ABOUT TO GIVE A TUBA RECITAL DURING HOMECOMING.

THE SOUND THAT EMITTED FROM THE TUBA WHEN HE PULLED HIS LIPS FREE WAS SO *INTENSE* THAT IT KNOCKED OVER A LADDER, CAUSING A MAN TO FALL AND GRAB ONTO A POWER LINE, WHICH PRODUCED *FLYING SPARKS*. A PASSING *DIESEL* DROVE THROUGH THE SPARKS AND SMASHED INTO AN *OIL REFINERY*.

A SLEEPING HOBO WAS AWAKENED BY THE NOISE. HE WAS *SO* ANNOYED AT THE DISRUPTION THAT HE SET A FIRE THAT BURNED DOWN *THE ENTIRE TOWN*!

JOURNEY TO THE CELLAR OF THE KWIK-E-MART

SCRIPT
ROBERT L. GRAFF AND JESSE LEON MCCANN

PENCILS
JULIUS PREITE AND ERICK TRAN

INKS
TIM BAVINGTON

LETTERS
JEANNINE BLACK

COLORS
NATHAN KANE

EDITS
BILL MORRISON

SUBURBAN LEGEND
MATT GROENING

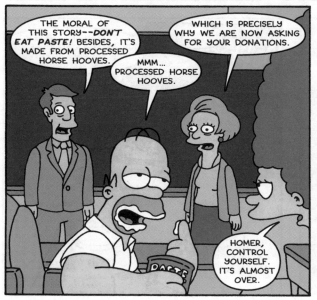

THE MORAL OF THIS STORY--*DON'T EAT PASTE!* BESIDES, IT'S MADE FROM PROCESSED HORSE HOOVES.

MMM... PROCESSED HORSE HOOVES.

WHICH IS PRECISELY WHY WE ARE NOW ASKING FOR YOUR DONATIONS.

HOMER, CONTROL YOURSELF. IT'S ALMOST OVER.

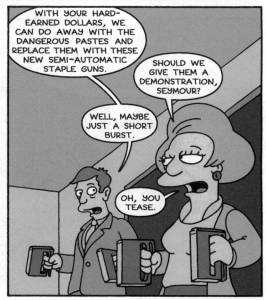

WITH YOUR HARD-EARNED DOLLARS, WE CAN DO AWAY WITH THE DANGEROUS PASTES AND REPLACE THEM WITH THESE NEW SEMI-AUTOMATIC STAPLE GUNS.

SHOULD WE GIVE THEM A DEMONSTRATION, SEYMOUR?

WELL, MAYBE JUST A SHORT BURST.

OH, YOU TEASE.

30 YEARS EARLIER...
RIIIING!
CLASS DISMISSED. AND DON'T FORGET TO TELL YOUR PARENTS TO DONATE TO OUR NEW, IMPROVED PASTE FUND. WE DON'T WANT TO END UP LIKE THAT OTHER TOWN IN A NEIGHBORING STATE.
YOU WANT TO GO OVER TO THAT NEW KWIK-E-MART FOR A SQUISHEE?
DO I?! I'VE HEARD THEY HAVE GREAT HOT DOGS! I CAN'T WAIT TO TRY ONE OF THEM.
KWIK-E-MART
COMING SOON
SQUISHZILLA
640 OZ
HOT DOG
5¢
OUT OF HOT DOGS AGAIN? HOW LONG WILL I HAVE TO WAIT?
I'M GONNA DRINK MY SQUISHEE WITH TWO STRAWS.
ME TOO!
WHAT THE?!?
WHAT'S GOIN' ON?
SLAP!
SPLAT!
DON'T YOU KNOW WHAT CAN HAPPEN WHEN YOU DRINK A SQUISHEE WITH TWO STRAWS? YOU'LL END LIKE BRAIN FREEZE STEVE, WHO'S HEAD SWELLED UP AND CRACKED OPEN!
Duff BEER
Foam it to me, baby!
OH MAN, I'LL NEVER BUY ANOTHER SQUISHEE! I'LL HAVE TO FIND SOMETHING ELSE TO DRINK.
EH, BRAIN FREEZE STEVE IS JUST A STUPID URBAN LEGEND.

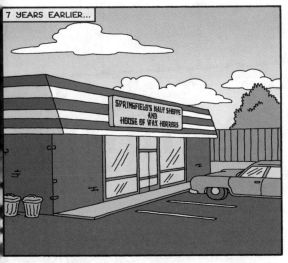

7 YEARS EARLIER...

SPRINGFIELD'S MALT SHOPPE AND HOUSE OF WAX HORRORS

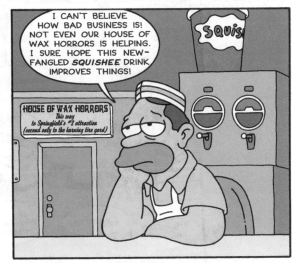

I CAN'T BELIEVE HOW BAD BUSINESS IS! NOT EVEN OUR HOUSE OF WAX HORRORS IS HELPING. I SURE HOPE THIS NEW-FANGLED *SQUISHEE* DRINK IMPROVES THINGS!!

SQUIS

HOUSE OF WAX HORRORS
This way
to Springfield's #2 attraction
(second only to the burning tire yard)

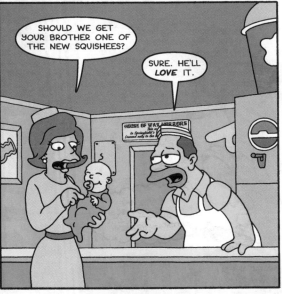

SHOULD WE GET YOUR BROTHER ONE OF THE NEW SQUISHEES?

SURE. HE'LL *LOVE* IT.

HOUSE OF WAX HORRORS
This way
to Springfield's
(second only to the

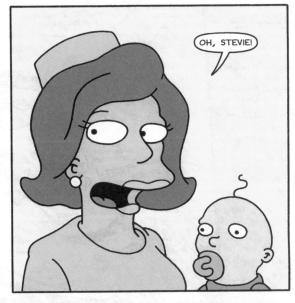

OH, STEVIE!

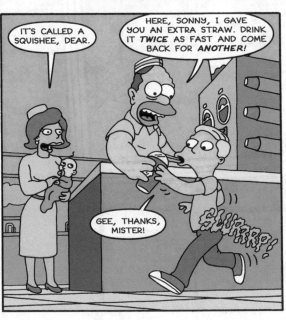

IT'S CALLED A SQUISHEE, DEAR.

HERE, SONNY, I GAVE YOU AN EXTRA STRAW. DRINK IT *TWICE* AS FAST AND COME BACK FOR *ANOTHER!*

GEE, THANKS, MISTER!

SQUORR!

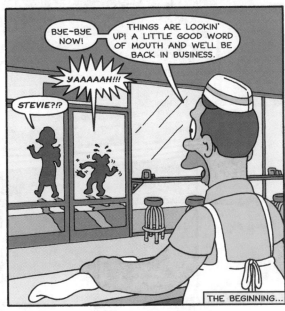

BYE-BYE NOW!

THINGS ARE LOOKIN' UP! A LITTLE GOOD WORD OF MOUTH AND WE'LL BE BACK IN BUSINESS.

YAAAAAH!!!

STEVIE?!?

THE BEGINNING...

Poochie Comics
JUNE #1
HE'S EXTREMELY LOVABLE--AND LOVABLY EXTREME!!!
Roger Meyers, Jr. presents
POOCHIE!
AH PITIES THE FOOL!
'EYYYYY!!!
I KNOW YOU ARE, BUT WHAT AM I?
SMASHING, BABY, YEAH!
EXCUUUUUUUSE ME!
KISS MAH GRITS!
I'M GOING COMPLETELY MENTAL, I MUST SAY!
EX-CELLENT!
SOCK IT TO ME!
WHAT'CHOO TALKIN' 'BOUT?
COWABUNGA, DUDES!
DON'T HAVE A COW, MAN!
COME BACK HERE, DOG-BOY!
YEAH, AS MEMBERS OF THE LEGION OF LAWYERS, WE HAVE A FEW BONES TO PICK WITH YOU!
...HMMM...COME BACK HERE, DOG-BOY! MAMA MIA! AT'SA SPICY CATCH'A-PHRASE!!!
SCOTT SHAW!
GROENING
AS SEEN ON TV'S ITCHY AND SCRATCHY AND POOCHIE SHOW!!!
CAN YOU IDENTIFY ALL OF POOCHIE'S PURLOINED CATCH-PHRASES? IF SO, THE LEGION OF LAWYERS WOULD LIKE TO SPEAK WITH YOU, TOO!

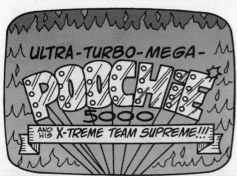

Poochie's kickin' tail and takin' dog tags in this **all-new**, in-yer-face animated series that's chock-full of the kind of white-knuckle action that **you**, the new breed of viewer, request, nay, **demand**!!!

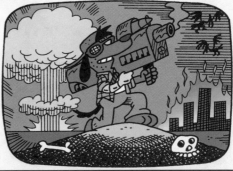

America's favorite cartoon canine cut-up is **trapped** in a post-apocalyptic **future-world** he never made! But **Poochie's** not alone...

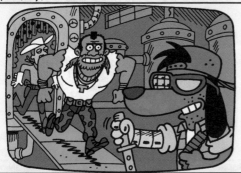

Discovering a **time machine** in the ruins of a scientific research lab, he assembles the greatest **pop cultural personalities** of all time to become his...
X-Treme Team Supreme!

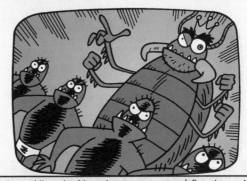

Meanwhile, the **Verminator**, a mutated flea that **rules** this irradiated wasteland, creates his **own** squad of evil underlings (each a major menace in its own right) to enforce his control!

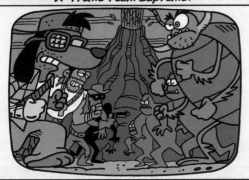

So tune in each week as **Poochie** and his power-pals face off against the Verminator and his evil forces as they battle for the **fate** of the future!

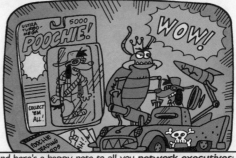

And here's a happy note to all you **network executives**: the **costs** of producing this exciting new **Poochie** cartoon series are completely covered by the (get **this**!) **advertising budget** for our new line of **Ultra-Turbo-Mega Poochie and His X-Treme Team Supreme** action figures, accessories and vehicles! !!

POOCHIE & the PUPPYDAWGZ on BREAKDANCE ISLAND!

Poochie's a funky dude with a street-wise 'tude in a 'toon with a beat that Today's Young People can really *relate* to!

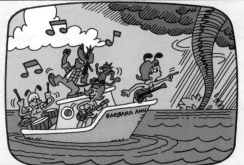

One day, *Poochie* and his all-girl band, *The Puppydawgz*, are chillin' on their *yacht*, en route to another gig, when suddenly, a *waterspout* appears on the horizon!

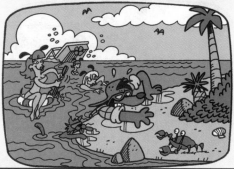

After the ferocious storm destroys their boat, *Poochie* and his *gal-pals* surf to safety, landing on the shore of an *uncharted tropical isle*!

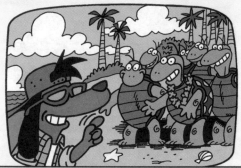

They're befriended by a friendly tribe of *turtles!* Years ago, a crate of breakdance records washed up on their island, and these naive natives have *worshipped* breakdancing ever since!

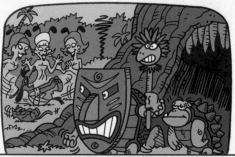

But there's a snake in every paradise, and Breakdance Island is *no* exception! His authority threatened by these newcomers, the tribe's witch-doctor *Snapper* (and his goofy side-kick *Sheldon*) vows to get *rid* of Poochie and his band in any way he *can*!

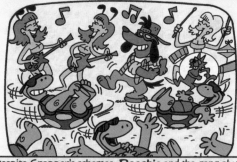

Despite Snapper's schemes, *Poochie* and the gang always manage to emerge victorious, thanks to the unstoppable power of *music*, as each week, we're treated to a funky-fresh slice of hip-hop served up piping hot by the *Puppydawgs* themselves!

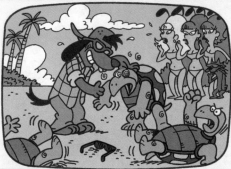

Of course, there's *also* always the task of helping the island's break-dancin' turtles get off their *backs* and onto their *feet!*

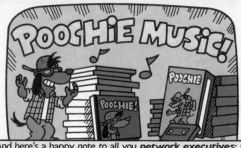

And here's a happy note to all you *network executives*: the *costs* of producing this exciting new Poochie cartoon series are *completely* covered by (yes, it's absolutely true) the *advertising budget* for the *Poochie and the Puppydawgz on Breakdance Island* soundtrack album on CD and cassette and *sing-along video*, on VHS and DVD, available wherever music and videos are sold!!!

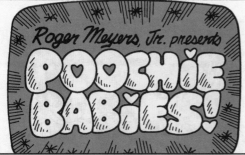

Roger Meyers, Jr. presents

POOCHIE BABIES!

Laff whilst you *learn* life's *hardest* lessons along with these irrepressibly lovable, mischief-makin' *Children of the Cornball!*

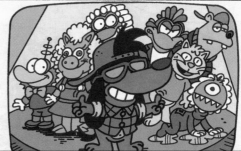

Meet *Li'l Poochie* and his pre-school pals-- **Whiney Swiney, Spazzy Bear, Alonzo the Whatchamacallit, Meowwlf, Baby Bestial** and the twins, **Skidmark** and **Scurvy!**

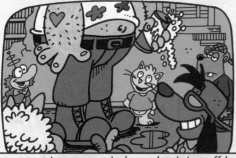

These cute tykes are watched over by their gruff-but-lovable guardian **Manny**, a man whose face we never clearly view (due to certain legal restrictions by the Government Witness Relocation Protection Program.)

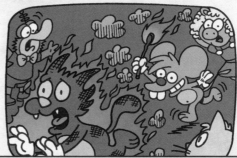

Then one day, their new friends *Li'l Itchy* and *Li'l Scratchy* come to visit! Oh, *my!* Despite Manny's efforts, things soon get out of hand!

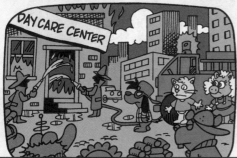

With their day-care center burnt to the ground, the *Poochie Babies* find themselves facing the **harsh realities** of a world without **food** or **shelter!**

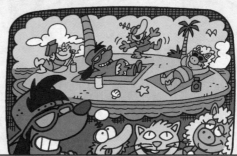

Our little friends may be **down** but they're **never** out! Using their powerful **imaginations**, the kids imagine that rather than being stranded on **Skid Row**, they're vacationing at sunny **Club Med!**

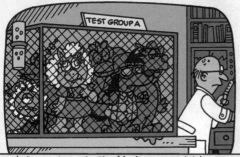

Instead, they wake up in **Med Lab**, a research laboratory that tests the toxic qualities of **cosmetics** on captive animals! Who **knows** where these plucky toddlers will wind up **next?**

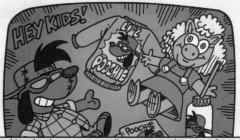

And here's a happy note to all you **network executives**: the **costs** of producing this exciting new **Poochie** cartoon series are **completely** covered by (can you **believe** it?) the **advertising budget** for our new line of **Roger Meyers, Jr.s' Poochie Babies** cuddle-dolls, activity books and sleepwear!!!

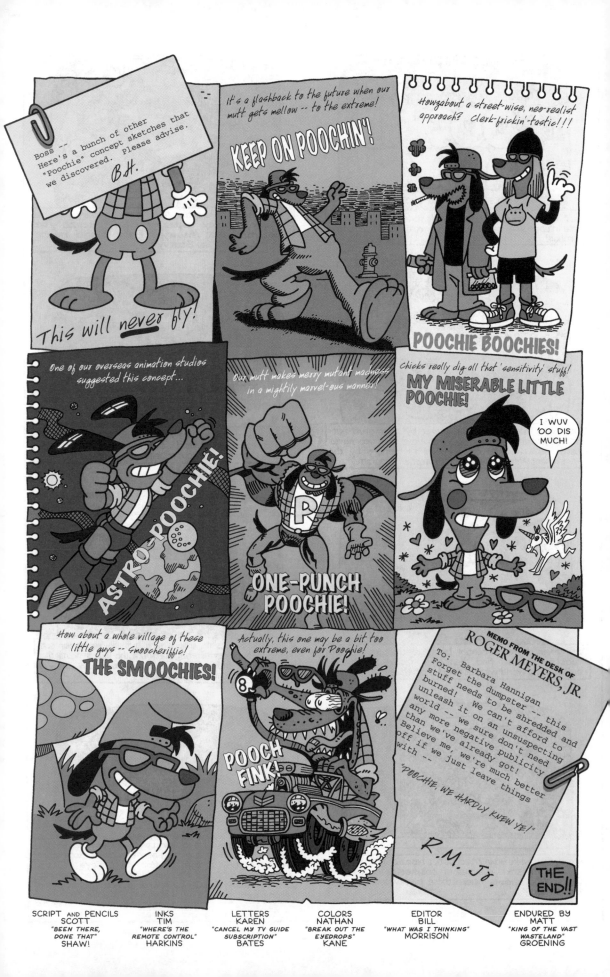

SCRIPT AND PENCILS
SCOTT
"BEEN THERE,
DONE THAT"
SHAW!

INKS
TIM
"WHERE'S THE
REMOTE CONTROL"
HARKINS

LETTERS
KAREN
"CANCEL MY TV GUIDE
SUBSCRIPTION"
BATES

COLORS
NATHAN
"BREAK OUT THE
EYEDROPS"
KANE

EDITOR
BILL
"WHAT WAS I THINKING"
MORRISON

ENDURED BY
MATT
"KING OF THE VAST
WASTELAND"
GROENING

SIMPSONS COMICS
#44
US $2.50
CAN $3.50
TODAY'S ASSIGNMENT- READ JANE EYRE AND WRITE A 40 PAGE REPORT
SUBSTITUTE TEACHER: LISA SIMPSON
APPLE SAUCE
GROENING
©1999 BONGO ENTERTAINMENT, INC. THE SIMPSONS ©&TM TWENTIETH CENTURY FOX FILM CORPORATION. ALL RIGHTS RESERVED.

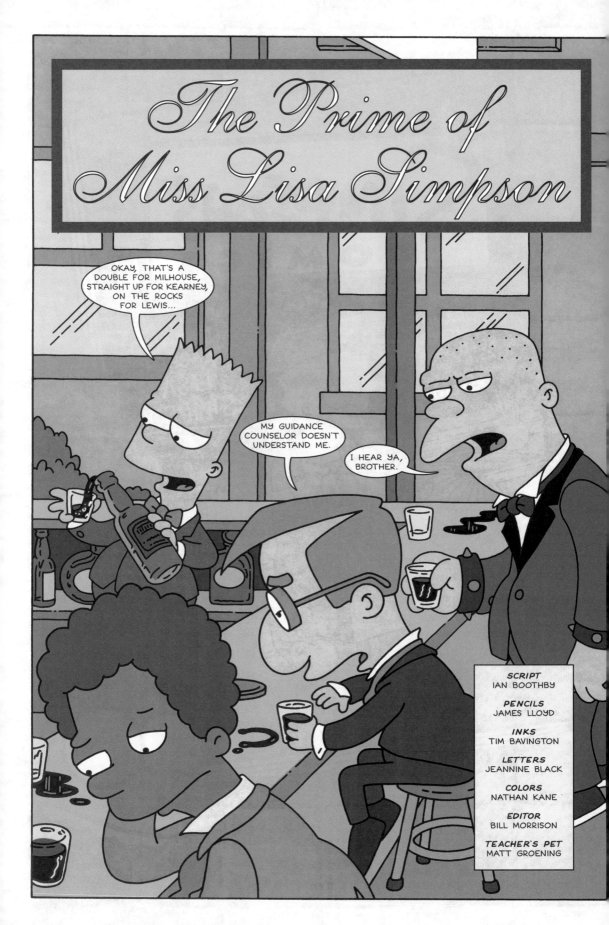

The Prime of Miss Lisa Simpson

OKAY, THAT'S A DOUBLE FOR MILHOUSE, STRAIGHT UP FOR KEARNEY, ON THE ROCKS FOR LEWIS...

MY GUIDANCE COUNSELOR DOESN'T UNDERSTAND ME.

I HEAR YA, BROTHER.

SCRIPT
IAN BOOTHBY

PENCILS
JAMES LLOYD

INKS
TIM BAVINGTON

LETTERS
JEANNINE BLACK

COLORS
NATHAN KANE

EDITOR
BILL MORRISON

TEACHER'S PET
MATT GROENING

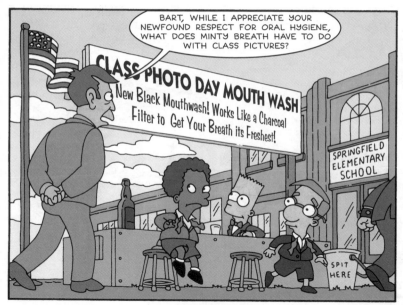

BART, WHILE I APPRECIATE YOUR NEWFOUND RESPECT FOR ORAL HYGIENE, WHAT DOES MINTY BREATH HAVE TO DO WITH CLASS PICTURES?

CLASS PHOTO DAY MOUTH WASH
New Black Mouthwash! Works Like a Charcoal Filter to Get Your Breath its Freshest!

SPRINGFIELD ELEMENTARY SCHOOL

SPIT HERE

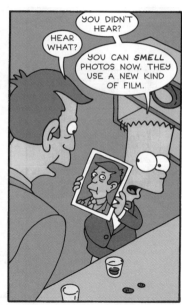

YOU DIDN'T HEAR?

HEAR WHAT?

YOU CAN SMELL PHOTOS NOW. THEY USE A NEW KIND OF FILM.

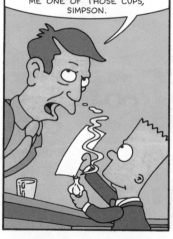

⸨SNIFF, SNIFF⸩ WHY, I DID HAVE MOTHER'S GARLIC OATMEAL THE MORNING THAT WAS TAKEN. GIVE ME ONE OF THOSE CUPS, SIMPSON.

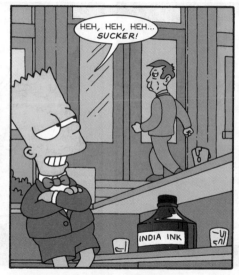

HEH, HEH, HEH... SUCKER!

INDIA INK

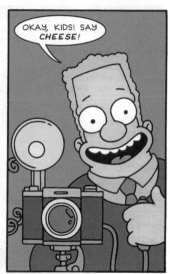

OKAY, KIDS! SAY CHEESE!

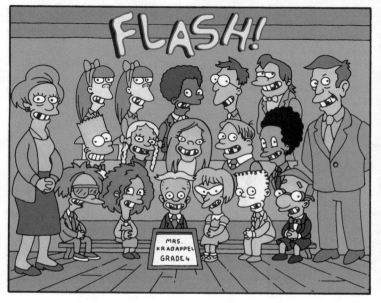

FLASH!

MRS. KRABAPPEL GRADE 4

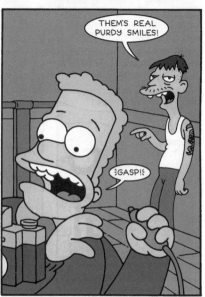

THEM'S REAL PURDY SMILES!

⸨GASP!⸩

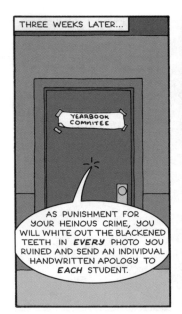

THREE WEEKS LATER...

YEARBOOK COMMITEE

AS PUNISHMENT FOR YOUR HEINOUS CRIME, YOU WILL WHITE OUT THE BLACKENED TEETH IN *EVERY* PHOTO YOU RUINED AND SEND AN INDIVIDUAL HANDWRITTEN APOLOGY TO *EACH* STUDENT.

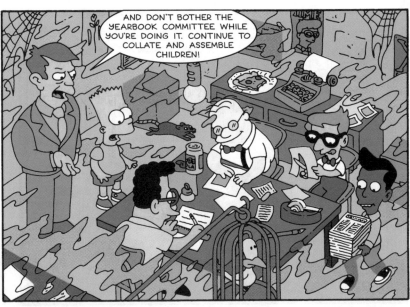

AND DON'T BOTHER THE YEARBOOK COMMITTEE WHILE YOU'RE DOING IT. CONTINUE TO COLLATE AND ASSEMBLE CHILDREN!

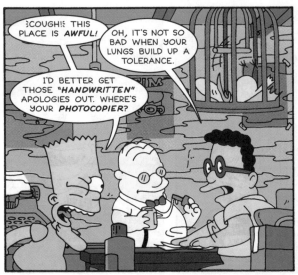

:COUGH!: THIS PLACE IS *AWFUL!*

OH, IT'S NOT SO BAD WHEN YOUR LUNGS BUILD UP A TOLERANCE.

I'D BETTER GET THOSE *"HANDWRITTEN"* APOLOGIES OUT. WHERE'S YOUR *PHOTOCOPIER?*

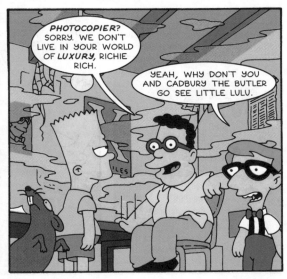

PHOTOCOPIER? SORRY. WE DON'T LIVE IN YOUR WORLD OF *LUXURY*, RICHIE RICH.

YEAH, WHY DON'T YOU AND CADBURY THE BUTLER GO SEE LITTLE LULU.

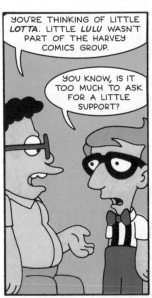

YOU'RE THINKING OF LITTLE *LOTTA.* LITTLE *LULU* WASN'T PART OF THE HARVEY COMICS GROUP.

YOU KNOW, IS IT TOO MUCH TO ASK FOR A LITTLE SUPPORT?

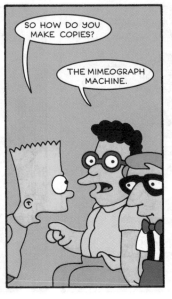

SO HOW DO YOU MAKE COPIES?

THE MIMEOGRAPH MACHINE.

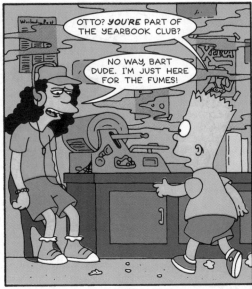

OTTO? *YOU'RE* PART OF THE YEARBOOK CLUB?

NO WAY, BART DUDE. I'M JUST HERE FOR THE FUMES!

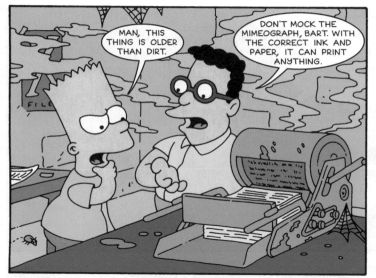

MAN, THIS THING IS OLDER THAN DIRT.

DON'T MOCK THE MIMEOGRAPH, BART. WITH THE CORRECT INK AND PAPER, IT CAN PRINT ANYTHING.

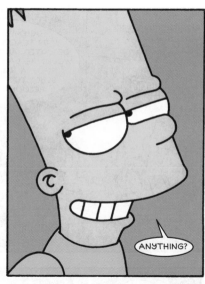

ANYTHING?

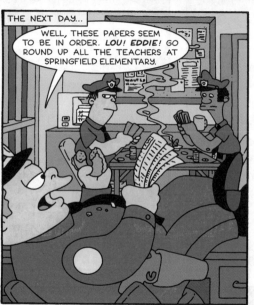

THE NEXT DAY...

WELL, THESE PAPERS SEEM TO BE IN ORDER. *LOU! EDDIE!* GO ROUND UP ALL THE TEACHERS AT SPRINGFIELD ELEMENTARY.

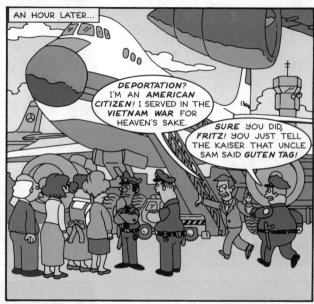

AN HOUR LATER...

DEPORTATION? I'M AN *AMERICAN CITIZEN!* I SERVED IN THE *VIETNAM WAR* FOR HEAVEN'S SAKE.

SURE YOU DID, *FRITZ!* YOU JUST TELL THE KAISER THAT UNCLE SAM SAID *GUTEN TAG!*

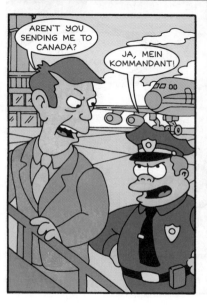

AREN'T YOU SENDING ME TO CANADA?

JA, MEIN KOMMANDANT!

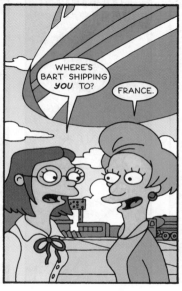

WHERE'S BART SHIPPING *YOU* TO?

FRANCE.

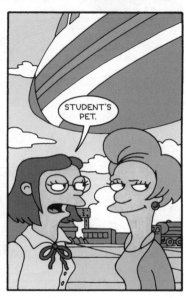

STUDENT'S PET.

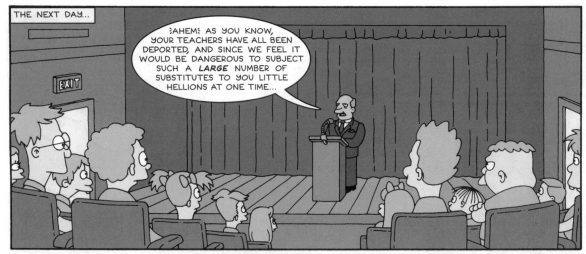

THE NEXT DAY...

AHEM AS YOU KNOW, YOUR TEACHERS HAVE ALL BEEN DEPORTED, AND SINCE WE FEEL IT WOULD BE DANGEROUS TO SUBJECT SUCH A *LARGE* NUMBER OF SUBSTITUTES TO YOU LITTLE HELLIONS AT ONE TIME...

EXIT

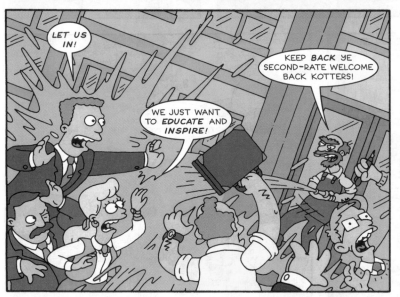

LET US IN!

KEEP *BACK* YE SECOND-RATE WELCOME BACK KOTTERS!

WE JUST WANT TO *EDUCATE* AND *INSPIRE!*

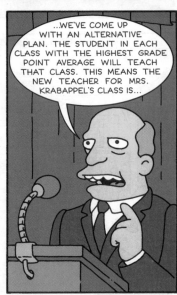

...WE'VE COME UP WITH AN ALTERNATIVE PLAN. THE STUDENT IN EACH CLASS WITH THE HIGHEST GRADE POINT AVERAGE WILL TEACH THAT CLASS. THIS MEANS THE NEW TEACHER FOR MRS. KRABAPPEL'S CLASS IS...

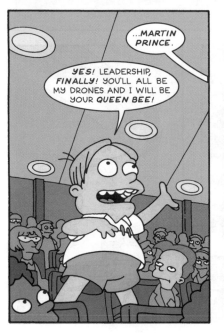

...MARTIN PRINCE.

YES! LEADERSHIP, *FINALLY!* YOU'LL ALL BE MY DRONES AND I WILL BE YOUR *QUEEN BEE!*

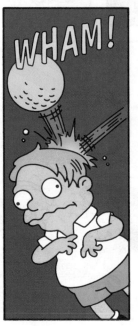

WHAM!

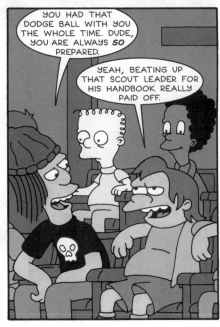

YOU HAD THAT DODGE BALL WITH YOU THE WHOLE TIME. DUDE, YOU ARE ALWAYS *SO* PREPARED.

YEAH, BEATING UP THAT SCOUT LEADER FOR HIS HANDBOOK REALLY PAID OFF.

AND THE NEW TEACHER FOR MISS HOOVER'S CLASS WILL BE LISA SIMPSON.
GASP!
THE REST OF THE LISTINGS WILL BE POSTED AS SOON AS WE GET THE MIMEOGRAPH MACHINE WORKING AGAIN.
LITTLE HELP?
LATER...
TO SCAR WITH LOVE
I AM YOUR NEW TEACHER
MR. SCRATCHY
SQUEAK! SQUEAK!
SSSS!

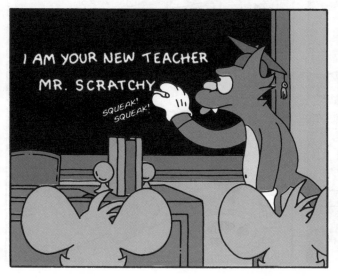

PSST!
AAAAAAH!
STING!
STING!
I AM Y
NEW T
THWIP!
GRIND!
GRIND!

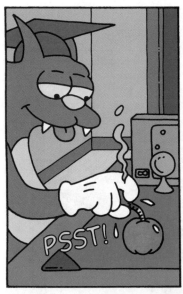

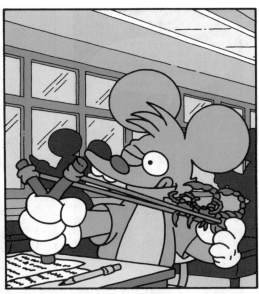

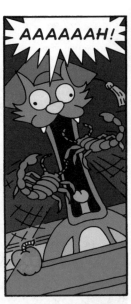

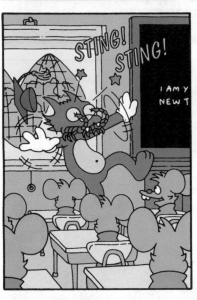

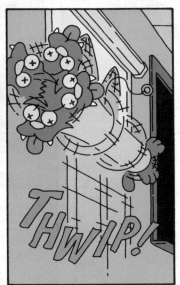

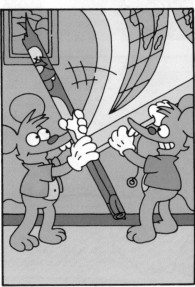

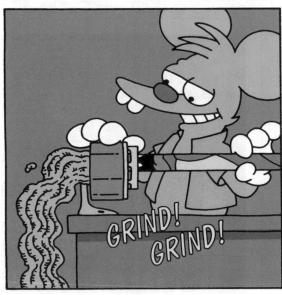

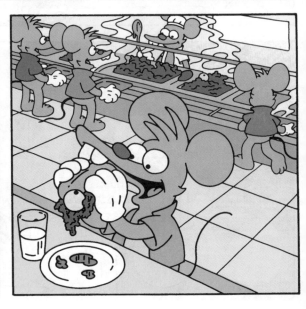

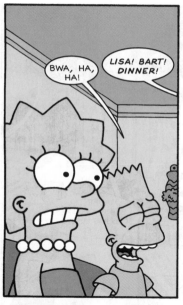

BWA, HA, HA!

LISA! BART! *DINNER!*

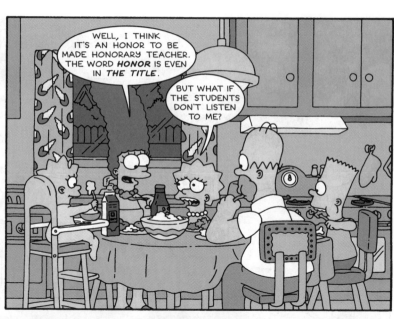

WELL, I THINK IT'S AN HONOR TO BE MADE HONORARY TEACHER. THE WORD *HONOR* IS EVEN IN *THE TITLE.*

BUT WHAT IF THE STUDENTS DON'T LISTEN TO ME?

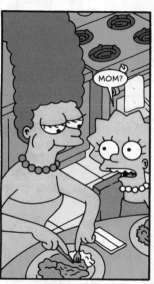

MOM?

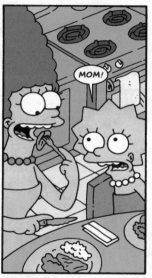

MOM!

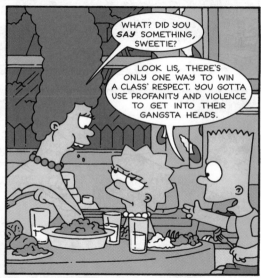

WHAT? DID YOU *SAY* SOMETHING, SWEETIE?

LOOK LIS, THERE'S ONLY ONE WAY TO WIN A CLASS' RESPECT. YOU GOTTA USE PROFANITY AND VIOLENCE TO GET INTO THEIR GANGSTA HEADS.

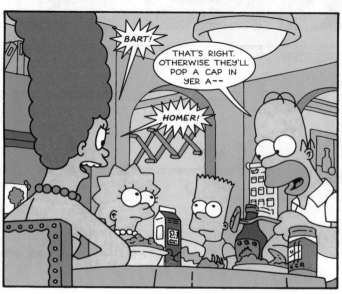

BART!

THAT'S RIGHT. OTHERWISE THEY'LL POP A CAP IN YER A--

HOMER!

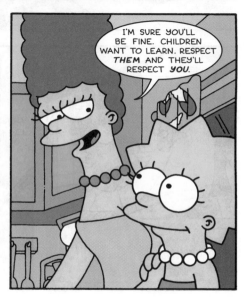

I'M SURE YOU'LL BE FINE. CHILDREN WANT TO LEARN. RESPECT *THEM* AND THEY'LL RESPECT *YOU.*

WISCONSIN CHEESE
SPRINGFIELD ELEM
ABANDON.. HOPE ALL YE WHO ENTER HEAR
MAYBE I'LL BRING UP THE SPELLING MISTAKE LATER.
GOOD MORNING, CLASS! LET'S UM... START WITH THE BASICS. WHO CAN TELL ME THE NAME OF OUR FIRST PRESIDENT?
HERE'S A HINT: HIS FIRST NAME WAS GEORGE.
KING GEORGE THE FIRST?
NO.
THEN WHY WAS HE CALLED THE FIRST?
HE WAS A **KING**. WE DON'T **HAVE** KINGS IN AMERICA.
SINCE WHEN?
BOOK!
SEPTEMBER

SINCE WHEN?!!
NO, WAIT, THAT'S A GOOD QUESTION.
WHEN DID WE DECIDE TO FREE OURSELVES FROM MONARCHICAL RULE?
OKAY! WHAT YEAR DID THE UNITED STATES BEGIN?
ONE.
ONE WHAT?
THE YEAR ONE. DUH!
I WONDER HOW MARTIN IS DOING?
I'VE ASKED YOU TO STAND ON YOUR DESKS FOR A REASON.
IT'S HARDER FOR US TO GET TO YOU?
THAT'S A SIDE BENEFIT, YES, BUT I ALSO WANT YOU TO OPEN YOUR MINDS TO THE POSSIBILITIES...

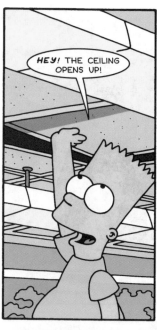

HEY! THE CEILING OPENS UP!

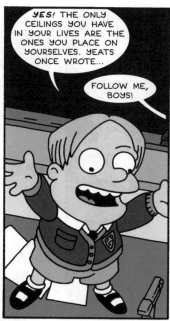

YES! THE ONLY CEILINGS YOU HAVE IN YOUR LIVES ARE THE ONES YOU PLACE ON YOURSELVES. YEATS ONCE WROTE...

FOLLOW ME, BOYS!

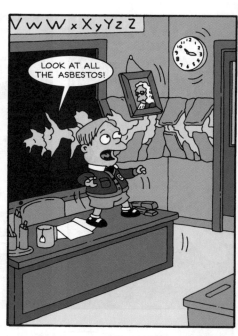

V w W x X y Y z Z

LOOK AT ALL THE ASBESTOS!

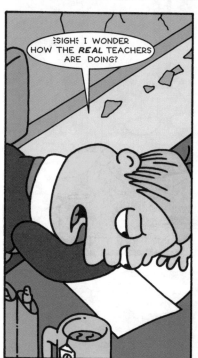

:SIGH: I WONDER HOW THE REAL TEACHERS ARE DOING?

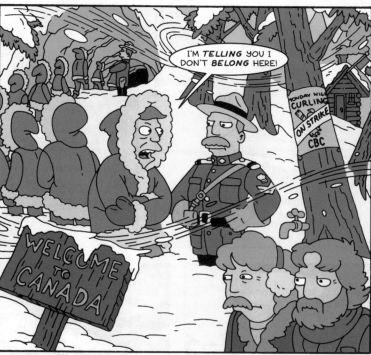

I'M TELLING YOU I DON'T BELONG HERE!

WELCOME TO CANADA

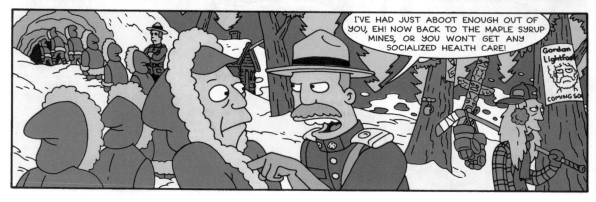

I'VE HAD JUST ABOOT ENOUGH OUT OF YOU, EH! NOW BACK TO THE MAPLE SYRUP MINES, OR YOU WON'T GET ANY SOCIALIZED HEALTH CARE!

OKAY, ONE MORE TIME. BRAZIL ISN'T A U.S. STATE.
THAT'S NOT PART OF THE UNITED STATES!
IT'S IN SOUTH AMERICA!
BUT NEW MEXICO IS?
GIVE AH HOOT READ AH BOOK!
CUCKOO!
OKAY, IT'S TIME FOR GYM. GO RUN AROUND...
...THE TOWN.
YAY!
RALPH, AM I A BAD TEACHER?
I DON'T GO TO GYM ANYMORE BECAUSE OF THE ACCIDENT WITH THE BASKETBALL PUMP.
NO.
DO I HAVE TO GO TO GYM IF I SAY YES?
LISA, YOU'RE SMART. WHATEVER YOU WANT TO DO YOU CAN DO. YOU'RE LIKE YODA, ONLY PRETTIER!

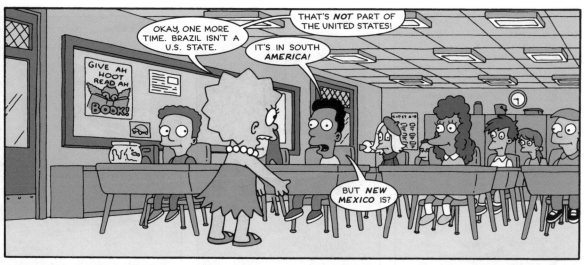

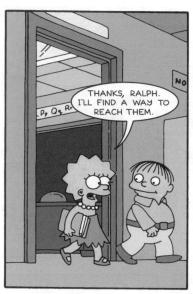

THANKS, RALPH. I'LL FIND A WAY TO REACH THEM.

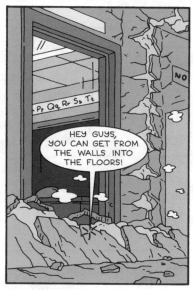

HEY GUYS, YOU CAN GET FROM THE WALLS INTO THE FLOORS!

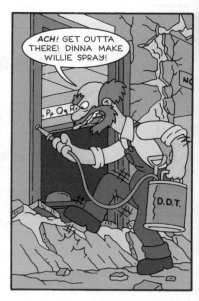

ACH! GET OUTTA THERE! DINNA MAKE WILLIE SPRAY!

D.D.T.

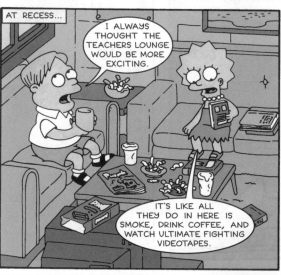

AT RECESS...

I ALWAYS THOUGHT THE TEACHERS LOUNGE WOULD BE MORE EXCITING.

IT'S LIKE ALL THEY DO IN HERE IS SMOKE, DRINK COFFEE, AND WATCH ULTIMATE FIGHTING VIDEOTAPES.

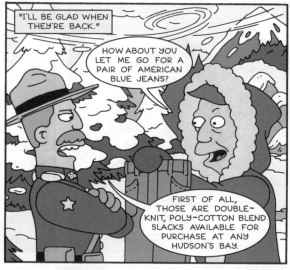

"I'LL BE GLAD WHEN THEY'RE BACK."

HOW ABOUT YOU LET ME GO FOR A PAIR OF AMERICAN BLUE JEANS?

FIRST OF ALL, THOSE ARE DOUBLE-KNIT, POLY-COTTON BLEND SLACKS AVAILABLE FOR PURCHASE AT ANY HUDSON'S BAY.

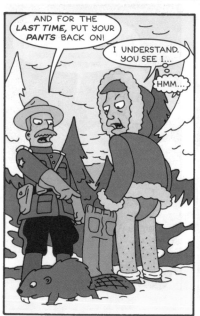

AND FOR THE LAST TIME, PUT YOUR PANTS BACK ON!

I UNDERSTAND. YOU SEE I...

HMM...

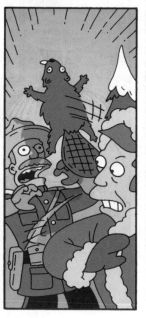

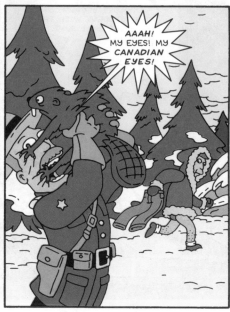

AAAH! MY EYES! MY CANADIAN EYES!

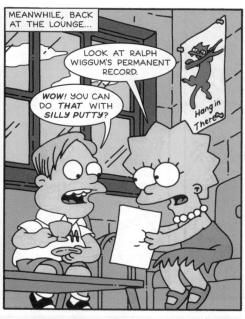

MEANWHILE, BACK AT THE LOUNGE...

LOOK AT RALPH WIGGUM'S PERMANENT RECORD.

WOW! YOU CAN DO *THAT* WITH *SILLY PUTTY?*

Hang in There

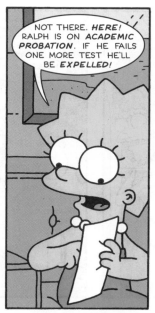

NOT THERE. *HERE!* RALPH IS ON *ACADEMIC PROBATION.* IF HE FAILS ONE MORE TEST HE'LL BE *EXPELLED!*

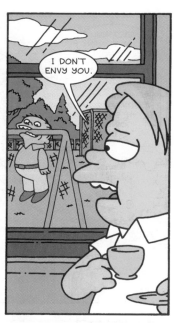

I DON'T ENVY YOU.

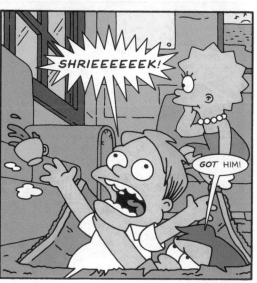

SHRIEEEEEEEK!

GOT HIM!

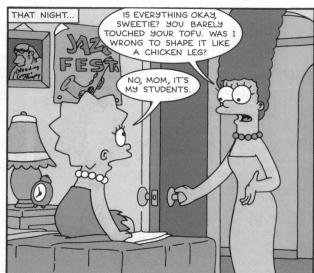

THAT NIGHT...

IS EVERYTHING OKAY, SWEETIE? YOU BARELY TOUCHED YOUR TOFU. WAS I WRONG TO SHAPE IT LIKE A CHICKEN LEG?

NO, MOM, IT'S MY STUDENTS.

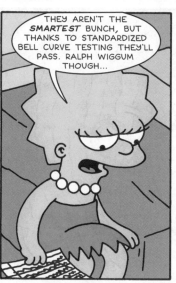

THEY AREN'T THE *SMARTEST* BUNCH, BUT THANKS TO STANDARDIZED BELL CURVE TESTING THEY'LL PASS. RALPH WIGGUM THOUGH...

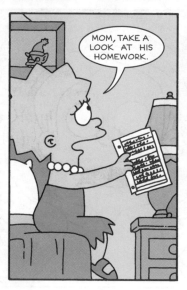

MOM, TAKE A LOOK AT HIS HOMEWORK.

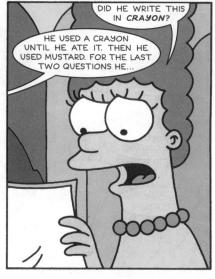

DID HE WRITE THIS IN *CRAYON?*

HE USED A CRAYON UNTIL HE ATE IT. THEN HE USED MUSTARD. FOR THE LAST TWO QUESTIONS HE...

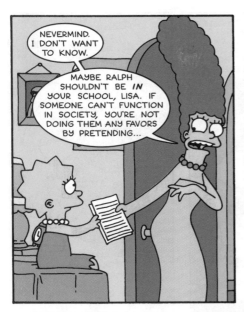

NEVERMIND. I DON'T WANT TO KNOW.

MAYBE RALPH SHOULDN'T BE *IN* YOUR SCHOOL, LISA. IF SOMEONE CAN'T FUNCTION IN SOCIETY, YOU'RE NOT DOING THEM ANY FAVORS BY PRETENDING...

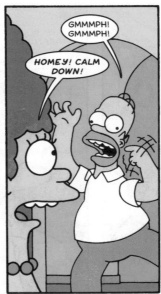

GMMMPH! GMMMPH!

HOMEY! CALM DOWN!

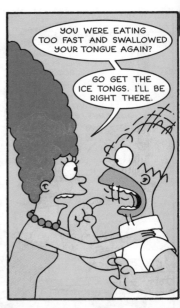

YOU WERE EATING TOO FAST AND SWALLOWED YOUR TONGUE AGAIN?

GO GET THE ICE TONGS. I'LL BE RIGHT THERE.

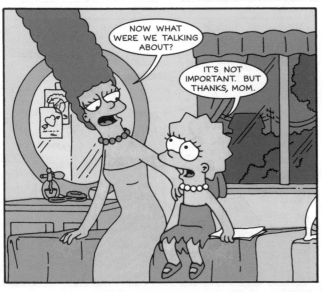

NOW WHAT WERE WE TALKING ABOUT?

IT'S NOT IMPORTANT. BUT THANKS, MOM.

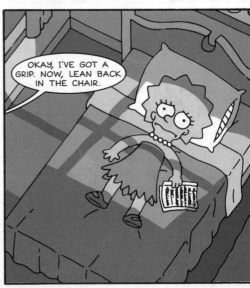

OKAY, I'VE GOT A GRIP. NOW, LEAN BACK IN THE CHAIR.

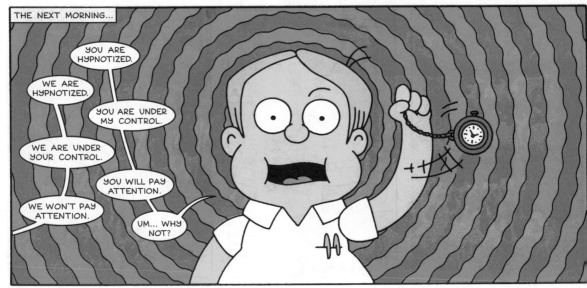

THE NEXT MORNING...

YOU ARE HYPNOTIZED.

WE ARE HYPNOTIZED.

YOU ARE UNDER MY CONTROL.

WE ARE UNDER YOUR CONTROL.

YOU WILL PAY ATTENTION.

WE WON'T PAY ATTENTION.

UM... WHY NOT?

WE'RE JUST LULLING YOU INTO A FALSE SENSE OF SECURITY.
NOW, RALPH, THE OTHER KIDS'LL BE BACK FROM GYM SOON. I WANT TO HELP YOU CRAM FOR TOMORROW'S TEST.
SHRIEEEEEEK!
I'M NOT ALLOWED TO CRAM ANYMORE SINCE I HAD TO GET MY NOSE PUMPED.
LET'S START WITH MATH.
MATH MAKES MY BRAIN STING.
25
+5
C'MON, RALPH. YOU CAN DO IT.
NO, I CAN'T.
RALPH, IF YOU FAIL THIS TEST YOU'LL BE EXPELLED. JUST TRY TO ANSWER.
IT'S...IT'S...
BUMP!
THREE HUNDRED AND SEVENTY TWO.
RALPH! YOU JUST COUNTED THOSE TOOTHPICKS! MAYBE THAT'S THE PROBLEM. YOU ARE A SAVANT. A REPRESSED GENIUS!
TOOTHPICKS?
YOU WERE ANSWERING THE QUESTION ON THE BOARD WEREN'T YOU RALPH?
SIGH
25
+5

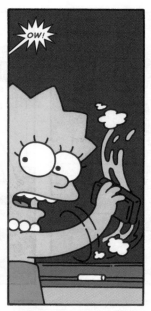

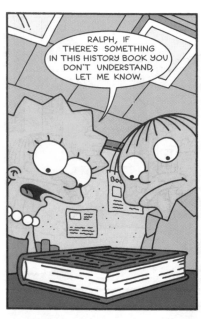

RALPH, IF THERE'S SOMETHING IN THIS HISTORY BOOK YOU DON'T UNDERSTAND, LET ME KNOW.

OW!

A QUICK AMBULANCE RIDE LATER...

AH, HEH, HEH, HEH! NEVER SEEN ANYTHING LIKE IT. 25 SIMULTANEOUS SECOND DEGREE PAPER CUTS.

WHY, IF I DIDN'T KNOW BETTER, I'D SAY THIS YOUNG MAN NEVER HELD A BOOK BEFORE.

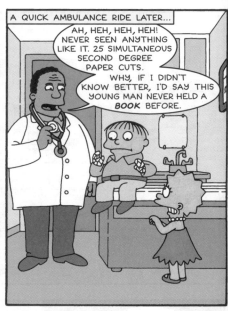

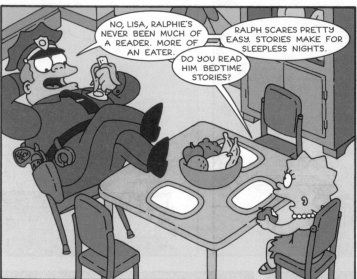

NO, LISA, RALPHIE'S NEVER BEEN MUCH OF A READER. MORE OF AN EATER.

DO YOU READ HIM BEDTIME STORIES?

RALPH SCARES PRETTY EASY. STORIES MAKE FOR SLEEPLESS NIGHTS.

I DON'T KNOW WHAT MADE HIM SO HIGH-STRUNG.

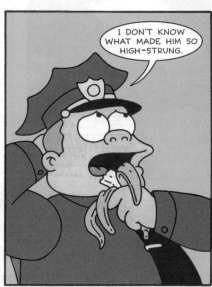

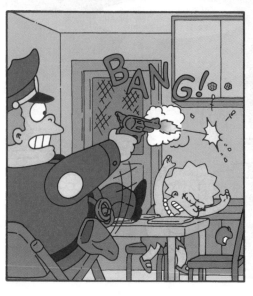

BANG!

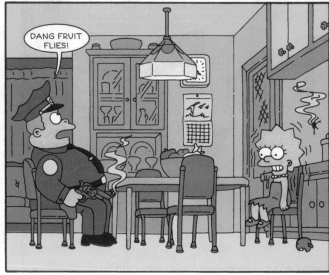

DANG FRUIT FLIES!

WHAT ARE YOU LOOKING AT, RALPH?
KRUSTY THE CLOWN.
BUT...THE TV IS OFF.
I'VE SEEN IT BEFORE SO I'M PLAYING IT IN MY HEAD. THAT WAY I CAN CHANGE THE COLORS AND MAKE THINGS MELT.
YOU REALLY REMEMBER THE WHOLE SHOW, RALPH?
YEP. NOW SHHHHH! ITCHY'S SHOOTING SCORPIONS AT SCRATCHY.
THE NEXT DAY...
SURE YOU CAN BORROW MY VIDEO CAMERA FOR YOUR CLASS PROJECT, LISA.
AND, UH...HERE'S A TAPE YOUR PARENTS SHOT AND LEFT IN THE CAMERA THE LAST TIME THEY BORROWED IT.
IS IT HOME MOVIES?
WELL... KIND OF.
I LOVE HOME MOVIES. I'LL WATCH IT WHEN I GET HOME.
NO!
I MEAN, JUST GIVE THEM THIS $5 TO REPLACE THE BROKEN TAPE.
BUT THAT TAPE'S NOT BROKEN.
OOPS! JUST CALL ME BUTTERFINGERLY-DINGLY.

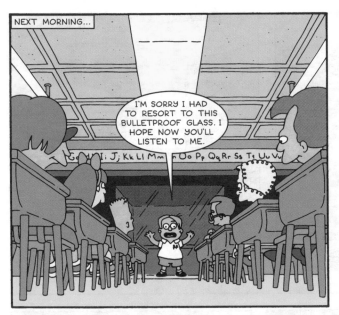

NEXT MORNING...

I'M SORRY I HAD TO RESORT TO THIS BULLETPROOF GLASS. I HOPE NOW YOU'LL LISTEN TO ME.

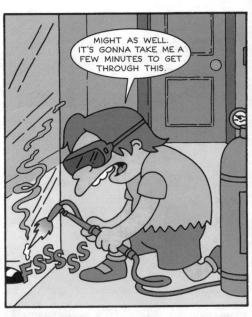

MIGHT AS WELL. IT'S GONNA TAKE ME A FEW MINUTES TO GET THROUGH THIS.

FSSSS

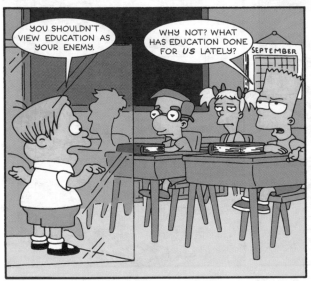

YOU SHOULDN'T VIEW EDUCATION AS YOUR ENEMY.

WHY NOT? WHAT HAS EDUCATION DONE FOR *US* LATELY?

SEPTEMBER

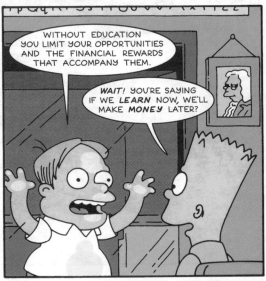

WITHOUT EDUCATION YOU LIMIT YOUR OPPORTUNITIES AND THE FINANCIAL REWARDS THAT ACCOMPANY THEM.

WAIT! YOU'RE SAYING IF WE *LEARN* NOW, WE'LL MAKE *MONEY* LATER?

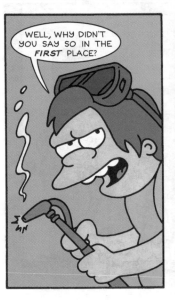

WELL, WHY DIDN'T YOU SAY SO IN THE *FIRST* PLACE?

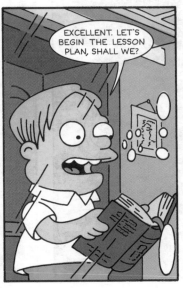

EXCELLENT. LET'S BEGIN THE LESSON PLAN, SHALL WE?

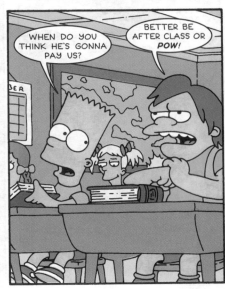

WHEN DO YOU THINK HE'S GONNA PAY US?

BETTER BE AFTER CLASS OR *POW!*

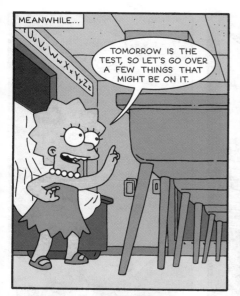

MEANWHILE...

TOMORROW IS THE TEST, SO LET'S GO OVER A FEW THINGS THAT MIGHT BE ON IT.

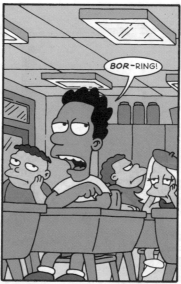

BOR-RING!

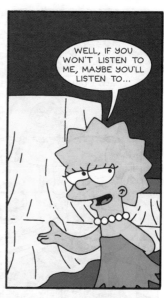

WELL, IF YOU WON'T LISTEN TO ME, MAYBE YOU'LL LISTEN TO...

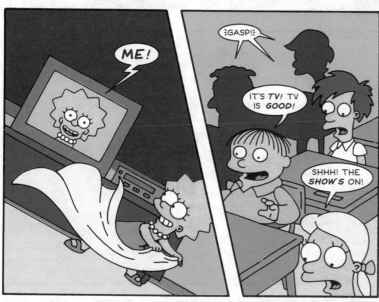

ME!

:GASP!:

IT'S TV! TV IS GOOD!

SHHH! THE SHOW'S ON!

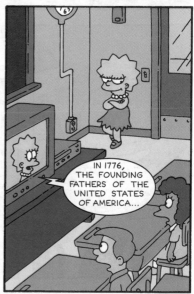

IN 1776, THE FOUNDING FATHERS OF THE UNITED STATES OF AMERICA...

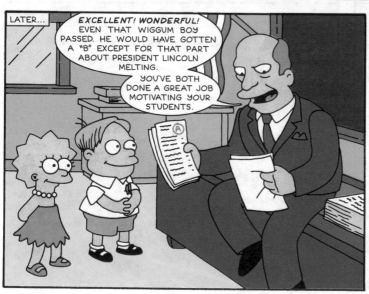

LATER...

EXCELLENT! WONDERFUL! EVEN THAT WIGGUM BOY PASSED. HE WOULD HAVE GOTTEN A "B" EXCEPT FOR THAT PART ABOUT PRESIDENT LINCOLN MELTING.

YOU'VE BOTH DONE A GREAT JOB MOTIVATING YOUR STUDENTS.

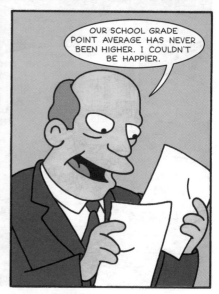

OUR SCHOOL GRADE POINT AVERAGE HAS NEVER BEEN HIGHER. I COULDN'T BE HAPPIER.

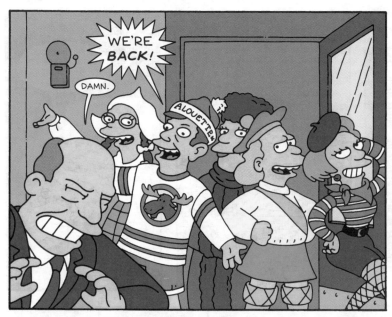

WE'RE *BACK!*

DAMN.

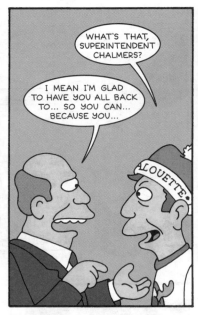

WHAT'S THAT, SUPERINTENDENT CHALMERS?

I MEAN I'M GLAD TO HAVE YOU ALL BACK TO... SO YOU CAN... BECAUSE YOU...

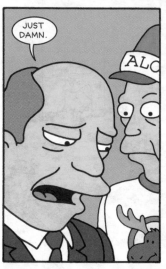

JUST DAMN.

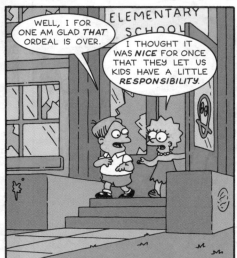

WELL, I FOR ONE AM GLAD *THAT* ORDEAL IS OVER.

I THOUGHT IT WAS *NICE* FOR ONCE THAT THEY LET US KIDS HAVE A LITTLE *RESPONSIBILITY.*

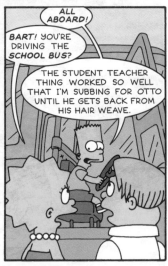

ALL ABOARD!

BART! YOU'RE DRIVING THE *SCHOOL BUS?*

THE STUDENT TEACHER THING WORKED SO WELL THAT I'M SUBBING FOR OTTO UNTIL HE GETS BACK FROM HIS HAIR WEAVE.

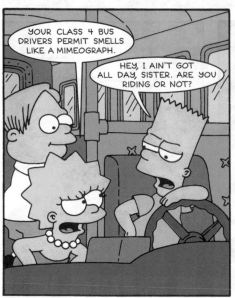

YOUR CLASS 4 BUS DRIVERS PERMIT SMELLS LIKE A MIMEOGRAPH.

HEY, I AIN'T GOT ALL DAY, SISTER. ARE YOU RIDING OR NOT?

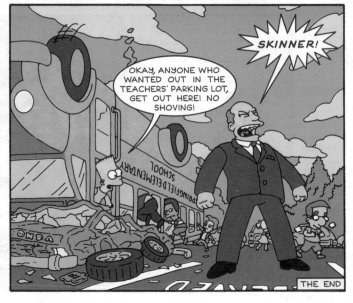

SKINNER!

OKAY, ANYONE WHO WANTED OUT IN THE TEACHERS' PARKING LOT, GET OUT HERE! NO SHOVING!

THE END

BARTMAN IN IDENTITY CRISIS

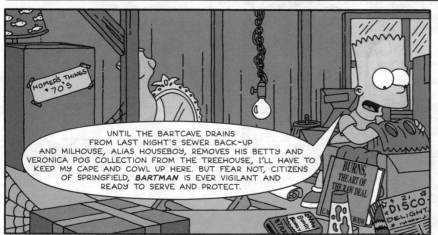

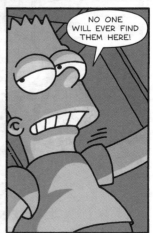

NO ONE WILL EVER FIND THEM HERE!

UNTIL THE BARTCAVE DRAINS FROM LAST NIGHT'S SEWER BACK-UP AND MILHOUSE, ALIAS HOUSEBOY, REMOVES HIS BETTY AND VERONICA POG COLLECTION FROM THE TREEHOUSE, I'LL HAVE TO KEEP MY CAPE AND COWL UP HERE. BUT FEAR NOT, CITIZENS OF SPRINGFIELD, *BARTMAN* IS EVER VIGILANT AND READY TO SERVE AND PROTECT.

HOMER'S THINGS '70S

BURNS, THE ART OF THE RAW DEAL

21 DISCO DELIGHT

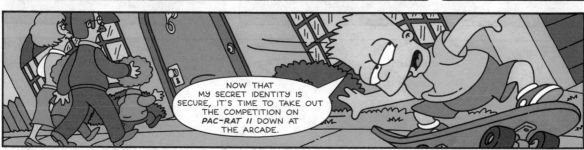

NOW THAT MY SECRET IDENTITY IS SECURE, IT'S TIME TO TAKE OUT THE COMPETITION ON *PAC-RAT II* DOWN AT THE ARCADE.

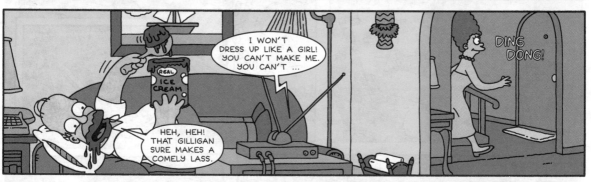

I WON'T DRESS UP LIKE A GIRL! YOU CAN'T MAKE ME. YOU CAN'T ...

REAL ICE CREAM

HEH, HEH! THAT GILLIGAN SURE MAKES A COMELY LASS.

DING DONG!

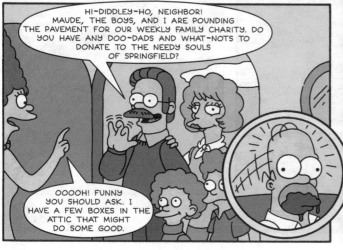

HI-DIDDLEY-HO, NEIGHBOR! MAUDE, THE BOYS, AND I ARE POUNDING THE PAVEMENT FOR OUR WEEKLY FAMILY CHARITY. DO YOU HAVE ANY DOO-DADS AND WHAT-NOTS TO DONATE TO THE NEEDY SOULS OF SPRINGFIELD?

OOOOH! FUNNY YOU SHOULD ASK. I HAVE A FEW BOXES IN THE ATTIC THAT MIGHT DO SOME GOOD.

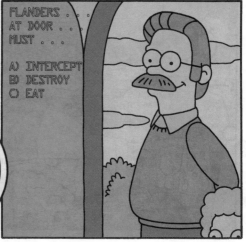

FLANDERS . . . AT DOOR . . . MUST . . .

A) INTERCEPT
B) DESTROY
C) EAT

CAN I CARRY A BOX FOR THE DOWNTRODDEN?
OF COURSE, LITTLE SOLDIER. JUST REMEMBER: HIS YOKE IS EASY, AND HIS BURDEN IS LIGHT.
WELCOME
FLANDERS, JUST WHERE DO YOU THINK YOU'RE GOING?
HOW-DO, HOMER. MARGE DONATED THESE WONDERFUL KNICK-KNACKS . . .
THAT HAPPENS TO BE MY STUFF.
BUT, HOMER . . . IT'S FOR THE PENNILESS.
SOOO . . . MY STUFF'S NOT GOOD ENOUGH FOR RESPECTABLE PEOPLE, EH?
YOU CAN HAVE WHAT'S LEFT, FLANDERS. MY COMPLIMENTS TO THE DESTITUTE!
DUKAKIS BENTSEN '88
Rich Man, Poor Wife
A Guide to Divorce
by Lionel Hutz
FOAMY STRING
SOON. . .
KNEAD! KNEAD!
MMMM... LAVA-EY!
On the Mend: The Daredevil Lance Murdock Story
BRIEFS IN A TUBE
MARGE, HOLD STILL! YOU'RE MAKING MY BRAIN THROB.
HMMM! HOMER SIMPSON, YOU'VE EMBARRASSED THE SIMPSON FAMILY FOR WHAT I CAN ONLY DREAM IS THE LAST TIME. THERE ARE GOING TO BE SOME CHANGES MADE, AND YOU CAN START BY WASHING THAT DIRTY OLD CAR!

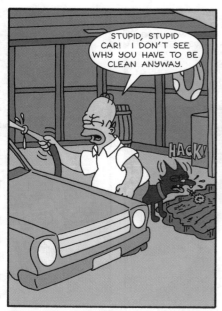

STUPID, STUPID CAR! I DON'T SEE WHY YOU HAVE TO BE CLEAN ANYWAY.

HACK!

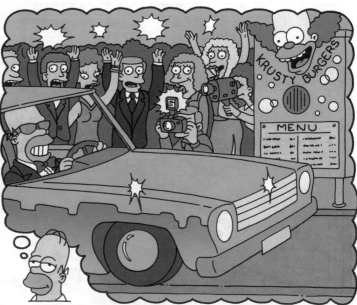

KRUSTY BURGERS

MENU

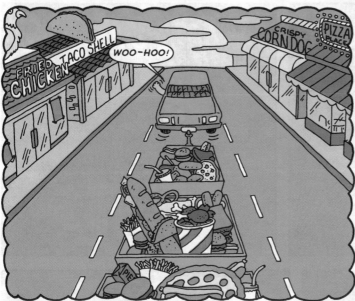

FRIED CHICKEN

TACO SHELL

WOO-HOO!

CRISPY CORNDOG

PIZZA PLACE

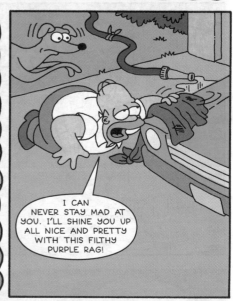

I CAN NEVER STAY MAD AT YOU. I'LL SHINE YOU UP ALL NICE AND PRETTY WITH THIS FILTHY PURPLE RAG!

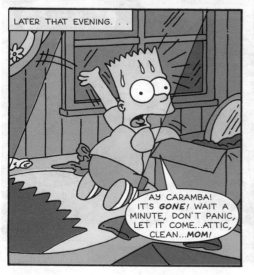

LATER THAT EVENING. . .

AY CARAMBA! IT'S **GONE**! WAIT A MINUTE, DON'T PANIC, LET IT COME...ATTIC, CLEAN...**MOM**!

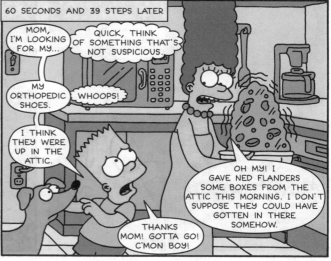

60 SECONDS AND 39 STEPS LATER

MOM, I'M LOOKING FOR MY...

QUICK, THINK OF SOMETHING THAT'S NOT SUSPICIOUS.

MY ORTHOPEDIC SHOES.

WHOOPS!

I THINK THEY WERE UP IN THE ATTIC.

OH MY! I GAVE NED FLANDERS SOME BOXES FROM THE ATTIC THIS MORNING. I DON'T SUPPOSE THEY COULD HAVE GOTTEN IN THERE SOMEHOW.

THANKS MOM! GOTTA GO! C'MON BOY!

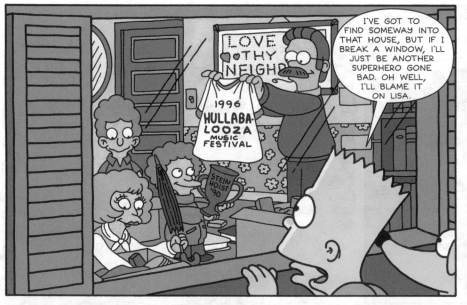

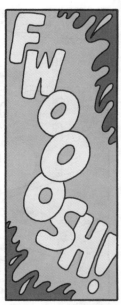

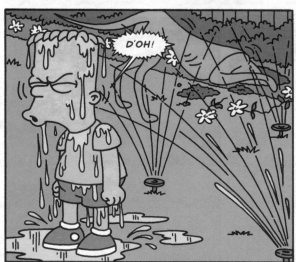

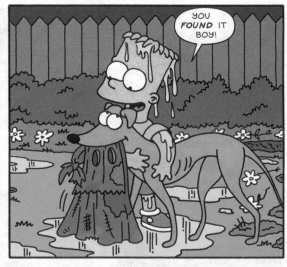

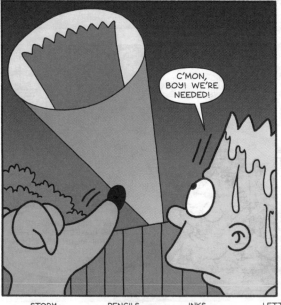

THE END

STORY
TERRY DELEGEANE

PENCILS
PHIL ORTIZ

INKS
TIM BAVINGTON

LETTERS
KAREN BATES

COLORS
NATHAN KANE

EDITOR
BILL MORRISON

BOY WONDER
MATT GROENING

HOT DOG ON A SCHTICK!
BONGO COMICS GROUP
SIMPSONS™ COMICS
#45
US $2.50
CAN $3.50
APPROVED BY THE COMICS CODE AUTHORITY
THE SIMPSONS ©&TM TWENTIETH CENTURY FOX FILM CORPORATION. ALL RIGHTS RESERVED

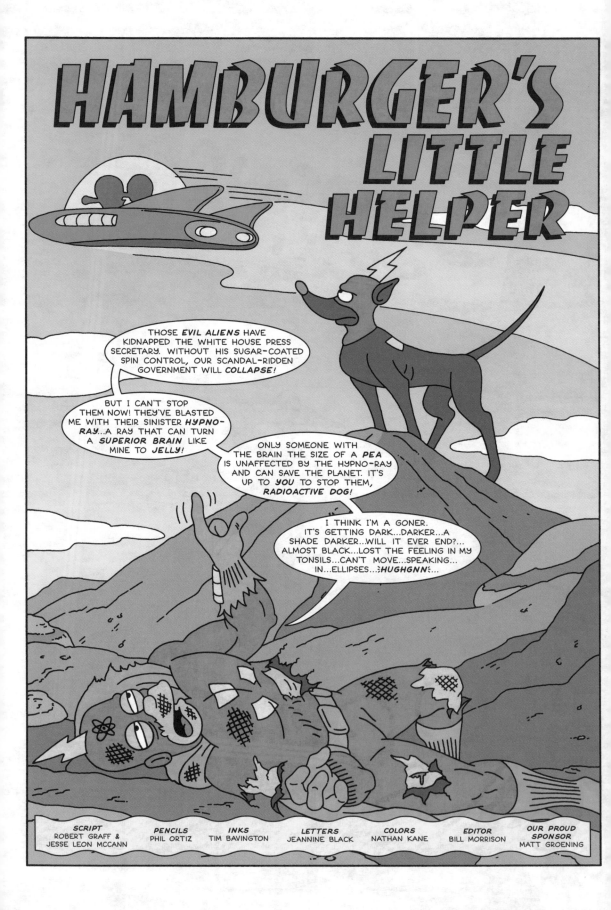

HAMBURGER'S LITTLE HELPER

THOSE *EVIL ALIENS* HAVE KIDNAPPED THE WHITE HOUSE PRESS SECRETARY. WITHOUT HIS SUGAR-COATED SPIN CONTROL, OUR SCANDAL-RIDDEN GOVERNMENT WILL *COLLAPSE!*

BUT I CAN'T STOP THEM NOW! THEY'VE BLASTED ME WITH THEIR SINISTER *HYPNO-RAY*...A RAY THAT CAN TURN A *SUPERIOR BRAIN* LIKE MINE TO *JELLY!*

ONLY SOMEONE WITH THE BRAIN THE SIZE OF A *PEA* IS UNAFFECTED BY THE HYPNO-RAY AND CAN SAVE THE PLANET. IT'S UP TO *YOU* TO STOP THEM, *RADIOACTIVE DOG!*

I THINK I'M A GONER. IT'S GETTING DARK...DARKER...A SHADE DARKER...WILL IT EVER END?... ALMOST BLACK...LOST THE FEELING IN MY TONSILS...CAN'T MOVE...SPEAKING... IN...ELLIPSES...GHUGHGNN§...

SCRIPT ROBERT GRAFF & JESSE LEON McCANN	**PENCILS** PHIL ORTIZ	**INKS** TIM BAVINGTON	**LETTERS** JEANNINE BLACK	**COLORS** NATHAN KANE	**EDITOR** BILL MORRISON	**OUR PROUD SPONSOR** MATT GROENING

OH, WAIT... IT'S GETTING LIGHTER NOW...NO, DARKER...NO, LIGHT...DARK...LIGHT...LIGHTER... I THINK I'LL SURVIVE!
DID YOU HEAR THAT, BOY? YOUR MASTER IS GOING TO BE OKAY!
RADIOACTIVE DOG?
HMMMM, HE WENT ON WITHOUT ME.
CONFOUND IT! THAT PESKY MUTT IS AFTER US!
NO MATTER! RELEASE COUNTER MEASURES!
IT'S NO USE! HE'S GAINING ON US!
BLAM!
KA-BOOM!
BA-BAM!
THANK GOODNESS! IT'S RADIOACTIVE DOG!
WAP!
OUR HYPNO-RAY IS USELESS AGAINST HIM. BLAST THAT PEA-SIZE BRAIN OF HIS!
STAY, BOY. HEEL! HEEL!
DOWN, BOY!
CHAKK!

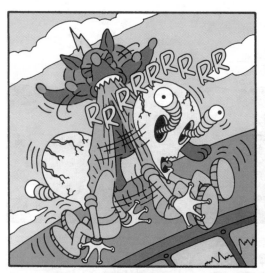

RRRRRRRR

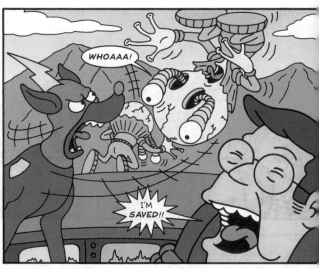

WHOAAA!

I'M SAVED!!

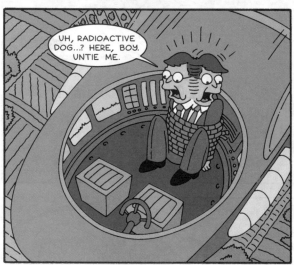

UH, RADIOACTIVE DOG...? HERE, BOY. UNTIE ME.

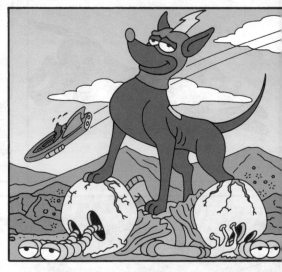

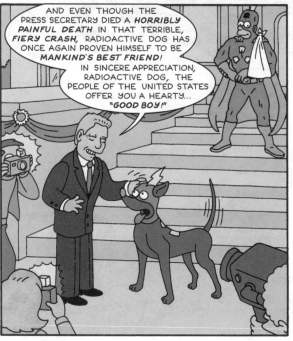

AND EVEN THOUGH THE PRESS SECRETARY DIED A *HORRIBLY PAINFUL DEATH* IN THAT TERRIBLE, *FIERY CRASH,* RADIOACTIVE DOG HAS ONCE AGAIN PROVEN HIMSELF TO BE *MANKIND'S BEST FRIEND!*
IN SINCERE APPRECIATION, RADIOACTIVE DOG, THE PEOPLE OF THE UNITED STATES OFFER YOU A HEARTY... *"GOOD BOY!"*

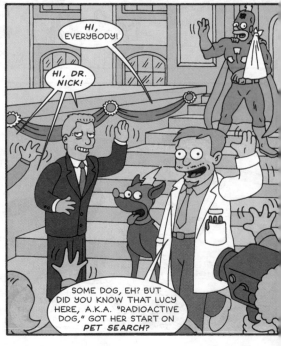

HI, EVERYBODY!

HI, DR. NICK!

SOME DOG, EH? BUT DID YOU KNOW THAT LUCY HERE, A.K.A. "RADIOACTIVE DOG," GOT HER START ON *PET SEARCH?*

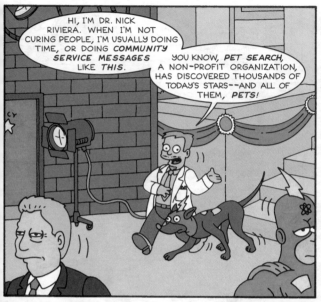

HI, I'M DR. NICK RIVIERA. WHEN I'M NOT CURING PEOPLE, I'M USUALLY DOING TIME, OR DOING *COMMUNITY SERVICE MESSAGES* LIKE *THIS*.

YOU KNOW, *PET SEARCH*, A NON-PROFIT ORGANIZATION, HAS DISCOVERED THOUSANDS OF TODAY'S STARS--AND ALL OF THEM, *PETS*!

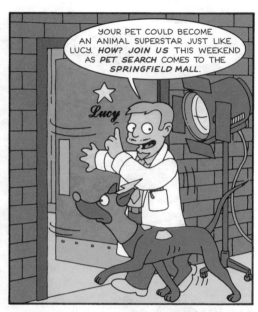

YOUR PET COULD BECOME AN ANIMAL SUPERSTAR JUST LIKE LUCY. *HOW? JOIN US* THIS WEEKEND AS *PET SEARCH* COMES TO THE *SPRINGFIELD MALL*.

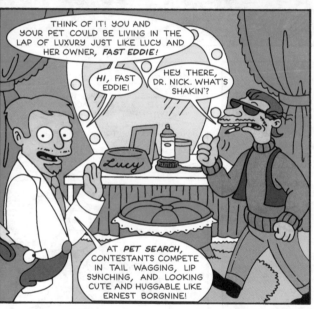

THINK OF IT! YOU AND YOUR PET COULD BE LIVING IN THE LAP OF LUXURY JUST LIKE LUCY AND HER OWNER, *FAST EDDIE!*

HI, FAST EDDIE!

HEY THERE, DR. NICK. WHAT'S SHAKIN'?

AT *PET SEARCH*, CONTESTANTS COMPETE IN TAIL WAGGING, LIP SYNCHING, AND LOOKING CUTE AND HUGGABLE LIKE ERNEST BORGNINE!

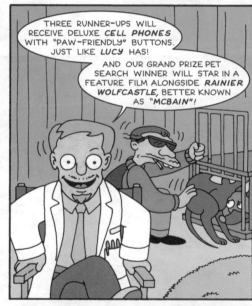

THREE RUNNER-UPS WILL RECEIVE DELUXE *CELL PHONES* WITH "PAW-FRIENDLY" BUTTONS. JUST LIKE *LUCY* HAS!

AND OUR GRAND PRIZE PET SEARCH WINNER WILL STAR IN A FEATURE FILM ALONGSIDE *RAINIER WOLFCASTLE*, BETTER KNOWN AS *"MCBAIN"!*

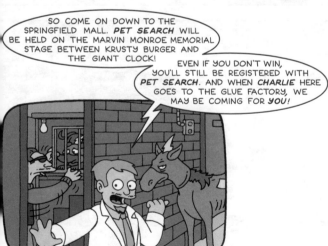

SO COME ON DOWN TO THE SPRINGFIELD MALL. *PET SEARCH* WILL BE HELD ON THE MARVIN MONROE MEMORIAL STAGE BETWEEN KRUSTY BURGER AND THE GIANT CLOCK!

EVEN IF YOU DON'T WIN, YOU'LL STILL BE REGISTERED WITH *PET SEARCH*. AND WHEN *CHARLIE* HERE GOES TO THE GLUE FACTORY, WE MAY BE COMING FOR *YOU!*

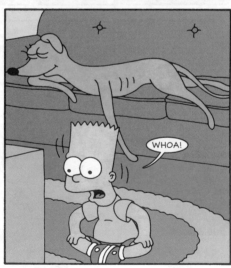

WHOA!

61

COME ON, BOY. WE'VE GOTTA BE FIRST IN LINE.
ACK COUGH
D'OH!
BUUURP!
MY KITTY TASTES LIKE CAT FOOD.
AAARG, 'TIS THE END OF THE LINE FOR YOU, MATEY.
IF YOU DON'T STOP SPOILING THAT ANIMAL, HE WONT EAT HIS FILET MIGNON FOR DINNER.
PET SEARCH
HI, EVERYBODY!
WELCOME TO PET SEARCH WHERE WE DISCOVER BIG STARS, AND WHERE I EARN COMMUNITY SERVICE CREDIT.
HI, DR. NICK!
AS YOU KNOW, THE PET SEARCH COMPETITION IS COMPOSED OF THREE RIGOROUS EVENTS, WITH CONTESTANTS CATEGORIZED BY THEIR ABILITIES AND TALENTS IN STRICT ACCORDANCE WITH PET SEARCH RULES!
BUT SINCE SO MANY OF YOU SHOWED UP TODAY, THE FIRE MARSHAL HAS GIVEN ME AN HOUR TO CLEAR THE PLACE. YOU EACH HAVE 10 SECONDS...STARTING NOW!
I'M A LI'L TEAPOT, SHORT AN' STOUT...
BURRRRP!
COME ON, BUDDY...YOU KNOW THE ROUTINE. DO IT FOR GIL! GIL NEEDS THIS GIG!

59 MINUTES LATER...
AT LAST! C'MON BOY, IT'S OUR TURN TO SHINE!
H-HURRY UP, BART! MY MONGOOSE GETS IRRITABLE IF HE DOESN'T GET HIS LUNCH ON TIME.
COOL, MAN! YOU BROUGHT A MONGOOSE? WHAT A COINCIDENCE...
GROWL!
HISSSSS!
...'CAUSE I BROUGHT MY COBRA!
IT SAYS HERE YOUR DOG DOES IMPRESSIONS! IS THAT RIGHT, SON?
THAT'S RIGHT, SIR. HERE'S HIS IMPRESSION OF CHEVY CHASE.
PANT PANT
HE'S GOOD! CAN HE DO FLORENCE HENDERSON, TOO?
YES, SIR!
I DON'T KNOW WHAT COULD POSSIBLY TOP THIS!
AYE, CARUMBA!
GROWL!
HISSSSS!
BARK!
AAAHOOOGA!
OINK!
HELLLLLP! SEND BACK-UP.
HONK!
MOO!
WHINNY!

KRUSTY, THIS COMMERCIAL MUST HAVE SOMETHING DIFFERENT --SOMETHING SPECIAL. WE WANT PEOPLE TO SAY, "I'LL DIE WITHOUT A KRUSTY BURGER!"
YEAH, YEAH, SURE. I'LL SAY WHATEVER YOU WANT. JUST DON'T MAKE ME EAT ONE OF THESE THINGS.
TV
AND ACTION!
HEY, HEY, KIDS! HAS THIS EVER HAPPENED TO YOU?
YOU'RE MINDING YOUR OWN BUSINESS, THEN SUDDENLY BOOM! IT HITS YOU.
YOU'RE HUNGRY FOR SOMETHING GOOD TO EAT! THAT'S WHEN I SAY...
SINK YOUR TEETH INTO SOMETHING KRUSTY!
CHOMP!
YEOWCH!
AND CUT!
THEY'RE COOL. THEY'RE TODAY!
PURE GENIUS, KRUSTY, THROWING A DOG IN LIKE THAT. DOGS ARE HIP.
UH, YEAH. CAN SOMEBODY REMOVE THIS MUTT.
OF COURSE, BUT FIRST LET'S PLAY THAT BACK ON THE OUTSIDE MONITORS.
THERE SEEMS TO BE A LARGE, AGITATED CROWD OUT THERE--THE PERFECT CHANCE FOR SOME INSTANT, UNSOLICITED TEST MARKETING!

SINK YOUR TEETH INTO SOMETHING KRUSTY!
YEOOWWWCH!
PET ROCK EMPORIUM
THAT COMMERCIAL IS FUN-DIDDILY-FUNNY!
I'M NIGEL, STAR DISCOVERER, FORTUNE MAKER, AND HAT BLOCKER. NO CLIENT TOO BIG OR TOO SMALL! PETS ARE MY SPECIALTY!
I THINK WE HAVE A HIT ON OUR HANDS.
HA-HA!
JA, DAS GOOD! NOW I'M EVEN HUNGRIER!
OH, NO! MY MONGOOSE IS LOOSE, AND HE HASN'T HAD HIS SHOTS!
I CAN NEVER GET ENOUGH OF THAT TALKING HORSE!
BURRP!
WE'VE GOT TO SIGN THAT DOG! HE'S GOING TO MAKE US MILLIONS WITH THAT QUIRKY, GO-GETTER ATTITUDE!
WHY, HE'LL BE BIGGER THAN WEBSTER!
HOLD THE PHONE!
OY!
THERE YOU ARE, SANTA'S LITTLE HELPER! I WAS SO WORRIED ABOUT YOU, BOY!
ICE
SO HE'S YOUR DOG! WELL, HAVE WE GOT A STACK OF RELEASE FORMS FOR YOU!
HOLD IT! THERE WON'T BE ANY SIGNINGS UNTIL WE TALK MONEY. ALLOW ME TO INTRODUCE MYSELF. I'M NIGEL, AGENT TO THE PET STARS.
I REPRESENT THIS BOY'S DOG HERE, SAMMY'S MIDDLE HOLSTER...
IT'S SANTA'S LITTLE HELPER.
...YES, OF COURSE IT IS. I WANT TO MAKE SURE MY CLIENT GETS HIS FAIR SHARE FOR BEING IN YOUR COMMERCIALS.
WE'LL GO TO MY OFFICE, SIGN A FEW CONTRACTS-- THEN I'LL DO ALL THE WORK WHILE YOU SPEND ALL YOUR PROFITS!
YOUNG BART, I THINK THIS IS THE START OF A BEAUTIFUL RELATIONSHIP!
COOL, MAN!

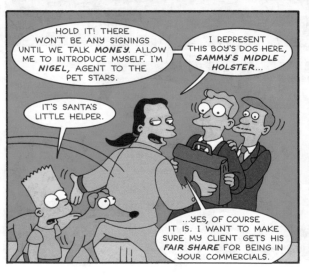

AND SO BEGINS THE SANTA'S LITTLE HELPER MEDIA BLITZ!

KENT BROCKMAN HERE WITH ARNIE PIE IN THE SKY. THE SPRINGFIELD AQUARIUM HAS *BURST* INTO FLAMES. WE ARE RACING THERE NOW AS PART OF A RESCUE ATTEMPT TO AIRLIFT *BABY BINGO* THE WHALE OUT OF THE FLAMES.

WHAT A TERRIBLE TRAGEDY, RIGHT, ARNIE?

YOU BETCHA, KENT. IT'S HORRIBLE TIMING. I'M SUPPOSED TO BE ON MY *LUNCH HOUR!*

WE'RE RIGHT ABOVE THE AQUARIUM NOW. THE SMOKE IS SO THICK, WE'VE LOST ALL VISUAL CONTACT.

NOT ONLY THAT, KENT, THIS FLAMING WHALE BLUBBER IS MAKING ME *HUNGRY.*

WE NEED HELP!

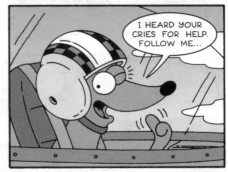

THANK GOODNESS, WE'RE *SAVED!*

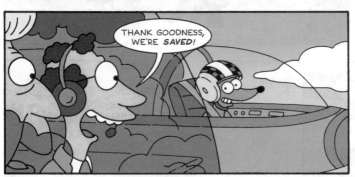

I HEARD YOUR CRIES FOR HELP. FOLLOW ME...

WOOO-YEAH!

...TO *KRUSTY BURGER!*

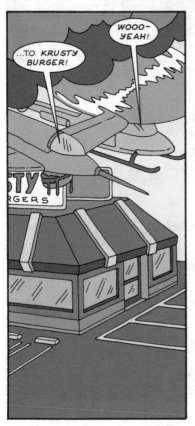

HEY, HEY, WHEN YOU'RE *LATE* FOR AN IMPORTANT DATE, AND YOU DON'T HAVE TIME TO *WAIT,* SINK YOUR TEETH INTO *SOMETHING KRUSTY!*

CHOMP!

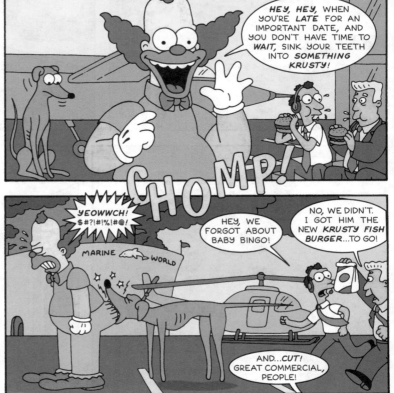

YEOWWCH! $#?!#!%!#@!

MARINE WORLD

HEY, WE FORGOT ABOUT BABY BINGO!

NO, WE DIDN'T. I GOT HIM THE NEW *KRUSTY FISH BURGER...*TO GO!

AND...*CUT!* GREAT COMMERCIAL, PEOPLE!

SANTA'S LITTLE HELPER'S COMMERCIALS ARE A BIG HIT--*REALLY* BIG--*MONTAGE* BIG!
GREAT TEETH, EH, PAUL? HEH, HEH, HEH.
SINK YOUR TEETH INTO SOMETHING KRUSTY
DAVID
...SOON, THE SIMPSON'S PET IS APPEARING ON EVERYTHING FROM T-SHIRTS TO TALK SHOWS!
SLH ON SNL
BEST USE OF BITTER IRONY IN A COMMERCIAL
GET THE JAWS OF LIFE--STAT!
...AND CAPTURING THE FICKLE, YET LUCRATIVE HEARTS OF THE NATION'S YOUTH.
Rolling Stone
THIS DOG'S COMMERCIAL REALLY BITES!
TACO BELL CHIHUAHUA: "Yo quiero career back!"
THIS WEEK, A VERY SPECIAL "ER"...

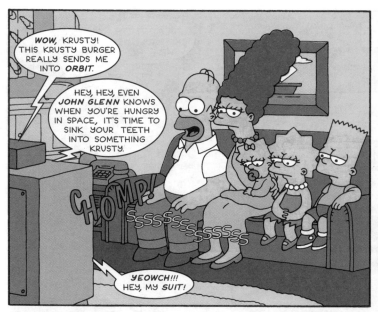

WOW, KRUSTY! THIS KRUSTY BURGER REALLY SENDS ME INTO *ORBIT.*

HEY, HEY, EVEN *JOHN GLENN* KNOWS WHEN YOU'RE HUNGRY IN SPACE, IT'S TIME TO SINK YOUR TEETH INTO SOMETHING KRUSTY.

CHOMP!

SSSSSSSSSSSS

YEOWCH!!! HEY, MY *SUIT!*

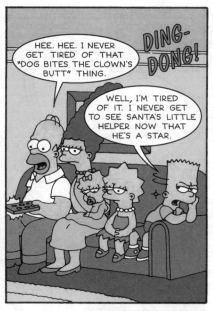

HEE. HEE. I NEVER GET TIRED OF THAT "DOG BITES THE CLOWN'S BUTT" THING.

WELL, I'M TIRED OF IT. I NEVER GET TO SEE SANTA'S LITTLE HELPER NOW THAT HE'S A STAR.

DING-DONG!

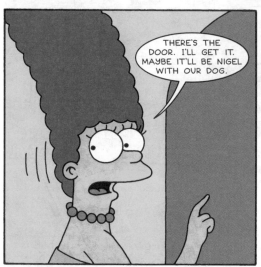

THERE'S THE DOOR. I'LL GET IT. MAYBE IT'LL BE NIGEL WITH OUR DOG.

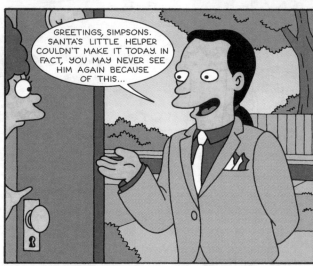

GREETINGS, SIMPSONS. SANTA'S LITTLE HELPER COULDN'T MAKE IT TODAY. IN FACT, YOU MAY NEVER SEE HIM AGAIN BECAUSE OF THIS...

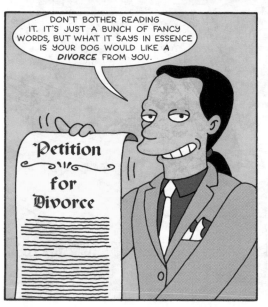

DON'T BOTHER READING IT. IT'S JUST A BUNCH OF FANCY WORDS, BUT WHAT IT SAYS IN ESSENCE IS YOUR DOG WOULD LIKE *A DIVORCE* FROM YOU.

Petition for Divorce

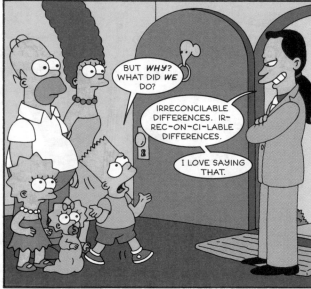

BUT *WHY*? WHAT DID *WE* DO?

IRRECONCILABLE DIFFERENCES. IR-REC-ON-CI-LABLE DIFFERENCES.

I LOVE SAYING THAT.

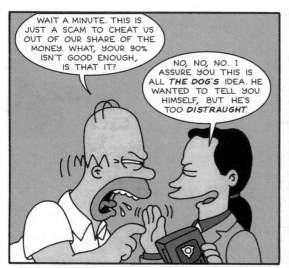

WAIT A MINUTE. THIS IS JUST A SCAM TO CHEAT US OUT OF OUR SHARE OF THE MONEY. WHAT, YOUR 90% ISN'T GOOD ENOUGH, IS THAT IT?

NO, NO, NO. I ASSURE YOU THIS IS ALL *THE DOG'S* IDEA. HE WANTED TO TELL YOU HIMSELF, BUT HE'S TOO *DISTRAUGHT*.

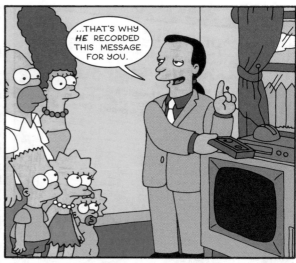

...THAT'S WHY *HE* RECORDED THIS MESSAGE FOR YOU.

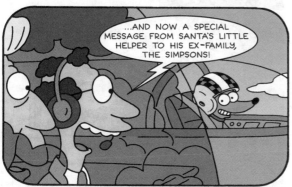

...AND NOW A SPECIAL MESSAGE FROM SANTA'S LITTLE HELPER TO HIS EX-FAMILY, THE SIMPSONS!

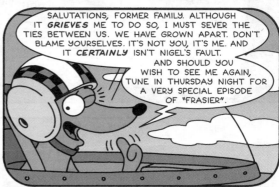

SALUTATIONS, FORMER FAMILY. ALTHOUGH IT *GRIEVES* ME TO DO SO, I MUST SEVER THE TIES BETWEEN US. WE HAVE GROWN APART. DON'T BLAME YOURSELVES. IT'S NOT YOU, IT'S ME. AND IT *CERTAINLY* ISN'T NIGEL'S FAULT. AND SHOULD YOU WISH TO SEE ME AGAIN, TUNE IN THURSDAY NIGHT FOR A VERY SPECIAL EPISODE OF "FRASIER".

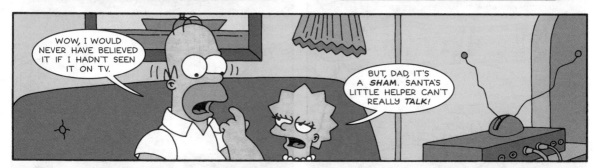

WOW, I WOULD NEVER HAVE BELIEVED IT IF I HADN'T SEEN IT ON TV.

BUT, DAD, IT'S A *SHAM*. SANTA'S LITTLE HELPER CAN'T REALLY *TALK*!

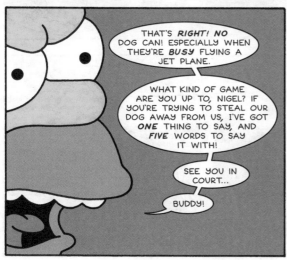

THAT'S *RIGHT!* *NO* DOG CAN! ESPECIALLY WHEN THEY'RE *BUSY* FLYING A JET PLANE.

WHAT KIND OF GAME ARE YOU UP TO, NIGEL? IF YOU'RE TRYING TO STEAL OUR DOG AWAY FROM US, I'VE GOT *ONE* THING TO SAY, AND *FIVE* WORDS TO SAY IT WITH!

SEE YOU IN COURT...

BUDDY!

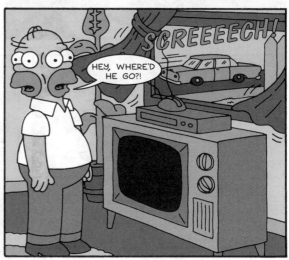

SCREEEECH!

HEY, WHERE'D HE GO?!

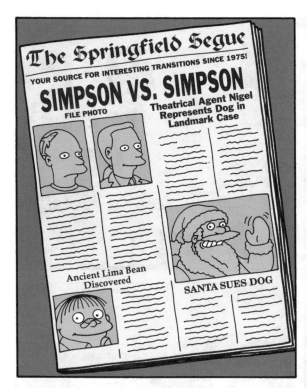

The Springfield Segue

YOUR SOURCE FOR INTERESTING TRANSITIONS SINCE 1975!

SIMPSON VS. SIMPSON

FILE PHOTO

Theatrical Agent Nigel Represents Dog in Landmark Case

Ancient Lima Bean Discovered

SANTA SUES DOG

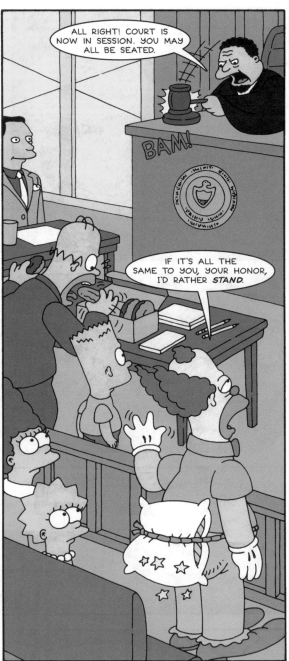

ALL RIGHT! COURT IS NOW IN SESSION. YOU MAY ALL BE SEATED.

BAM!

IF IT'S ALL THE SAME TO YOU, YOUR HONOR, I'D RATHER *STAND*.

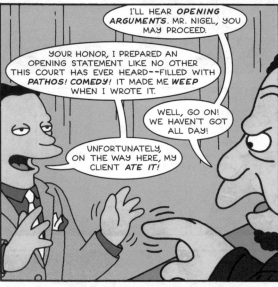

I'LL HEAR *OPENING ARGUMENTS*. MR. NIGEL, YOU MAY PROCEED.

YOUR HONOR, I PREPARED AN OPENING STATEMENT LIKE NO OTHER THIS COURT HAS EVER HEARD--FILLED WITH *PATHOS! COMEDY!* IT MADE ME *WEEP* WHEN I WROTE IT.

WELL, GO ON! WE HAVEN'T GOT ALL DAY!

UNFORTUNATELY, ON THE WAY HERE, MY CLIENT *ATE IT!*

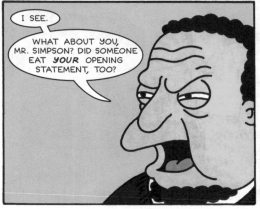

I SEE. WHAT ABOUT YOU, MR. SIMPSON? DID SOMEONE EAT *YOUR* OPENING STATEMENT, TOO?

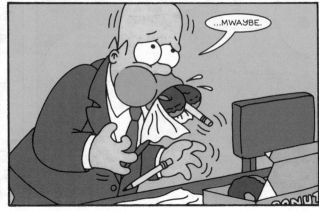

...MWAYBE.

YOUR HONOR! AT THIS TIME I WOULD LIKE TO CALL A SURPRISE WITNESS.
WHO?
IF I TOLD YOU, IT WOULDN'T BE A SURPRISE, NOW WOULD IT?
AY, CHIHUAHUA!
IS IT MATLOCK?
GASP!
GASP!
OH, DEAR!
OH, MY GOD... IT'S CHARLIE SHEEN! BACK AGAIN?!?
MURMUR!
MUMBLE! MUMBLE!
NOW, TO OVERCOME THE LANGUAGE BARRIER, WE'LL NEED TO USE SIMPLE SIGNALS. AFTER I ASK A QUESTION, IF YOU WANT TO ANSWER "YES," SIMPLY...PANT. OKAY?
PANT PANT
VERY GOOD. AND TO SAY "NO," YOU NEED TO...HMMM, LET'S SEE...JUMP UP, STAND ON YOUR FRONT PAWS, THEN DO A SOMERSAULT. PANT IF YOU AGREE.
PANT PANT
THAT'S ENOUGH NONSENSE. I HATE IT WHEN CLIENTS REPRESENT THEMSELVES.
I THINK WE SHOULD JUST CUT TO THE CHASE HERE. LET THE DOG DECIDE WHO HE WANTS TO LIVE WITH.
BAM!
COME HERE, BOY. COME ON.
WHO LOVES YOU, SNOOKUMS? COME TO DADDY.

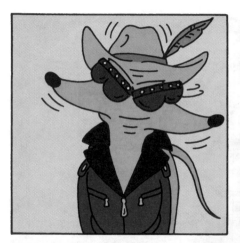

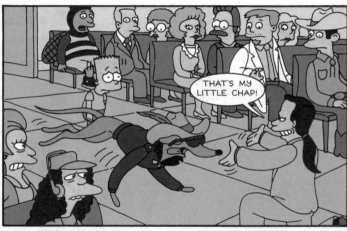

THAT'S MY LITTLE CHAP!

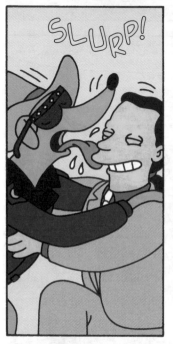

SLURP!

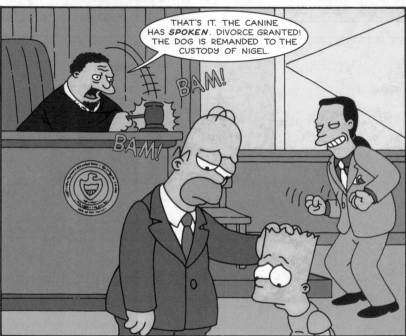

THAT'S IT. THE CANINE HAS *SPOKEN*. DIVORCE GRANTED! THE DOG IS REMANDED TO THE CUSTODY OF NIGEL.

BAM!

BAM!

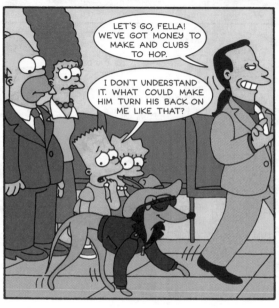

LET'S GO, FELLA! WE'VE GOT MONEY TO MAKE AND CLUBS TO HOP.

I DON'T UNDERSTAND IT. WHAT COULD MAKE HIM TURN HIS BACK ON ME LIKE THAT?

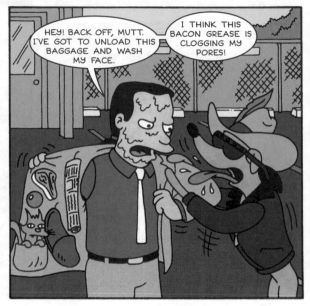

HEY! BACK OFF, MUTT. I'VE GOT TO UNLOAD THIS BAGGAGE AND WASH MY FACE.

I THINK THIS BACON GREASE IS CLOGGING MY PORES!

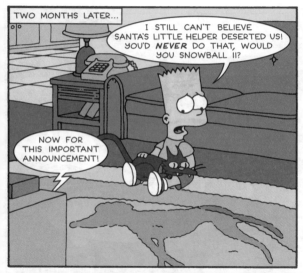

TWO MONTHS LATER...

I STILL CAN'T BELIEVE SANTA'S LITTLE HELPER DESERTED US! YOU'D *NEVER* DO THAT, WOULD YOU SNOWBALL II?

NOW FOR THIS IMPORTANT ANNOUNCEMENT!

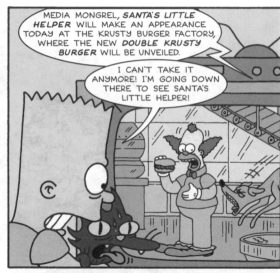

MEDIA MONGREL, *SANTA'S LITTLE HELPER* WILL MAKE AN APPEARANCE TODAY AT THE KRUSTY BURGER FACTORY, WHERE THE NEW *DOUBLE KRUSTY BURGER* WILL BE UNVEILED.

I CAN'T TAKE IT ANYMORE! I'M GOING DOWN THERE TO SEE SANTA'S LITTLE HELPER!

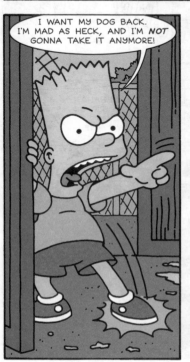

I SWEAR BY MY CAT, I'LL GET MY DOG BACK!

GURK!

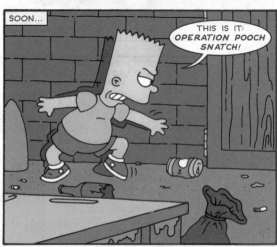

SOON...

THIS IS IT: *OPERATION POOCH SNATCH!*

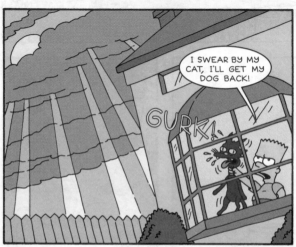

I WANT MY DOG BACK. I'M MAD AS HECK, AND I'M *NOT* GONNA TAKE IT ANYMORE!

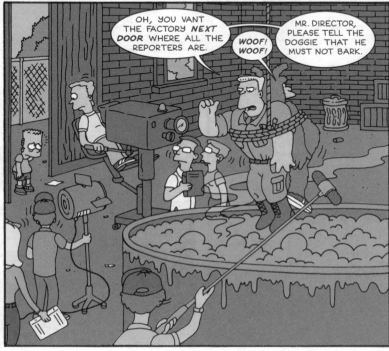

OH, YOU VANT THE FACTORY *NEXT DOOR* WHERE ALL THE REPORTERS ARE.

WOOF! WOOF!

MR. DIRECTOR, PLEASE TELL THE DOGGIE THAT HE MUST NOT BARK.

KRUSTY BURGER FACTORY
(Formerly known as the Krusty Burger Slaughterhouse)
KRUSTY! KRUSTY, IS IT TRUE ABOUT YOU AND PAMELA?
DOES TOMMY LEE KNOW IT'S NOT HIS?
HEY, HEY, HEY, YOU'LL HAVE TO WATCH MY BARBARA WALTERS SPECIAL IF YOU WANT TO HEAR ABOUT THAT.
TODAY WE'RE UNVEILING MY NEW DOUBLE KRUSTY BURGER, MADE FROM THE FINEST ANIMALS ON EARTH! JUST LIKE THESE!
IF YOU ENJOY THE MOUTH-PLEASING EXPERIENCE OF MY REGULAR KRUSTY BURGERS--AND WHO DOESN'T?--YOU'LL HAVE TWICE THE FUN WITH MY NEW DOUBLE KRUSTY BURGER.
SO REMEMBER...
OH, BOY, HERE WE GO AGAIN.
SINK YOUR TEETH INTO SOMETHING...
CHOMP!
YEOOOWW!
YOU STUPID MONGREL! YOU DIDN'T EVEN WAIT FOR YOUR CUE!
CLOWN CHASES DOG! WHATTA SCOOP! QUICK, GET A SHOT.
IF I GET MY HANDS ON YOU, I'LL RIP YOU SCRAWNY LIMB FROM SCRAWNY LIMB!
YELP!
YELP!
YELP!

HEY, LEAVE MY DOG ALONE. COME HERE, BOY. YOU'RE SAFE NOW!
I DEMAND YOU RELEASE MY **MEAL TICKET**... ER, **CLIENT!**
NO WAY, MAN! DON'T YOU SEE HE'S NOT HAPPY WITH YOU?
CAN'T YOU SEE HE BELONGS WITH ME? I NEED HIM. WHO AM I GOING TO THROW THE BALL FOR? WHO'S GOING TO CHEW UP MY SOCKS? WHO AM I GOING TO BLAME FOR EATING MY HOMEWORK?
CAN I TAKE HIM BACK, NIGEL? CAN I?
GOOD HEAVENS, I NEVER THOUGHT ABOUT IT LIKE THAT! LET ME THINK. HMMMM...
...NO.
BUT I'LL TELL YOU WHAT--IN THE INTEREST OF FAIR PLAY, I'LL MAKE YOU A DEAL. IF SANTA'S LITTLE HELPER DOESN'T WANT TO GO WITH ME AND WANTS TO STAY WITH YOU, I WON'T FIGHT IT.
I'LL JUST STAND OVER HERE WITH THIS DELICIOUS **DOUBLE KRUSTY BURGER** WHILE HE DECIDES.
SNIFF SNIFF
NO, BOY! DON'T DO IT!

THAT'S RIGHT, FELLA! I KNEW YOU'D MAKE THE RIGHT DECISION.
OH, MAN!
GULP!
HACK-KOFF!
STAND BACK! HE'S GONNA BLOW!
BAAARRRRF!
DOG BARFS UP BURGER! WHAT A SCOOP! QUICK, JIMMY, GET A SHOT OF IT!
EWWWW!
OH, NO! NOT ON MY CLEAN SLAUGHTER-HOUSE FLOOR!
IF A DOG COULDN'T KEEP ONE OF MY DOUBLE KRUSTY BURGERS DOWN, HOW AM I SUPPOSED TO SELL THEM TO PEOPLE? IF THE PAPERS PRINT A STORY ABOUT THIS, I'LL BE RUINED!
PRINT A STORY ABOUT THIS? THAT'S A GREAT IDEA!

YOU STUPID MUTT! YOUR CONTRACT WITH KRUSTY BURGER INC. IS OVER! KAPUT! FINISHED!
RIP!
TEAR!
SHRED!
AND YOUR CONTRACT WITH ME IS NULL AND VOID!
RIP!
TEAR!
SHRED!
BADGES?! WE DON'T NEED NO STINKING BADGES! THEY CAN TAKE AWAY OUR LIVES, BUT THEY CAN NEVER TAKE AWAY OUR FREEDOM! ALBA GU BRATH!
WHAT ARE YOU DOING, YOU YUTZ?! HOW DID YOU GET IN HERE!?! HEY, THAT'S MY WALLET!
RIP!
TEAR!
SHRED!
TIME TO SETTLE THIS LIKE MEN. I'M SUING THE PANTS OFF THE BOTH OF YA!
THAT'S RIGHT! YOU CAN EXPECT TO HEAR FROM US IN THE MORNING!
OUT! OUT! OUT! MY ARTIFICIAL HEART CAN'T TAKE ANY MORE OF THIS! I'M GONNA BURST A SPRING!
EXIT
I KNEW YOU'D COME BACK TO ME SOMEDAY.

VHAT ARE YOU DOING WITH MY DOG?
BONK!
OOF!
YOU WOULD NOT BE PRACTICING CRUELTY TO ANIMALS, WOULD YOU?
WELL, THAT IS...ER...I...
DON'T WORRY. I SAW THE WHOLE THING. I'M NIGEL, PROFESSIONAL WITNESS AND AGENT. ARE YOU IN NEED OF REPRESENTATION, MR. WOLFCASTLE?
CLOWNS LIKE YOU MAKE ME SICK. I AM ALSO UNHAPPY WITH YOU, KRUSTY. I THINK I AM LOSING MY TEMPER.
THERE, IT IS *LOST*.
EXCUSE ME, I THINK I HEAR MY MUM CALLING.
SIC 'EM, BOY.
YEESH, WHAT A DAY!
ALL'S WELL THAT *ENDS* WELL! EH, BOY?
YEEEEOWCH!
THE BIG END!

SPARKLE MANGA PUBLISHING CORPORATION
HE IS DISRESPECTFUL TO DIRT!!!
ミスタ
スパーコル
TASTE THE ZESTFUL BUBBLING FOAM OF MY VENGEANCE!
I AM THE HARSH NEMESIS OF ALL THAT IS UNCLEAN!!!
DRAGONBRAWLER X! SAILOR MOOSE! PIKKANOZE AND THE PORKYMEN! WITNESS MR. SPARKLE IN CONFLICT WITH THE MANGA MINIONS OF THE EVIL INKY HAND!
AIEEE!! WE ARE UNDONE!
ONE WAY
GROENING SHAW!

HERE'S A SOMEWHAT AMUSING LITTLE ITEM I DISCOVERED IN THE ANDROID'S DUNGEON'S QUARTER BOX! I BELIEVE IT TO BE A RARE GIVEAWAY PROMOTIONAL COMIC BOOK--OR MANGA--FROM JAPAN, EXTOLLING THE VIRTUES OF A POPULAR JAPANESE HOME CLEANING PRODUCT!
PERSONALLY, I FIND IT DIFFICULT TO JUSTIFY WASTING ONE'S INCOME ON SUCH UNNECESSARY NOTIONS AS CLEANSERS, SOAP, SHAVING CREAM, TOOTHPASTE OR DEODORANT--ESPECIALLY WHEN SAID FUNDS COULD PAY FOR A COMPLETE SET OF VINTAGE DEVIL DINOSAUR COMIC BOOKS IN MINT CONDITION--BUT THE JAPANESE ARE A NOTORIOUSLY FUSSY PEOPLE!
IN ANY EVENT, IT IS MY VAGUE PLEASURE TO PRESENT, TRANSLATED FOR YOUR READING ENJOYMENT--
Mr. Sparkle in "DESTROY ALL MANGA!"
ALL-TOO SCRUTIBLE STORY, SCRIPT AND PENCIL ART BY SCOTT SHAW!
BENEVOLENT, NON-MESSY INKS BY DAN NAKROSIS
CONTRACTION-LESS LETTERING BY CHRIS UNGAR
TRANQUILLY TASTEFUL COLORS BY NATHAN KANE
PLACIDLY EDITED BY BILL MORRISON
SUSHI CATERED BY MATT GROENING
THESE DIRTY DISHES AND EATING UTENSILS ARE FESTOONED WITH UNPLEASANT RESIDUE FROM OUR MOST RECENT MEAL! HOW WILL I EVER RENDER THEM CLEAN AND WASABI-FREE?
PERHAPS THIS AMUSINGLY-DECORATED BOX OF CLEANSING PRODUCT CAN ALLEVIATE MY PREDICAMENT!
WHAT--!?!
PLEASE GET OUT OF MY WAY, ATTRACTIVE LADY! I AM ON A HIGH-PRIORITY MISSION TO DECIMATE HOUSEHOLD FILTH!
TWINKLE!
IT IS TIME TO EXCHANGE PLEASANTRIES WITH OBLIVION, OBSTINATE PARTICLES OF UNCLEANLINESS!
AIEEE!!!
SPARKLE!
AHH, MY COMPUTER-GENERATED EARS ARE HAPPY TO RECEIVE THE DEATH-CRIES OF MY DISEASE-LADEN ADVERSARIES!
MY DISHES AND I ARE HONORED TO THANK YOU, MR. SPARKLE! YOU ARE ONE GO-GETTING CORPORATE ICON!
NOW, PERMIT ME TO INTRODUCE YOU TO OUR ROOM OF PORCELAIN DELIGHTS!
HA! I'D WAGER THAT IT CONTAINS MUCH UNCLEANLINESS WAITING T SAVOR MY UNFALTERING PUNISHMENT! LET US BE--EH?
AIEEEE!!!

THAT WAS THE CRY OF MY MANGA-ARTIST HUSBAND! WHAT DIRE CALAMITY HAS BEFALLEN YOU HERE IN THE SACROSANCT SOLITUDE OF YOUR STUDIO?
THE FORCES OF GRAVITY HAVE CONSPIRED TO ACCIDENTALLY SPILL THIS BLACK DRAWING INK ALL OVER MYSELF! I AM DISGRACED BY SUCH A SLOVENLY DEMEANOR!
MY VERY MOLECULES ARE BRISTLING WITH RAGE AT THE MERE SIGHT OF SUCH RAMPANT UNTIDYNESS! I AM FEELING MOST DISRESPECTFUL!!!
AVENGE MY HUSBAND'S REPUTATION FOR CLEANLINESS! MOVE WITH SPEED AND SERIOUS INTENTION! THUS DO I COMMAND YOU, MR. SPARKLE!
I HASTEN TO OBEY, FOR I AM LIKE A MINTY-FRESH FORCE OF NATURE!
BEHOLD MY UNFORTUNATE CONDITION! I AM INK-SMUDGED BEYOND RECOGNITION! I AM INDEED BLESSED TO HAVE SUCH A BUBBLY BENEFACTOR IN YOU, MR. SPARKLE!
WHAT?! THE OFFENDING PIGMENT DISPLAYS A MALEVOLENT PERSONALITY?!?
THAT IS YOUR MISCONCEPTION, FOOLISH HUMAN! MR. SPARKLE MUST DIE!!!
ARISE, MY INKY BRETHREN! I HEREBY RELEASE YOU FROM YOUR TWO DIMENSIONAL INCARCERATION! ATTACK AND DESTROY MR. SPARKLE!
WE SPRING TO LIFE AT YOUR COMMAND, O DIGIT-BOUND DICTATOR! WE VOW TO SHAME YOUR ANAL-RETENTIVE ADVERSARY!

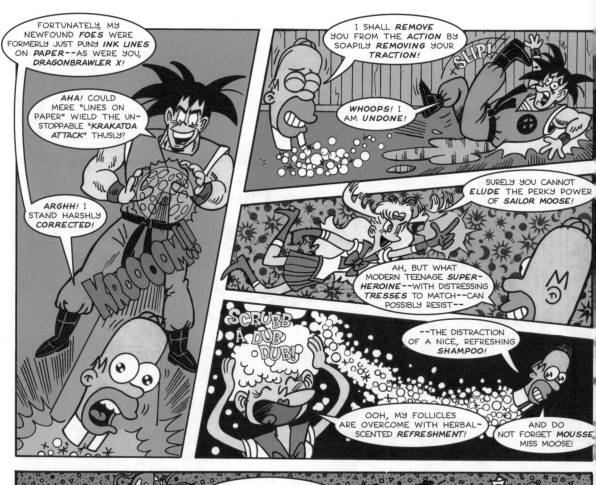

FORTUNATELY, MY NEWFOUND *FOES* WERE FORMERLY JUST PUNY *INK LINES* ON *PAPER*--AS WERE YOU, DRAGONBRAWLER X!

AHA! COULD MERE "LINES ON PAPER" WIELD THE UN-STOPPABLE "KRAKATOA ATTACK" THUSLY?

ARGHH! I STAND HARSHLY *CORRECTED!*

KROOOOM!

I SHALL *REMOVE* YOU FROM THE *ACTION* BY SOAPILY *REMOVING* YOUR TRACTION!

SLIP!

WHOOPS! I AM *UNDONE!*

SURELY YOU CANNOT *ELUDE* THE PERKY POWER OF *SAILOR MOOSE!*

AH, BUT WHAT MODERN TEENAGE *SUPER-HEROINE*--WITH DISTRESSING *TRESSES* TO MATCH--CAN POSSIBLY RESIST--

SCRUBB A DUB DUB!

--THE DISTRACTION OF A NICE, REFRESHING *SHAMPOO!*

OOH, MY FOLLICLES ARE OVERCOME WITH HERBAL-SCENTED *REFRESHMENT!*

AND DO NOT FORGET *MOUSSE*, MISS MOOSE!

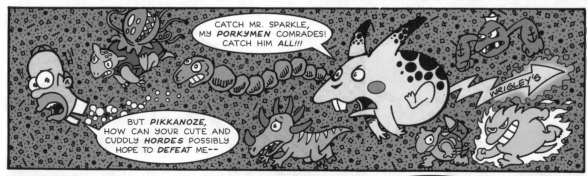

CATCH MR. SPARKLE, MY *PORKYMEN* COMRADES! CATCH HIM *ALL!!!*

BUT *PIKKANOZE*, HOW CAN YOUR CUTE AND CUDDLY *HORDES* POSSIBLY HOPE TO *DEFEAT* ME--

WRIGLEY'S

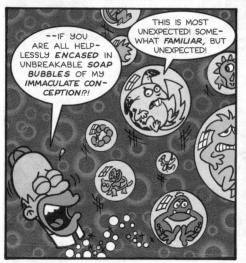

--IF YOU ARE ALL HELP-LESSLY *ENCASED* IN UNBREAKABLE *SOAP BUBBLES* OF MY *IMMACULATE CON-CEPTION?!*

THIS IS MOST UNEXPECTED! SOME-WHAT *FAMILIAR*, BUT UNEXPECTED!

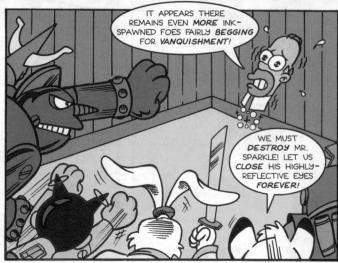

IT APPEARS THERE REMAINS EVEN *MORE* INK-SPAWNED FOES FAIRLY *BEGGING* FOR *VANQUISHMENT!*

WE MUST *DESTROY* MR. SPARKLE! LET US *CLOSE* HIS HIGHLY-REFLECTIVE EYES *FOREVER!*

THIS IS ONE FEISTY CORPORATE ICON WHO WILL NOT BE DISGRACED!
IT IS TIME TO ACTIVATE MY SPARKLING SPIC-AND SPAN COUNTER-ATTACK--
--THE ULTIMATE WHITE-OUT!
EXIT
AIEEE!!!
ANCESTORS, RECEIVE US!!!
WE ARE DIS-PATCHED TO OSAMU TEZUKA, THE GOD OF CARTOONS!
AND WITHOUT MUSS NOR FUSS!
YOU HAVE TRIUMPHED ONCE AGAIN, MR. SPARKLE! MY HUSBAND AND HIS STUDIO ARE ONCE AGAIN FREE OF THE BLIGHT OF LOOSE INK! WE ARE IN YOUR DEBT!
DEBT IS CORRECT! MR. SPARKLE NOT ONLY CLEANED UP THE SPILLED INK, BUT HE ALSO REMOVED ALL THE INK FROM THE PAGES OF MANGA I WAS DRAWING--NOW THEY ARE COM-PLETELY BLANK! MY EDITOR WILL DISRESPECT ME WITH TERMINATION OF EMPLOYMENT! WE WILL BE WITHOUT A SINGLE YEN!
THANKS TO THAT BELOVED CORPORATE SYMBOL, I MUST RENOUNCE MY CAREER IN UTTER SHAME! NOW I AM FORCED TO BECOME A LOWLY SALARY-MAN!!!
ONCE AGAIN, MR. SPARKLE HAS TRIUMPHED OVER THE FORCES OF UNCLEANLINESS! I BASK IN MY OWN SUCCESS! BANZAI!
I CURSE YOU, MR. SPARKLE! YOU HAVE DESTROYED OUR LIVES! NOW I MUST COMMIT THE CLEANSING FINAL RITUAL OF SEPPUKU!
IN THAT EVENTUALITY, PLEASE MAKE AN EFFORT NOT TO BLEED ALL OVER YOUR FLOOR, FORMER MR. MANGA ARTIST! THAT WOULD BE MOST UNCLEAN! SAYONARA!
SO ENDS ANOTHER ADVENTURE OF MR. SPARKLE, ENEMY OF THE UNCLEAN! AND DON'T NEGLECT TO PICK UP MANY MR. SPARKLE BRAND CLEANSING PRODUCTS IMMEDIATELY!
HMPH! WORST GIVEAWAY PROMOTIONAL MANGA EVER!
THE END!

TOGETHER AGAIN FOR THEIR FIRST CRIME!
BONGO COMICS GROUP
#46
US $2.50
CAN $3.50
SIMPSONS™
COMICS
APPROVED BY THE COMICS CODE AUTHORITY
El Barto
GROENING
Ortiz
Rote

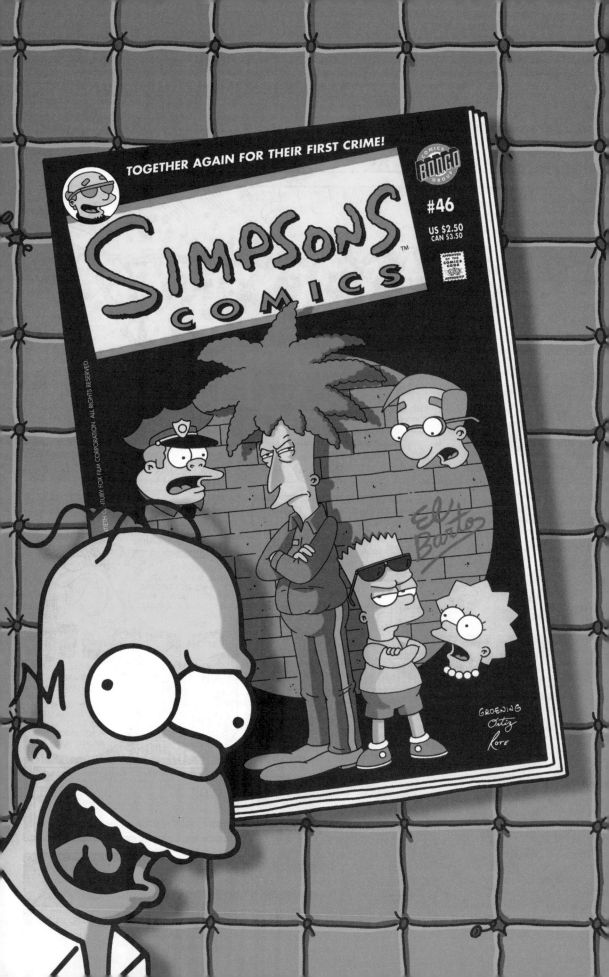

ANGELS WITH YELLOW FACES
KZZAAAK!
SCRIPT
ERIC ROGERS
PENCILS
PHIL ORTIZ
INKS
TIM BAVINGTON
EDITOR
BILL MORRISON
LETTERS
JEANNINE BLACK
JUDGE, JURY AND EXECUTIONER
MATT GROENING

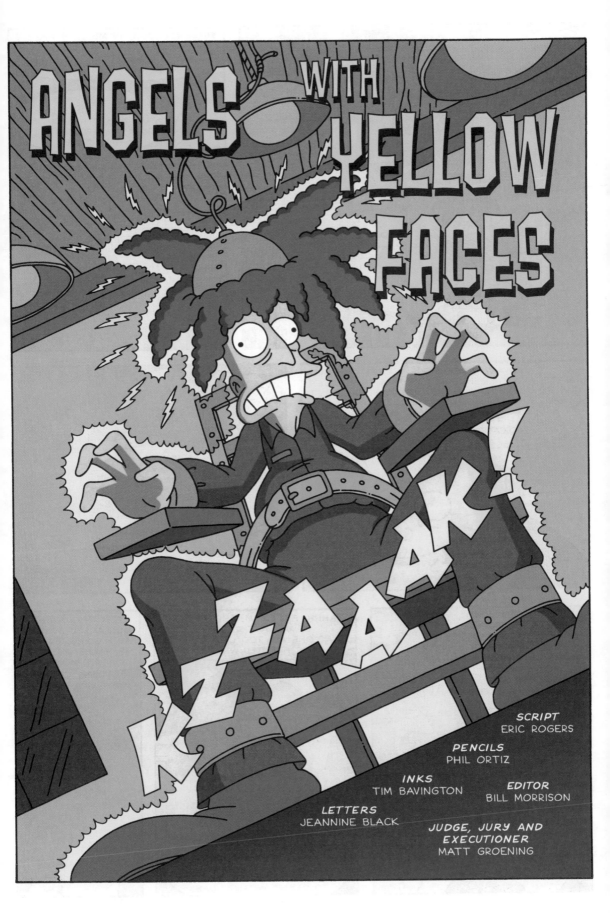

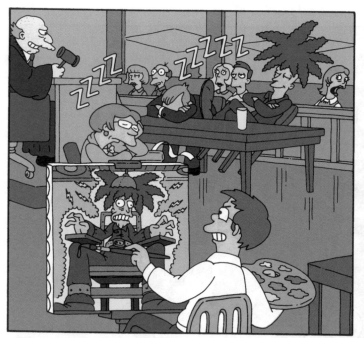

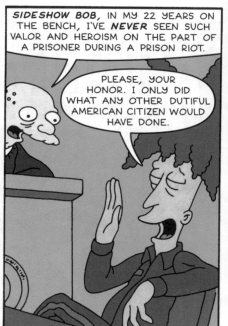
SIDESHOW BOB, IN MY 22 YEARS ON THE BENCH, I'VE NEVER SEEN SUCH VALOR AND HEROISM ON THE PART OF A PRISONER DURING A PRISON RIOT.

PLEASE, YOUR HONOR. I ONLY DID WHAT ANY OTHER DUTIFUL AMERICAN CITIZEN WOULD HAVE DONE.

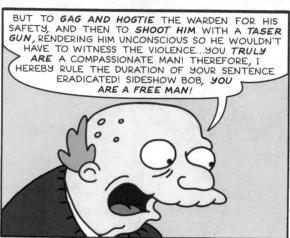
BUT TO GAG AND HOGTIE THE WARDEN FOR HIS SAFETY, AND THEN TO SHOOT HIM WITH A TASER GUN, RENDERING HIM UNCONSCIOUS SO HE WOULDN'T HAVE TO WITNESS THE VIOLENCE...YOU TRULY ARE A COMPASSIONATE MAN! THEREFORE, I HEREBY RULE THE DURATION OF YOUR SENTENCE ERADICATED! SIDESHOW BOB, YOU ARE A FREE MAN!

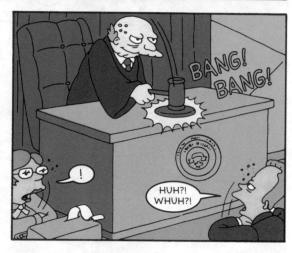
BANG! BANG!

HUH?! WHUH?!

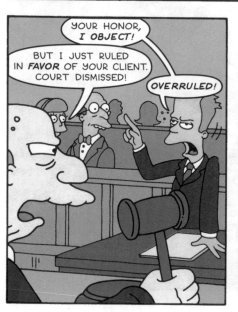
YOUR HONOR, I OBJECT!

BUT I JUST RULED IN FAVOR OF YOUR CLIENT. COURT DISMISSED!

OVERRULED!

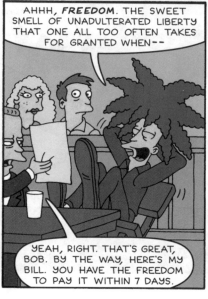
AHHH, FREEDOM. THE SWEET SMELL OF UNADULTERATED LIBERTY THAT ONE ALL TOO OFTEN TAKES FOR GRANTED WHEN--

YEAH, RIGHT. THAT'S GREAT, BOB. BY THE WAY, HERE'S MY BILL. YOU HAVE THE FREEDOM TO PAY IT WITHIN 7 DAYS.

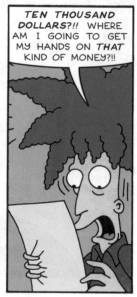
TEN THOUSAND DOLLARS?!! WHERE AM I GOING TO GET MY HANDS ON THAT KIND OF MONEY?!!

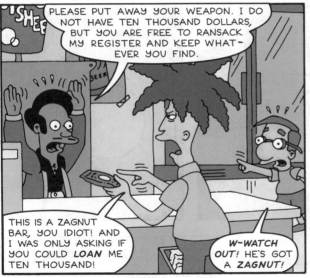

PLEASE PUT AWAY YOUR WEAPON. I DO NOT HAVE TEN THOUSAND DOLLARS, BUT YOU ARE FREE TO RANSACK MY REGISTER AND KEEP WHAT-EVER YOU FIND.

THIS IS A ZAGNUT BAR, YOU IDIOT! AND I WAS ONLY ASKING IF YOU COULD *LOAN* ME TEN THOUSAND!

W-WATCH *OUT!* HE'S GOT A *ZAGNUT!*

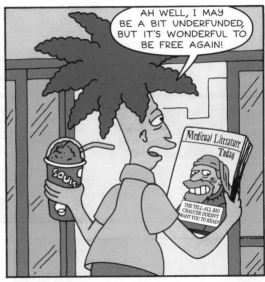

AH WELL, I MAY BE A BIT UNDERFUNDED, BUT IT'S WONDERFUL TO BE FREE AGAIN!

Medieval Literature Today

THE TELL-ALL BIO CHAUCER DOESN'T WANT YOU TO READ!

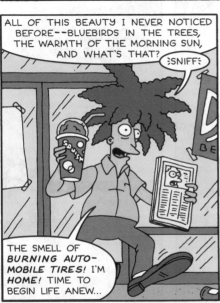

ALL OF THIS BEAUTY I NEVER NOTICED BEFORE--BLUEBIRDS IN THE TREES, THE WARMTH OF THE MORNING SUN, AND WHAT'S THAT?

:SNIFF:

THE SMELL OF *BURNING AUTO-MOBILE TIRES!* I'M *HOME!* TIME TO BEGIN LIFE ANEW...

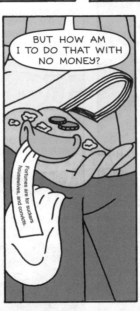

BUT HOW AM I TO DO THAT WITH NO MONEY?

Fortunes are for suckers, housewives, and convicts.

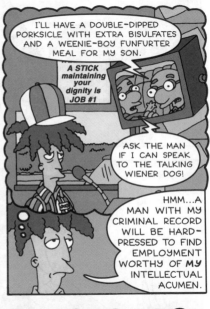

I'LL HAVE A DOUBLE-DIPPED PORKSICLE WITH EXTRA BISULFATES AND A WEENIE-BOY FUNFURTER MEAL FOR MY SON.

A STICK maintaining your dignity is JOB #1

ASK THE MAN IF I CAN SPEAK TO THE TALKING WIENER DOG!

HMM...A MAN WITH MY CRIMINAL RECORD WILL BE HARD-PRESSED TO FIND EMPLOYMENT WORTHY OF *MY* INTELLECTUAL ACUMEN.

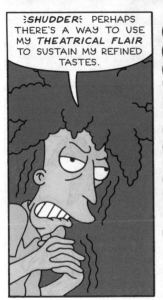

:SHUDDER: PERHAPS THERE'S A WAY TO USE MY *THEATRICAL FLAIR* TO SUSTAIN MY REFINED TASTES.

"I COULD BE A *STREET PERFORMER*..."

YES, WE'RE OPEN

MACBETH

IF IT WERE DONE WHEN 'TIS DONE, THEN 'TWERE WELL IT WERE DONE QUICKLY.

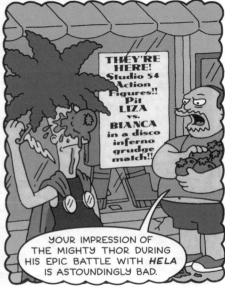

THEY'RE HERE! Studio 54 Action figures!! Pit LIZA vs. BIANCA in a disco inferno grudge match!!

YOUR IMPRESSION OF THE MIGHTY THOR DURING HIS EPIC BATTLE WITH *HELA* IS ASTOUNDINGLY BAD.

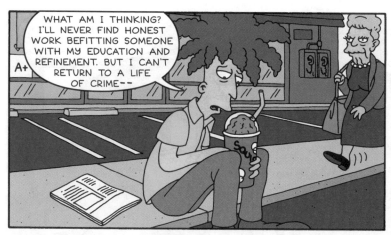

WHAT AM I THINKING? I'LL NEVER FIND HONEST WORK BEFITTING SOMEONE WITH MY EDUCATION AND REFINEMENT. BUT I CAN'T RETURN TO A LIFE OF CRIME--

A+

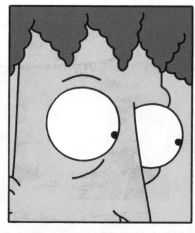

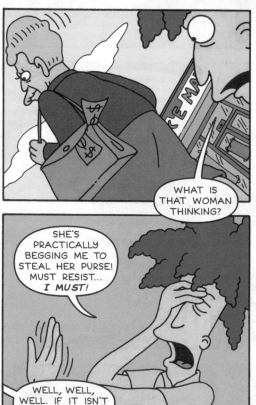

WHAT IS THAT WOMAN THINKING?

SHE'S PRACTICALLY BEGGING ME TO STEAL HER PURSE! MUST RESIST... *I MUST!*

WELL, WELL, WELL. IF IT ISN'T SIDESHOW BOB!

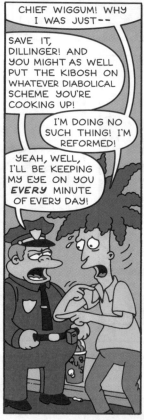

CHIEF WIGGUM! WHY I WAS JUST--

SAVE IT, DILLINGER! AND YOU MIGHT AS WELL PUT THE KIBOSH ON WHATEVER DIABOLICAL SCHEME YOU'RE COOKING UP!

I'M DOING NO SUCH THING! I'M REFORMED!

YEAH, WELL, I'LL BE KEEPING MY EYE ON YOU *EVERY* MINUTE OF EVERY DAY!

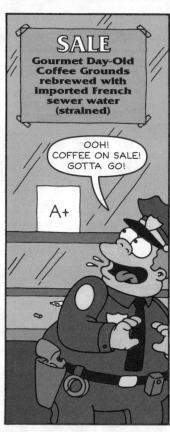

SALE
Gourmet Day-Old Coffee Grounds rebrewed with imported French sewer water (strained)

A+

OOH! COFFEE ON SALE! GOTTA GO!

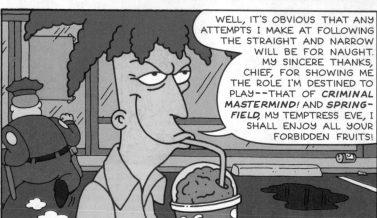

WELL, IT'S OBVIOUS THAT ANY ATTEMPTS I MAKE AT FOLLOWING THE STRAIGHT AND NARROW WILL BE FOR NAUGHT. MY SINCERE THANKS, CHIEF, FOR SHOWING ME THE ROLE I'M DESTINED TO PLAY--THAT OF *CRIMINAL MASTERMIND!* AND *SPRINGFIELD,* MY TEMPTRESS EVE, I SHALL ENJOY ALL YOUR FORBIDDEN FRUITS!

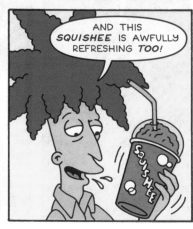

AND THIS *SQUISHEE* IS AWFULLY REFRESHING *TOO!*

THE FOLLOWING DAY...
CAN I HELP YOU, SIR?
THIS IS A STICKUP. I WANT YOU TO VERY QUIETLY AND CALMLY--
HEY, DON'T LET HER SUCKER YOU INTO THAT BOGUS "FREE CHECKING" DEAL!
IT'S ABOUT AS FREE AS A *TIBETAN IN JAPAN!*
THAT'S *CHINA,* YOU IDIOT.
WHAT WAS THAT?
OH, HELLO OFFICER. ER, I WAS JUST SAYING THAT...UM, I'D FEEL LIKE AN IDIOT FOR OPENING AN ACCOUNT AT ANY BANK THAT DIDN'T GIVE AWAY FREE CHINA!
LATER...
WHY, YES...I DO FIND MYSELF *ALLURING*...*AND* SASSY!
AS WILL YOUR WIFE, CHIEF, WHICH MAKES IT THE PERFECT ANNIVERSARY GIFT.
ER... UH, RIGHT. ANNIVERSARY GIFT. *SOLD!*
JIM'S
GENUINE GEMS AND CHEAP IMITATIONS
We can't tell the difference and neither can you!
D'OH!
AND...
NOW WHO ARE *YOU* SUPPOSED TO BE?
I'M A ROGUE COP IN THE WRONG PLACE AT THE WRONG TIME.
AH, FORGET IT!

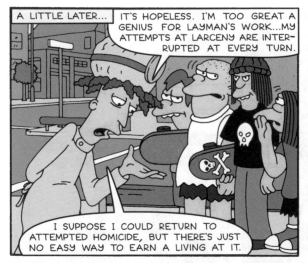

A LITTLE LATER...

IT'S HOPELESS. I'M TOO GREAT A GENIUS FOR LAYMAN'S WORK...MY ATTEMPTS AT LARCENY ARE INTERRUPTED AT EVERY TURN.

I SUPPOSE I COULD RETURN TO ATTEMPTED HOMICIDE, BUT THERE'S JUST NO EASY WAY TO EARN A LIVING AT IT.

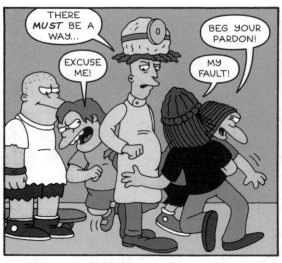

THERE *MUST* BE A WAY...

EXCUSE ME!

BEG YOUR PARDON!

MY FAULT!

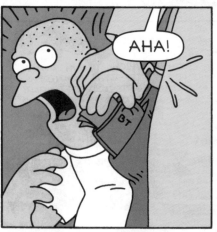

AHA!

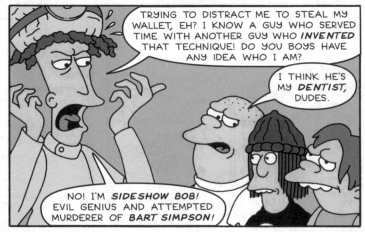

TRYING TO DISTRACT ME TO STEAL MY WALLET, EH? I KNOW A GUY WHO SERVED TIME WITH ANOTHER GUY WHO *INVENTED* THAT TECHNIQUE! DO YOU BOYS HAVE ANY IDEA WHO I AM?

I THINK HE'S MY *DENTIST*, DUDES.

NO! I'M *SIDESHOW BOB!* EVIL GENIUS AND ATTEMPTED MURDERER OF *BART SIMPSON!*

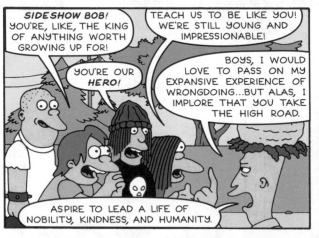

SIDESHOW BOB! YOU'RE, LIKE, THE KING OF ANYTHING WORTH GROWING UP FOR!

YOU'RE OUR *HERO!*

TEACH US TO BE LIKE YOU! WE'RE STILL YOUNG AND IMPRESSIONABLE!

BOYS, I WOULD LOVE TO PASS ON MY EXPANSIVE EXPERIENCE OF WRONGDOING...BUT ALAS, I IMPLORE THAT YOU TAKE THE HIGH ROAD.

ASPIRE TO LEAD A LIFE OF NOBILITY, KINDNESS, AND HUMANITY.

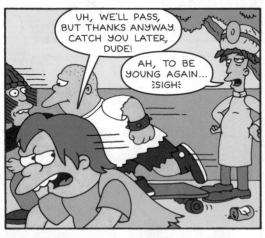

UH, WE'LL PASS, BUT THANKS ANYWAY. CATCH YOU LATER, DUDE!

AH, TO BE YOUNG AGAIN... ⸗SIGH⸗

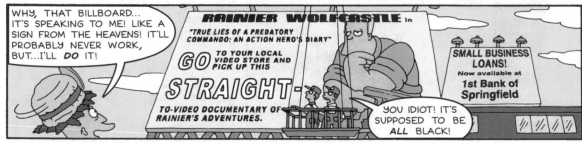

WHY, THAT BILLBOARD... IT'S SPEAKING TO ME! LIKE A SIGN FROM THE HEAVENS! IT'LL PROBABLY NEVER WORK, BUT...I'LL *DO* IT!

RAINIER WOLFCASTLE In

"TRUE LIES OF A PREDATORY COMMANDO: AN ACTION HERO'S DIARY"

GO TO YOUR LOCAL VIDEO STORE AND PICK UP THIS

STRAIGHT-

TO-VIDEO DOCUMENTARY OF RAINIER'S ADVENTURES.

SMALL BUSINESS LOANS! Now available at 1st Bank of Springfield

YOU IDIOT! IT'S SUPPOSED TO BE *ALL* BLACK!

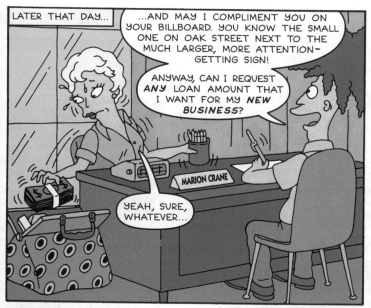

LATER THAT DAY...

...AND MAY I COMPLIMENT YOU ON YOUR BILLBOARD. YOU KNOW THE SMALL ONE ON OAK STREET NEXT TO THE MUCH LARGER, MORE ATTENTION-GETTING SIGN!

ANYWAY, CAN I REQUEST *ANY* LOAN AMOUNT THAT I WANT FOR MY *NEW BUSINESS*?

YEAH, SURE, WHATEVER...

MARION CRANE

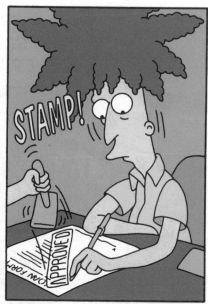

STAMP!

APPROVED

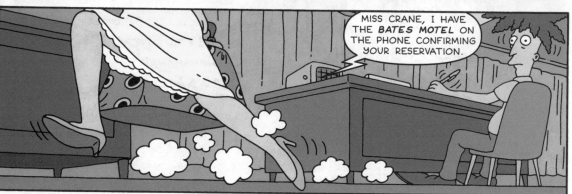

MISS CRANE, I HAVE THE *BATES MOTEL* ON THE PHONE CONFIRMING YOUR RESERVATION.

TWO WEEKS LATER...

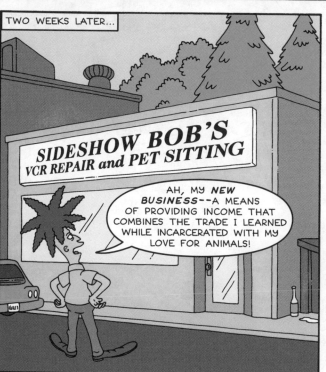

SIDESHOW BOB'S
VCR REPAIR and PET SITTING

AH, MY *NEW BUSINESS*--A MEANS OF PROVIDING INCOME THAT COMBINES THE TRADE I LEARNED WHILE INCARCERATED WITH MY LOVE FOR ANIMALS!

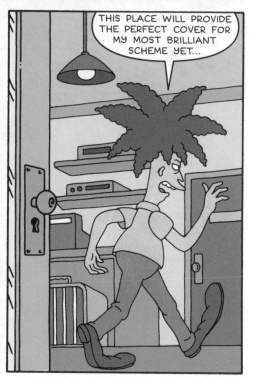

THIS PLACE WILL PROVIDE THE PERFECT COVER FOR MY MOST BRILLIANT SCHEME YET...

...MY SCHOOL OF CRIME!!!
A-ARSON B-BURGLARY C-CRIME BOSS
INSTRUCTOR: BOB TERWILLIGER
AL
BLACK-JACKS
SUCTION CUPS
BRASS KNUCKLES
TEAR GAS
SHIVS
HEATERS
I'LL TEACH MY STUDENTS THE FINE ART OF CRIME! THEN, WHILE I REMAIN HERE, THEY'LL GO OUT AND PILLAGE SPRINGFIELD! I'LL REAP THE REWARDS OF THEIR EFFORTS AND I'LL NEVER BE SUSPECTED OF THE CRIMES!
HAHAHAHAHA!!!
MELON
GULLET
TICKER
PRIVATES
MITTS
PINS
TIPS FOR JUNIOR THIEVES
MAKING CRIME PAY

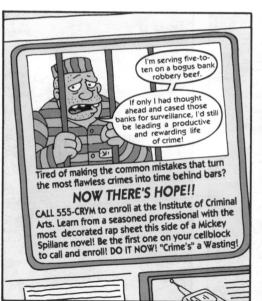

I'm serving five-to-ten on a bogus bank robbery beef.

If only I had thought ahead and cased those banks for surveillance, I'd still be leading a productive and rewarding life of crime!

Tired of making the common mistakes that turn the most flawless crimes into time behind bars?

NOW THERE'S HOPE!!

CALL 555-CRYM to enroll at the Institute of Criminal Arts. Learn from a seasoned professional with the most decorated rap sheet this side of a Mickey Spillane novel! Be the first one on your cellblock to call and enroll! DO IT NOW! "Crime's" a Wasting!

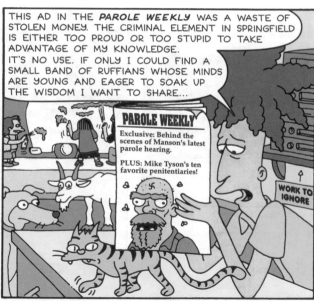

THIS AD IN THE *PAROLE WEEKLY* WAS A WASTE OF STOLEN MONEY. THE CRIMINAL ELEMENT IN SPRINGFIELD IS EITHER TOO PROUD OR TOO STUPID TO TAKE ADVANTAGE OF MY KNOWLEDGE.
IT'S NO USE. IF ONLY I COULD FIND A SMALL BAND OF RUFFIANS WHOSE MINDS ARE YOUNG AND EAGER TO SOAK UP THE WISDOM I WANT TO SHARE...

PAROLE WEEKLY

Exclusive: Behind the scenes of Manson's latest parole hearing.

PLUS: Mike Tyson's ten favorite penitentiaries!

WORK TO IGNORE

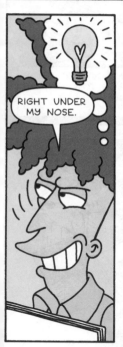

RIGHT UNDER MY NOSE.

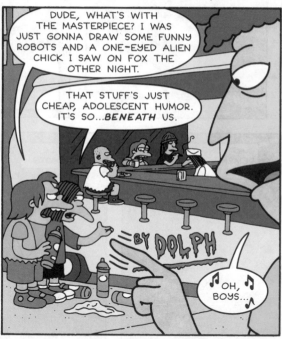

DUDE, WHAT'S WITH THE MASTERPIECE? I WAS JUST GONNA DRAW SOME FUNNY ROBOTS AND A ONE-EYED ALIEN CHICK I SAW ON FOX THE OTHER NIGHT.

THAT STUFF'S JUST CHEAP, ADOLESCENT HUMOR. IT'S SO...*BENEATH* US.

BY DOLPH

♪ OH, BOYS... ♪

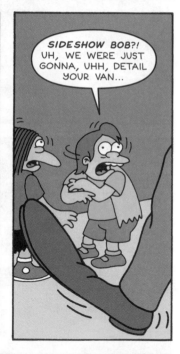

SIDESHOW BOB?! UH, WE WERE JUST GONNA, UHH, DETAIL YOUR VAN...

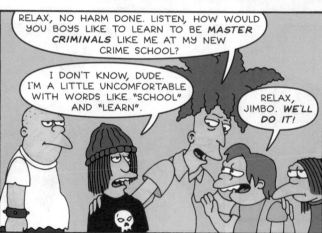

RELAX, NO HARM DONE. LISTEN, HOW WOULD YOU BOYS LIKE TO LEARN TO BE *MASTER CRIMINALS* LIKE ME AT MY NEW CRIME SCHOOL?

I DON'T KNOW, DUDE. I'M A LITTLE UNCOMFORTABLE WITH WORDS LIKE "SCHOOL" AND "LEARN".

RELAX, JIMBO. *WE'LL DO IT!*

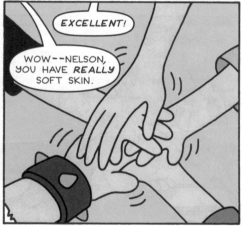

EXCELLENT!

WOW--NELSON, YOU HAVE *REALLY* SOFT SKIN.

-ARSON B-BURGLARY C-CRIME BOS
MIRANDA RIGHTS
PROBATION
ALIBI
"THERE'S NO CRIME TOO BIG...
...NO CRIME TOO IMPOSSIBLE TO PULL OFF...
...NO AMOUNT OF PROTECTION GREAT ENOUGH TO KEEP YOUR TARGET ONE HUNDRED PERCENT SAFE...
...AS LONG AS YOU REMEMBER ONE THING ALWAYS...
...PEOPLE ARE *IDIOTS*...
...JUST BE LESS OF AN IDIOT THAN EVERYONE ELSE, AND YOU'LL NEVER BE CAUGHT."
MELON
TICKER
MITTS
EXCELLENT, BOYS. NOW LET'S PUT WHAT YOU'VE LEARNED TO THE TEST!

OHH, THE PAIN! I THINK MY STOMACH'S GONNA EXPLODE!
OH PLEASE! BLOW YOUR GUTS OUT SOMEPLACE ELSE! NOT IN MY STORE!
DUFF BEER SALE
JERKY LOGS
SABLE WOULD KILL MISS ELIZABETH!
IN YOUR DREAMS!
EVEN GOD CAN'T SAVE YOU NOW!! EVERYBODY, RUN FOR YOUR LIVES!
DEMON HORDES ARE USING MY BODY AS A GATEWAY TO EARTH!
I'VE GOT THE DEVIL IN ME!
AT THE END OF THE DAY...
CONGRATULATIONS, BOYS! YOU'VE LEARNED YOUR LESSONS WELL. WHY DON'T YOU TAKE SOME LOOT AND BUY YOURSELVES A FEW HUNDRED SQUISHEES WHILE I PLAN OUR NEXT HEIST!
EVERYTHING'S FINALLY GOING MY WAY! NOBODY CAN POSSIBLY STOP ME NOW. NOT EVEN...

BART SIMPSON!!!

COOL! RANCH-FLAVORED PUDDING POPS! LIFE IS SWEET!

JIMBO AND HIS GANG HAVE STOPPED BEATING ME UP EVERY DAY AFTER SCHOOL. MY DOCTOR SAYS THAT THE INTERNAL BLEEDING MAY HAVE A CHANCE TO HEAL ON ITS OWN NOW!

YOU SURE ARE A PEPPY POLLYANNA TODAY. WHAT GIVES?

HMM...SOMETHING'S NOT RIGHT WITH THIS PICTURE. I JUST CAN'T PUT MY FINGER ON IT YET.

LATER THAT DAY...

HEH, HEH, HEH.

SUNDAY'S SERVICE:

"WINDOWS, THE INTERNET, AND RELIGION.COM--Y2K SALVATION OR JUST THE CONTROL-ALT-DELETE OF YOUR SOUL?"

5 MINUTES LATER...

CAUGHT RED-HANDED!

SUNDAY'S SERV

"LOVEJOY CAN KISS MY LITTLE YELLOW

CHIEF WIGGUM! I WAS JUST FIXING THE WORK OF SOME NOGOODNIK--

TELL IT TO THE JUDGE, SIMPSON!

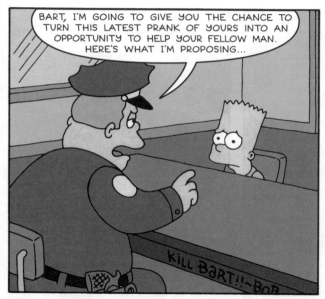

BART, I'M GOING TO GIVE YOU THE CHANCE TO TURN THIS LATEST PRANK OF YOURS INTO AN OPPORTUNITY TO HELP YOUR FELLOW MAN. HERE'S WHAT I'M PROPOSING...

KILL BART!!!~BOB

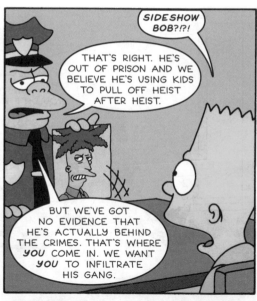

SIDESHOW BOB?!?!

THAT'S RIGHT. HE'S OUT OF PRISON AND WE BELIEVE HE'S USING KIDS TO PULL OFF HEIST AFTER HEIST.

BUT WE'VE GOT NO EVIDENCE THAT HE'S ACTUALLY BEHIND THE CRIMES. THAT'S WHERE *YOU* COME IN. WE WANT *YOU* TO INFILTRATE HIS GANG.

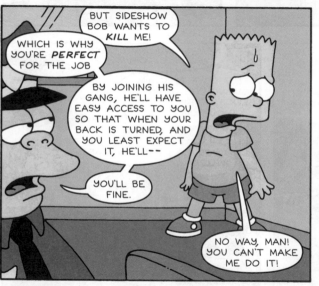

BUT SIDESHOW BOB WANTS TO *KILL* ME!

WHICH IS WHY YOU'RE *PERFECT* FOR THE JOB

BY JOINING HIS GANG, HE'LL HAVE EASY ACCESS TO YOU SO THAT WHEN YOUR BACK IS TURNED, AND YOU LEAST EXPECT IT, HE'LL--

YOU'LL BE FINE.

NO WAY, MAN! YOU CAN'T MAKE ME DO IT!

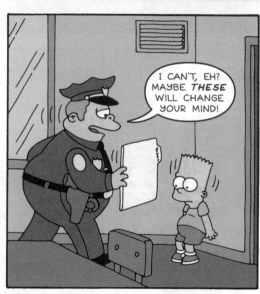

I CAN'T, EH? MAYBE *THESE* WILL CHANGE YOUR MIND!

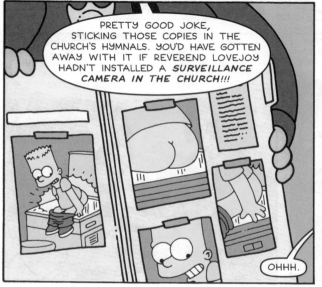

PRETTY GOOD JOKE, STICKING THOSE COPIES IN THE CHURCH'S HYMNALS. YOU'D HAVE GOTTEN AWAY WITH IT IF REVEREND LOVEJOY HADN'T INSTALLED A *SURVEILLANCE CAMERA IN THE CHURCH!!!*

OHHH.

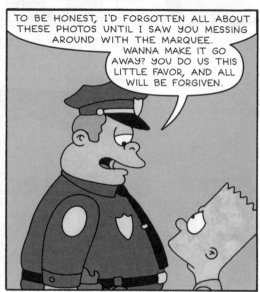

TO BE HONEST, I'D FORGOTTEN ALL ABOUT THESE PHOTOS UNTIL I SAW YOU MESSING AROUND WITH THE MARQUEE. WANNA MAKE IT GO AWAY? YOU DO US THIS LITTLE FAVOR, AND ALL WILL BE FORGIVEN.

97

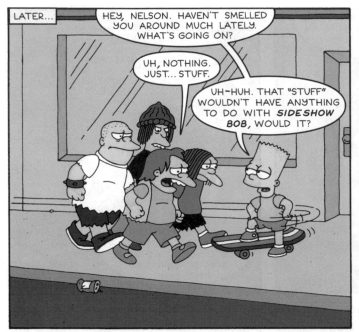

LATER...

HEY, NELSON. HAVEN'T SMELLED YOU AROUND MUCH LATELY. WHAT'S GOING ON?

UH, NOTHING. JUST... STUFF.

UH-HUH. THAT "STUFF" WOULDN'T HAVE ANYTHING TO DO WITH *SIDESHOW BOB*, WOULD IT?

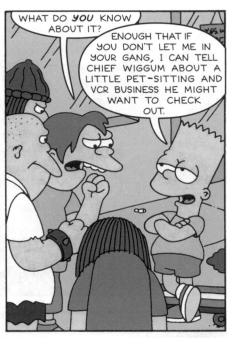

WHAT DO *YOU* KNOW ABOUT IT?

ENOUGH THAT IF YOU DON'T LET ME IN YOUR GANG, I CAN TELL CHIEF WIGGUM ABOUT A LITTLE PET-SITTING AND VCR BUSINESS HE MIGHT WANT TO CHECK OUT.

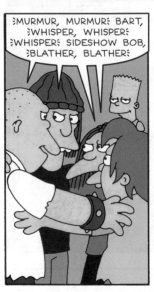

:MURMUR, MURMUR: BART, :WHISPER, WHISPER: :WHISPER: SIDESHOW BOB, :BLATHER, BLATHER:

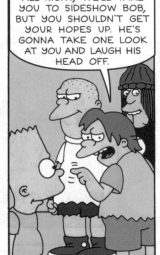

ALL RIGHT, WE'LL TAKE YOU TO SIDESHOW BOB, BUT YOU SHOULDN'T GET YOUR HOPES UP. HE'S GONNA TAKE ONE LOOK AT YOU AND LAUGH HIS HEAD OFF.

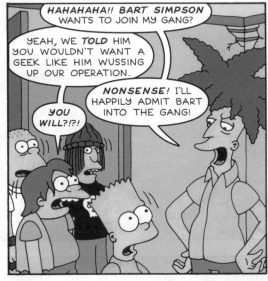

HAHAHAHA!! BART SIMPSON WANTS TO JOIN MY GANG?

YEAH, WE *TOLD* HIM YOU WOULDN'T WANT A GEEK LIKE HIM WUSSING UP OUR OPERATION.

NONSENSE! I'LL HAPPILY ADMIT BART INTO THE GANG!

YOU WILL?!?!

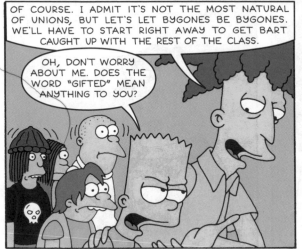

OF COURSE. I ADMIT IT'S NOT THE MOST NATURAL OF UNIONS, BUT LET'S LET BYGONES BE BYGONES. WE'LL HAVE TO START RIGHT AWAY TO GET BART CAUGHT UP WITH THE REST OF THE CLASS.

OH, DON'T WORRY ABOUT ME. DOES THE WORD "GIFTED" MEAN ANYTHING TO YOU?

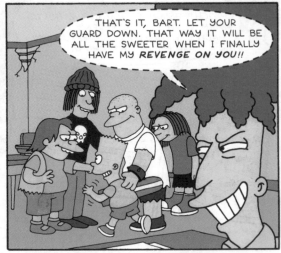

THAT'S IT, BART. LET YOUR GUARD DOWN. THAT WAY IT WILL BE ALL THE SWEETER WHEN I FINALLY HAVE MY *REVENGE ON YOU!!*

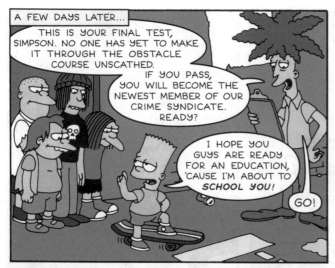

A FEW DAYS LATER...

THIS IS YOUR FINAL TEST, SIMPSON. NO ONE HAS YET TO MAKE IT THROUGH THE OBSTACLE COURSE UNSCATHED.

IF YOU PASS, YOU WILL BECOME THE NEWEST MEMBER OF OUR CRIME SYNDICATE. READY?

I HOPE YOU GUYS ARE READY FOR AN EDUCATION, 'CAUSE I'M ABOUT TO *SCHOOL YOU!*

GO!

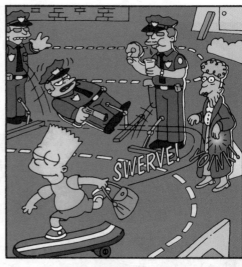

SWERVE!

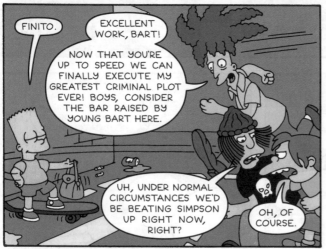

FINITO.

EXCELLENT WORK, BART!

NOW THAT YOU'RE UP TO SPEED WE CAN FINALLY EXECUTE MY GREATEST CRIMINAL PLOT EVER! BOYS, CONSIDER THE BAR RAISED BY YOUNG BART HERE.

UH, UNDER NORMAL CIRCUMSTANCES WE'D BE BEATING SIMPSON UP RIGHT NOW, RIGHT?

OH, OF COURSE.

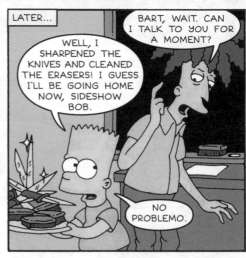

LATER...

BART, WAIT. CAN I TALK TO YOU FOR A MOMENT?

WELL, I SHARPENED THE KNIVES AND CLEANED THE ERASERS! I GUESS I'LL BE GOING HOME NOW, SIDESHOW BOB.

NO PROBLEMO.

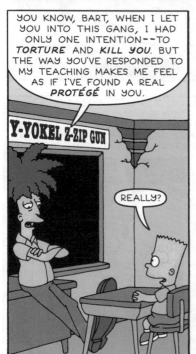

YOU KNOW, BART, WHEN I LET YOU INTO THIS GANG, I HAD ONLY ONE INTENTION--TO *TORTURE* AND *KILL YOU.* BUT THE WAY YOU'VE RESPONDED TO MY TEACHING MAKES ME FEEL AS IF I'VE FOUND A REAL *PROTÉGÉ* IN YOU.

Y-YOKEL Z-ZIP GUN

REALLY?

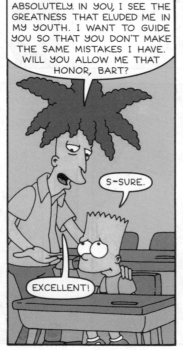

ABSOLUTELY. IN YOU, I SEE THE GREATNESS THAT ELUDED ME IN MY YOUTH. I WANT TO GUIDE YOU SO THAT YOU DON'T MAKE THE SAME MISTAKES I HAVE. WILL YOU ALLOW ME THAT HONOR, BART?

S-SURE.

EXCELLENT!

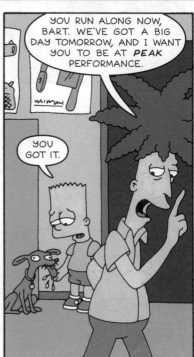

YOU RUN ALONG NOW, BART. WE'VE GOT A BIG DAY TOMORROW, AND I WANT YOU TO BE AT *PEAK* PERFORMANCE.

YOU GOT IT.

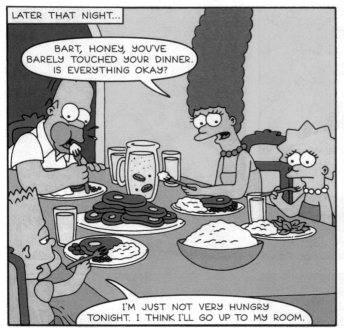

LATER THAT NIGHT...

BART, HONEY, YOU'VE BARELY TOUCHED YOUR DINNER. IS EVERYTHING OKAY?

I'M JUST NOT VERY HUNGRY TONIGHT. I THINK I'LL GO UP TO MY ROOM.

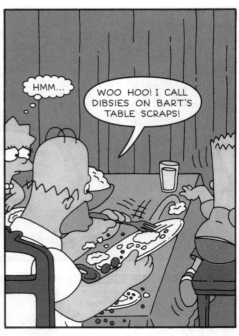

HMM...

WOO HOO! I CALL DIBSIES ON BART'S TABLE SCRAPS!

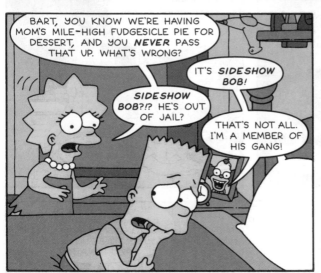

BART, YOU KNOW WE'RE HAVING MOM'S MILE-HIGH FUDGESICLE PIE FOR DESSERT, AND YOU *NEVER* PASS THAT UP. WHAT'S WRONG?

IT'S *SIDESHOW BOB!*

SIDESHOW BOB?!? HE'S OUT OF JAIL?

THAT'S NOT ALL. I'M A MEMBER OF HIS GANG!

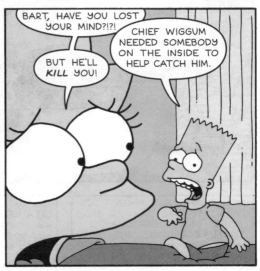

BART, HAVE YOU LOST YOUR MIND?!?!

BUT HE'LL *KILL* YOU!

CHIEF WIGGUM NEEDED SOMEBODY ON THE INSIDE TO HELP CATCH HIM.

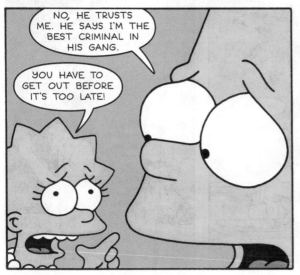

NO, HE TRUSTS ME. HE SAYS I'M THE BEST CRIMINAL IN HIS GANG.

YOU HAVE TO GET OUT BEFORE IT'S TOO LATE!

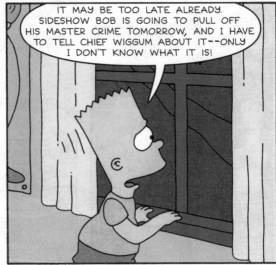

IT MAY BE TOO LATE ALREADY. SIDESHOW BOB IS GOING TO PULL OFF HIS MASTER CRIME TOMORROW, AND I HAVE TO TELL CHIEF WIGGUM ABOUT IT--ONLY I DON'T KNOW WHAT IT IS!

THE NEXT DAY...
WHAT DO YOU MEAN YOU DON'T KNOW WHAT IT IS?
WELL, YOU SEE, UHH...
DONUTS
CHIEF CLANKY WIGGUM
BART, DO YOU KNOW WHAT THE PENALTY IS FOR MAKING COPIES OF YOUR BUTT ON CHURCH PROPERTY?
NO.
OH. I THOUGHT MAYBE YOU COULD TELL ME. THAT MEANS I'M GOING TO HAVE TO MAKE UP THE PUNISHMENT MYSELF!
OH, UHH, NOW I REMEMBER WHAT THE PLAN IS--SIDESHOW BOB IS, UH, GOING TO STEAL A, UM, PRICELESS EXHIBIT FROM THE, UH...ART MUSEUM! THAT'S IT!
EXCELLENT WORK, SIMPSON.
UH, CHIEF, DOES SPRINGFIELD EVEN HAVE AN ART MUSEUM?
IT DOES NOW!
DONUTS

LATER...
GET INTO COSTUME, MY LITTLE OUTLAWS! TODAY'S THE DAY ALL YOUR HARD WORK AND PREPARATION PAY OFF, AS WE EXECUTE MY MOST DASTARDLY SCHEME YET--KIDNAPPING THE RICHEST MAN IN SPRINGFIELD!!!
OH, MAN! CHIEF WIGGUM BOUGHT MY PHONY STORY, BUT WHAT WILL HAPPEN WHEN HE FINDS OUT I DOUBLE-CROSSED HIM?
Dedication of the C. MONTGOMERY BURNS Children's Hospital
...AND THAT IS WHY I HAVE GIVEN SO GENEROUSLY OF MY MONEY AND TIME TO SEE THAT THE SPRINGFIELD HOSPITAL HAS A NEW CHILDREN'S WING.
THANK YOU, AND MAY GOD BLESS.
I NEVER KNEW YOU HAD SO MUCH COMPASSION FOR CHILDREN, SIR.
IF BY "COMPASSION" YOU MEAN A VESTED INTEREST IN THEIR RIPE, TENDER ORGANS...
COME AGAIN, SIR?
CLAP! CLAP! CLAP!
SMITHERS, I'M AN OLD MAN WHOSE BODY IS IN CONSTANT NEED OF REPLACEMENT PARTS.
THIS NEW CHILDREN'S WING WILL SERVE AS MY OWN PERSONAL ORGAN BANK.
EXCUSE ME, MISTER BURNS. CAN I HAVE A LITTLE MONEY TO BUY SOME FOOD?
NOT ON YOUR LIFE, TINY TIM! I WON'T HAVE MY FUTURE BODY PARTS SULLIED WITH YOUR "NEAR BEER" AND "CANDY CIGARETTES!"
FROM NOW ON, YOU'LL EAT NOTHING BUT KALE AND KIDNEY PIE!
GET BENT, SIR!
MR. BURNS!
AMBULA
WHAM!
GREETINGS, MR. BURNS. I'D LIKE TO CORDIALLY WELCOME YOU TO YOUR KIDNAPPING. I'M SIDESHOW BOB, AND I'LL BE YOUR GUIDE.

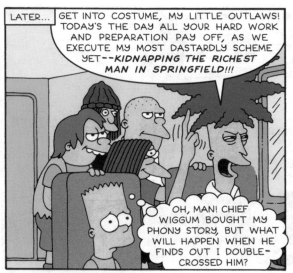

WHAT IS THE MEANING OF THIS? I'LL HAVE YOUR STETHOSCOPE FOR SUCH IMPROPRIETY!
QUIET!
BART, HURRY AND TIE HIM UP!
PLEASE, LITTLE BOY. THERE'S A SHILLING IN IT FOR YOU IF YOU'LL LAY DOWN YOUR LIFE FOR ME WHILST I MAKE MY ESCAPE.
SORRY, MR. BURNS.
IT'S NO USE, SIDESHOW BOB, I CAN'T DO IT. JUST LET ME OUT, AND I'LL NEVER TELL ANYONE ABOUT THE CRIME SCHOOL, OKAY?
YOU CAN'T QUIT NOW, BART!
LET'S JUST GET OUT OF HERE, AND EVERYTHING WILL BE--
SIDESHOW BOB, WE'VE GOT YOU SURROUNDED! YOU'VE GOT UNTIL THE COUNT OF THREE TO COME OUT!
YOU DID THIS! YOU BETRAYED ME!
I SWEAR I DIDN'T DO IT!
ONCE I BLOCK THE DOORS TO KEEP OUT THOSE MEDDLESOME COPS, I'LL DEAL WITH YOU!
AMBULANCE
SKREEECH!
THIS MAY BE MY LAST STAND BART SIMPSON, BUT IF I'M GOING DOWN, I'M GOING TO DO THE ONE THING THAT MATTERS MOST TO ME... KILL YOU!!!
STRYCHNINE

SLAM
I GOTTA GET OUT OF HERE!
OH...CHEST PAINS-- TOO...MUCH... EXCITEMENT!
ON
YOU'RE TRAPPED, SIMPSON. IT WILL BE A PITY MURDERING YOU. YOU HAD SUCH POTENTIAL.
STAY BACK, OR I'LL FRY YOU!
YOU CAN'T RUN FOREVER!
WHOA! I'M GETTING DIZZY.
WHOOPS!
WHO? WHA--?...
KA-ZAK!
OH NO!
GOODBYE, SIMPSON. I GUESS YOU COULD SAY YOU'RE FINALLY GOING TO GET MY "POINT!"
EAT VOLTAGE, TERWILLIGER!
KA-ZZZAK!
TWO AND A QUARTER...TWO AND A HALF...I'M NOT KIDDING HERE, BOB! TWO AND THREE QUARTERS...
I'M SERIOUS AS A HEART ATTACK...

YOU CAN RELAX, CHIEF. HERE'S YOUR MAN!
WHY'D YOU DO IT, BOB?
IT'S FOREVER WHO I AM--MY RAISON D'ÊTRE. I JUST HOPE THAT THE YOUTHS I SO WRONGLY INVOLVED IN MY PLAN HAVE LEARNED THEIR LESSON AND SEE WHAT A MISGUIDED PATH I ALMOST LED THEM DOWN.
HA, HA!
POL
BUT HOW'D THE POLICE KNOW WHERE TO FIND US? I GAVE THEM THE *WRONG* INFORMATION!
I THOUGHT YOU MIGHT DO THAT, SO I FOLLOWED YOU THIS MORNING AND CALLED CHIEF WIGGUM WHEN YOU GOT TO THE HOSPITAL.
I GUESS THIS SQUARES US, SIMPSON. I'LL DESTROY THOSE SURVEILLANCE PHOTOS, BUT YOU STAY OUT OF TROUBLE. I'M GOING TO BE WATCHING YOUR ACTIONS VERY CLOSELY FROM NOW ON.
DON'T WORRY CHIEF. FROM NOW ON, I PROMISE YOU WON'T SEE ME DOING ANYTHING I SHOULDN'T.
THERE'S A GOOD BOY!
HEY, LOU, GET THAT MANGY MUTT OUT OF THE SQUAD CAR. HE'S EATING MY LUNCH!
AS SEEN ON THE FOX SPECIAL, WORLD'S MOST DANGEROUS POLICE BUTTS
THE END

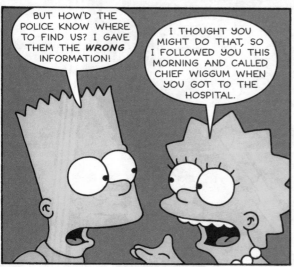

BART
#47
US $2.50
CAN $3.50
COMICS
JOURNEY TO THE FUTURE AND BACK AGAIN TO WITNESS...
...THE RISE AND FALL OF BART SIMPSON!
GROENING

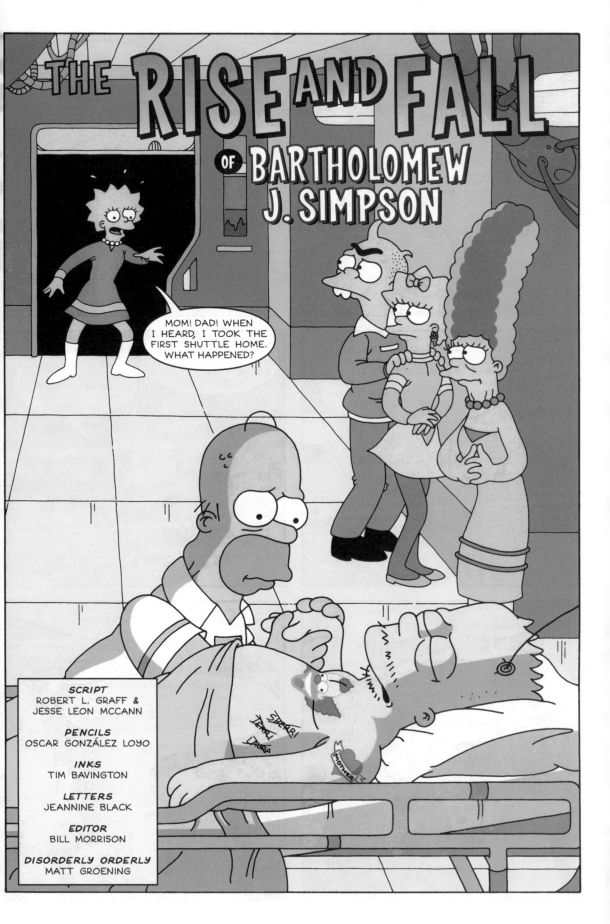

THE RISE AND FALL

OF BARTHOLOMEW J. SIMPSON

MOM! DAD! WHEN I HEARD, I TOOK THE FIRST SHUTTLE HOME. WHAT HAPPENED?

SCRIPT
ROBERT L. GRAFF &
JESSE LEON MCCANN

PENCILS
OSCAR GONZÁLEZ LOYO

INKS
TIM BAVINGTON

LETTERS
JEANNINE BLACK

EDITOR
BILL MORRISON

DISORDERLY ORDERLY
MATT GROENING

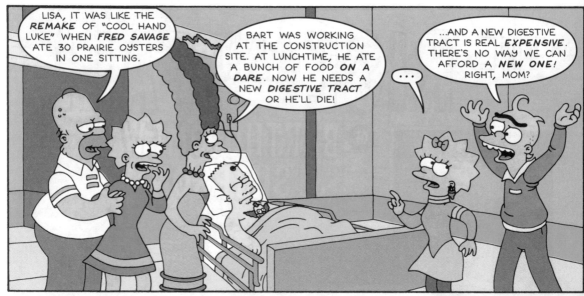

LISA, IT WAS LIKE THE *REMAKE* OF "COOL HAND LUKE" WHEN *FRED SAVAGE* ATE 30 PRAIRIE OYSTERS IN ONE SITTING.

BART WAS WORKING AT THE CONSTRUCTION SITE. AT LUNCHTIME, HE ATE A BUNCH OF FOOD *ON A DARE*. NOW HE NEEDS A NEW *DIGESTIVE TRACT* OR HE'LL DIE!

...

...AND A NEW DIGESTIVE TRACT IS REAL *EXPENSIVE*. THERE'S NO WAY WE CAN AFFORD A *NEW ONE*! RIGHT, MOM?

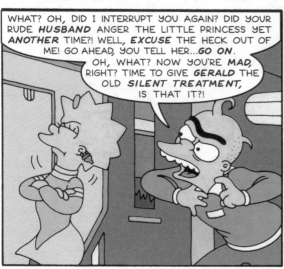

WHAT? OH, DID I INTERRUPT YOU AGAIN? DID YOUR RUDE *HUSBAND* ANGER THE LITTLE PRINCESS YET *ANOTHER* TIME?! WELL, *EXCUSE* THE HECK OUT OF ME! GO AHEAD, YOU TELL HER...*GO ON*. OH, WHAT? NOW YOU'RE *MAD*, RIGHT? TIME TO GIVE *GERALD* THE OLD *SILENT TREATMENT*, IS THAT IT?!

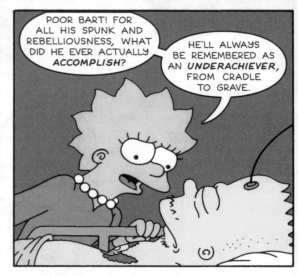

POOR BART! FOR ALL HIS SPUNK AND REBELLIOUSNESS, WHAT DID HE EVER ACTUALLY *ACCOMPLISH*?

HE'LL ALWAYS BE REMEMBERED AS AN *UNDERACHIEVER*, FROM CRADLE TO GRAVE.

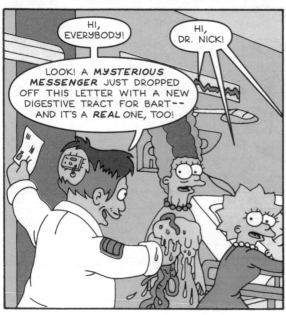

HI, EVERYBODY!

HI, DR. NICK!

LOOK! A *MYSTERIOUS MESSENGER* JUST DROPPED OFF THIS LETTER WITH A NEW DIGESTIVE TRACT FOR BART-- AND IT'S A *REAL* ONE, TOO!

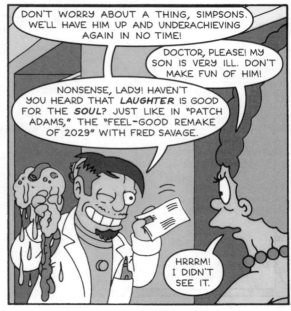

DON'T WORRY ABOUT A THING, SIMPSONS. WE'LL HAVE HIM UP AND UNDERACHIEVING AGAIN IN NO TIME!

DOCTOR, PLEASE! MY SON IS VERY ILL. DON'T MAKE FUN OF HIM!

NONSENSE, LADY! HAVEN'T YOU HEARD THAT *LAUGHTER* IS GOOD FOR THE *SOUL*? JUST LIKE IN "PATCH ADAMS," THE "FEEL-GOOD REMAKE OF 2029" WITH FRED SAVAGE.

HRRRM! I DIDN'T SEE IT.

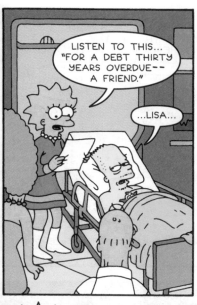

LISTEN TO THIS... "FOR A DEBT THIRTY YEARS OVERDUE-- A FRIEND."

...LISA...

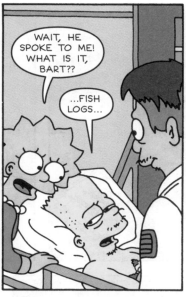

WAIT, HE SPOKE TO ME! WHAT IS IT, BART??

...FISH LOGS...

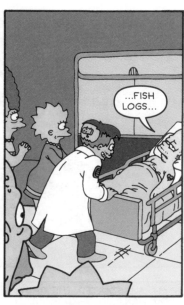

...FISH LOGS...

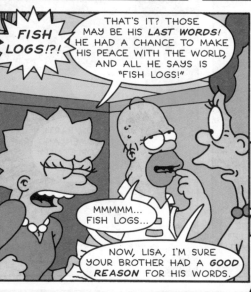

FISH LOGS!?!

THAT'S IT? THOSE MAY BE HIS *LAST WORDS*! HE HAD A CHANCE TO MAKE HIS PEACE WITH THE WORLD, AND ALL HE SAYS IS "FISH LOGS!"

MMMMM... FISH LOGS...

NOW, LISA, I'M SURE YOUR BROTHER HAD A *GOOD REASON* FOR HIS WORDS.

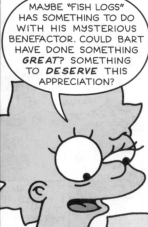

MAYBE "FISH LOGS" HAS SOMETHING TO DO WITH HIS MYSTERIOUS BENEFACTOR. COULD BART HAVE DONE SOMETHING *GREAT*? SOMETHING TO *DESERVE* THIS APPRECIATION?

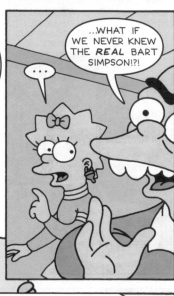

...WHAT IF WE NEVER KNEW THE *REAL* BART SIMPSON!?!

...

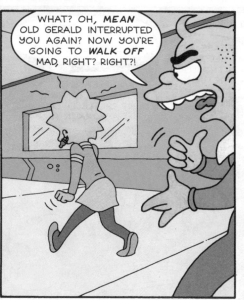

WHAT? OH, *MEAN* OLD GERALD INTERRUPTED YOU AGAIN? NOW YOU'RE GOING TO *WALK OFF* MAD, RIGHT? RIGHT?!

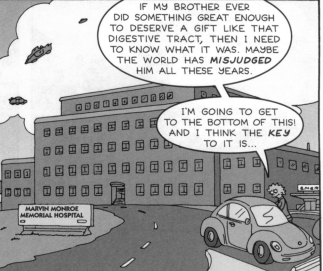

IF MY BROTHER EVER DID SOMETHING GREAT ENOUGH TO DESERVE A GIFT LIKE THAT DIGESTIVE TRACT, THEN I NEED TO KNOW WHAT IT WAS. MAYBE THE WORLD HAS *MISJUDGED* HIM ALL THESE YEARS.

I'M GOING TO GET TO THE BOTTOM OF THIS! AND I THINK THE *KEY* TO IT IS...

MARVIN MONROE MEMORIAL HOSPITAL

EMER

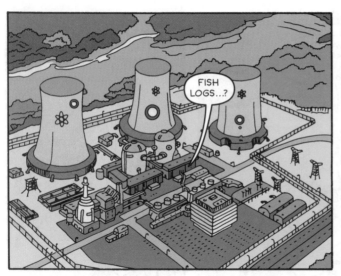

FISH LOGS...?

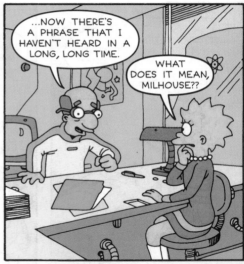

...NOW THERE'S A PHRASE THAT I HAVEN'T HEARD IN A LONG, LONG TIME.

WHAT DOES IT MEAN, MILHOUSE??

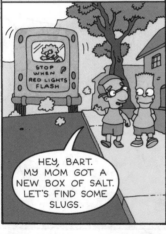

"I—IT ALL STARTED THE DAY YOU WENT TO SAXOPHONE CAMP FOR TWO WEEKS. ME AND BART WERE WALKING DOWN THE STREET, DOING OUR USUAL *COOL GUY* STUFF..."

HEY, BART. MY MOM GOT A NEW BOX OF SALT. LET'S FIND SOME SLUGS.

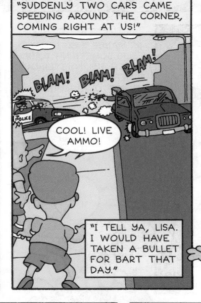

"SUDDENLY TWO CARS CAME SPEEDING AROUND THE CORNER, COMING RIGHT AT US!"

BLAM! BLAM! BLAM!

COOL! LIVE AMMO!

"I TELL YA, LISA. I WOULD HAVE TAKEN A BULLET FOR BART THAT DAY."

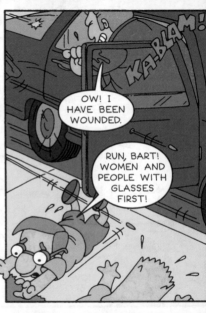

KA-BLAM!

OW! I HAVE BEEN WOUNDED.

RUN, BART! WOMEN AND PEOPLE WITH GLASSES FIRST!

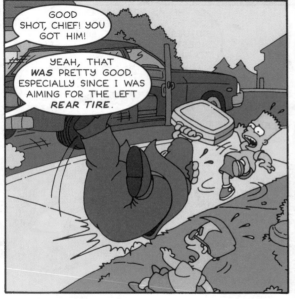

GOOD SHOT, CHIEF! YOU GOT HIM!

YEAH, THAT *WAS* PRETTY GOOD. ESPECIALLY SINCE I WAS AIMING FOR THE LEFT *REAR TIRE*.

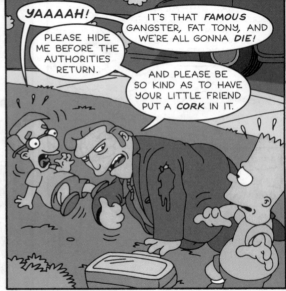

YAAAAH!

PLEASE HIDE ME BEFORE THE AUTHORITIES RETURN.

IT'S THAT *FAMOUS* GANGSTER, FAT TONY, AND WE'RE ALL GONNA *DIE*!

AND PLEASE BE SO KIND AS TO HAVE YOUR LITTLE FRIEND PUT A *CORK* IN IT.

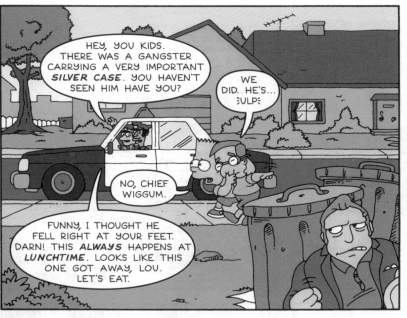

HEY, YOU KIDS. THERE WAS A GANGSTER CARRYING A VERY IMPORTANT *SILVER CASE.* YOU HAVEN'T SEEN HIM HAVE YOU?

WE DID...HE'S... ≥ULP≥

NO, CHIEF WIGGUM.

FUNNY, I THOUGHT HE FELL RIGHT AT YOUR FEET. DARN! THIS *ALWAYS* HAPPENS AT *LUNCHTIME.* LOOKS LIKE THIS ONE GOT AWAY, LOU. LET'S EAT.

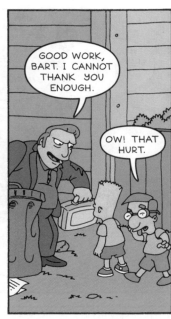

GOOD WORK, BART. I CANNOT THANK YOU ENOUGH.

OW! THAT HURT.

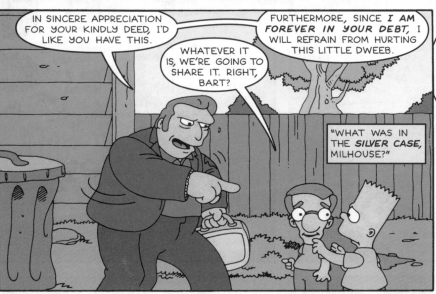

IN SINCERE APPRECIATION FOR YOUR KINDLY DEED, I'D LIKE YOU HAVE THIS.

FURTHERMORE, SINCE *I AM FOREVER IN YOUR DEBT,* I WILL REFRAIN FROM HURTING THIS LITTLE DWEEB.

WHATEVER IT IS, WE'RE GOING TO SHARE IT. RIGHT, BART?

"WHAT WAS IN THE *SILVER CASE,* MILHOUSE?"

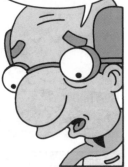

I-I'LL TELL YOU, LISA, BUT FIRST I'VE GOT SOMETHING *IMPORTANT* TO SAY. Y-YOU SEE, I'VE ALWAYS LOVED YOU, L-LISA... I JUST NEVER HAD THE COURAGE TO TELL YOU... WE'RE BOTH ADULTS NOW. SO...W-W-WILL YOU MARRY ME, LISA?

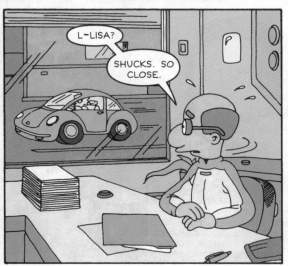

L-LISA?

SHUCKS. SO CLOSE.

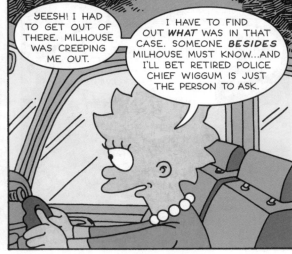

YEESH! I HAD TO GET OUT OF THERE. MILHOUSE WAS CREEPING ME OUT.

I HAVE TO FIND OUT *WHAT* WAS IN THAT CASE. SOMEONE *BESIDES* MILHOUSE MUST KNOW...AND I'LL BET RETIRED POLICE CHIEF WIGGUM IS JUST THE PERSON TO ASK.

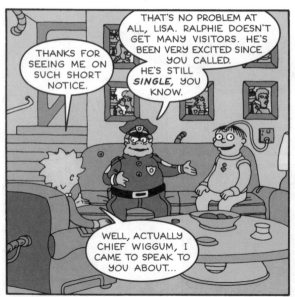

THANKS FOR SEEING ME ON SUCH SHORT NOTICE.

THAT'S NO PROBLEM AT ALL, LISA. RALPHIE DOESN'T GET MANY VISITORS. HE'S BEEN VERY EXCITED SINCE YOU CALLED. HE'S STILL *SINGLE*, YOU KNOW.

WELL, ACTUALLY CHIEF WIGGUM, I CAME TO SPEAK TO YOU ABOUT...

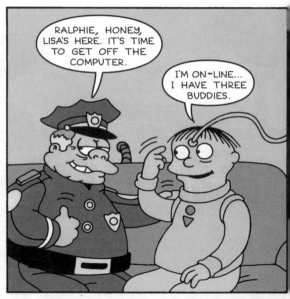

RALPHIE, HONEY, LISA'S HERE. IT'S TIME TO GET OFF THE COMPUTER.

I'M ON-LINE... I HAVE THREE BUDDIES.

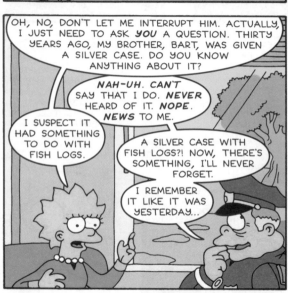

OH, NO, DON'T LET ME INTERRUPT HIM. ACTUALLY, I JUST NEED TO ASK *YOU* A QUESTION. THIRTY YEARS AGO, MY BROTHER, BART, WAS GIVEN A SILVER CASE. DO YOU KNOW ANYTHING ABOUT IT?

NAH-UH. CAN'T SAY THAT I DO. *NEVER* HEARD OF IT. *NOPE. NEWS* TO ME.

I SUSPECT IT HAD SOMETHING TO DO WITH FISH LOGS.

A SILVER CASE WITH FISH LOGS?! NOW, THERE'S SOMETHING, I'LL NEVER FORGET.

I REMEMBER IT LIKE IT WAS YESTERDAY...

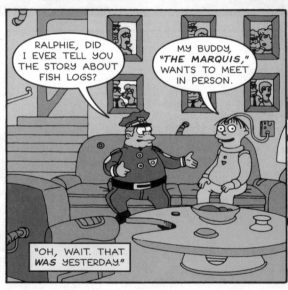

RALPHIE, DID I EVER TELL YOU THE STORY ABOUT FISH LOGS?

MY BUDDY, *"THE MARQUIS,"* WANTS TO MEET IN PERSON.

"OH, WAIT. THAT *WAS* YESTERDAY."

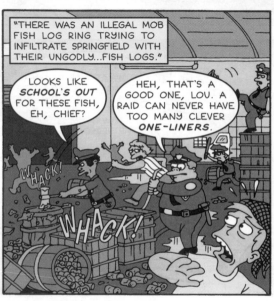

"THERE WAS AN ILLEGAL MOB FISH LOG RING TRYING TO INFILTRATE SPRINGFIELD WITH THEIR UNGODLY...FISH LOGS."

LOOKS LIKE *SCHOOL'S OUT* FOR THESE FISH, EH, CHIEF?

HEH, THAT'S A GOOD ONE, LOU. A RAID CAN NEVER HAVE TOO MANY CLEVER *ONE-LINERS.*

WHACK!

WHACK!

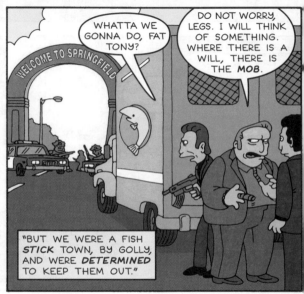

WHATTA WE GONNA DO, FAT TONY?

DO NOT WORRY, LEGS. I WILL THINK OF SOMETHING. WHERE THERE IS A WILL, THERE IS THE *MOB.*

WELCOME TO SPRINGFIELD

"BUT WE WERE A FISH *STICK* TOWN, BY GOLLY, AND WERE *DETERMINED* TO KEEP THEM OUT."

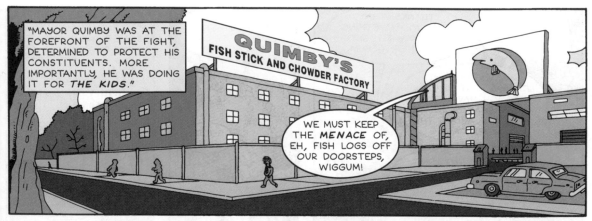

"MAYOR QUIMBY WAS AT THE FOREFRONT OF THE FIGHT, DETERMINED TO PROTECT HIS CONSTITUENTS. MORE IMPORTANTLY, HE WAS DOING IT FOR *THE KIDS*."

QUIMBY'S FISH STICK AND CHOWDER FACTORY

WE MUST KEEP THE *MENACE* OF, EH, FISH LOGS OFF OUR DOORSTEPS, WIGGUM!

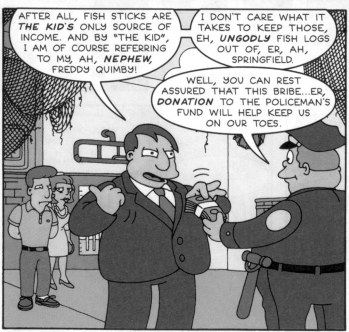

AFTER ALL, FISH STICKS ARE *THE KID'S* ONLY SOURCE OF INCOME. AND BY "THE KID", I AM OF COURSE REFERRING TO MY, AH, *NEPHEW*, FREDDY QUIMBY!

I DON'T CARE WHAT IT TAKES TO KEEP THOSE, EH, *UNGODLY* FISH LOGS OUT OF, ER, AH, SPRINGFIELD.

WELL, YOU CAN REST ASSURED THAT THIS BRIBE...ER, *DONATION* TO THE POLICEMAN'S FUND WILL HELP KEEP US ON OUR TOES.

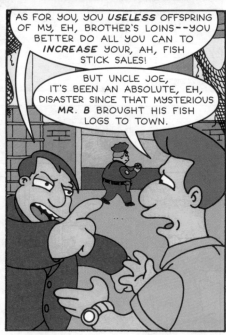

AS FOR YOU, YOU *USELESS* OFFSPRING OF MY, EH, BROTHER'S LOINS--YOU BETTER DO ALL YOU CAN TO *INCREASE* YOUR, AH, FISH STICK SALES!

BUT UNCLE JOE, IT'S BEEN AN ABSOLUTE, EH, DISASTER SINCE THAT MYSTERIOUS *MR. B* BROUGHT HIS FISH LOGS TO TOWN.

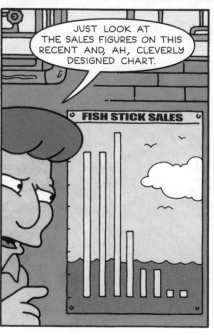

JUST LOOK AT THE SALES FIGURES ON THIS RECENT AND, AH, CLEVERLY DESIGNED CHART.

FISH STICK SALES

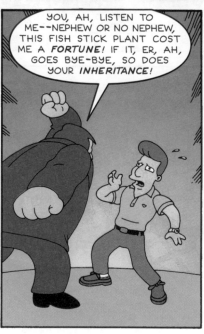

YOU, AH, LISTEN TO ME--NEPHEW OR NO NEPHEW, THIS FISH STICK PLANT COST ME A *FORTUNE*! IF IT, ER, AH, GOES BYE-BYE, SO DOES YOUR *INHERITANCE*!

I WANT THOSE SCHOOL KIDS EATING, AH, FISH STICKS WHENEVER POSSIBLE! FIVE DAYS A WEEK, THREE MEALS A DAY, MORNING, LUNCH AND, EH, SNACK TIME, TOO!

WHOEVER THIS MR. B IS, I WANT HIS HEAD ON A PLATTER...WITH, EH, *TARTAR SAUCE*!

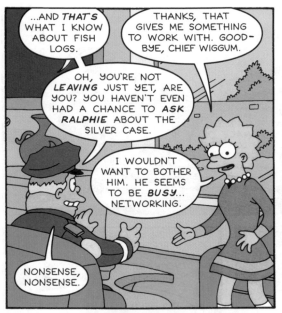

...AND *THAT'S* WHAT I KNOW ABOUT FISH LOGS.

THANKS, THAT GIVES ME SOMETHING TO WORK WITH. GOOD-BYE, CHIEF WIGGUM.

OH, YOU'RE NOT *LEAVING* JUST YET, ARE YOU? YOU HAVEN'T EVEN HAD A CHANCE TO *ASK RALPHIE* ABOUT THE SILVER CASE.

I WOULDN'T WANT TO BOTHER HIM. HE SEEMS TO BE *BUSY*... NETWORKING.

NONSENSE, NONSENSE.

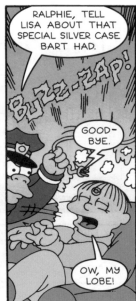

RALPHIE, TELL LISA ABOUT THAT SPECIAL SILVER CASE BART HAD.

BUZZ-ZAP!

GOOD-BYE.

OW, MY LOBE!

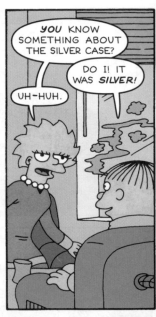

YOU KNOW SOMETHING ABOUT THE SILVER CASE?

DO I! IT WAS *SILVER!*

UH-HUH.

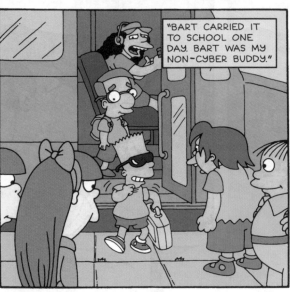

"BART CARRIED IT TO SCHOOL ONE DAY. BART WAS MY NON-CYBER BUDDY."

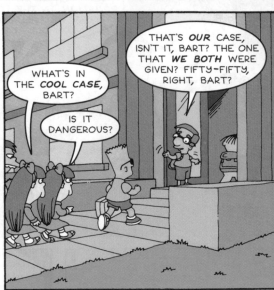

WHAT'S IN THE *COOL CASE*, BART?

IS IT DANGEROUS?

THAT'S *OUR* CASE, ISN'T IT, BART? THE ONE THAT *WE BOTH* WERE GIVEN? FIFTY-FIFTY, RIGHT, BART?

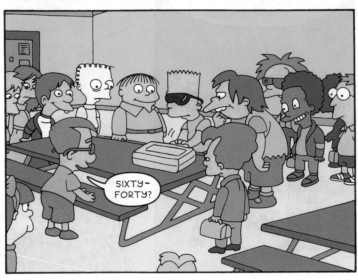

SIXTY-FORTY?

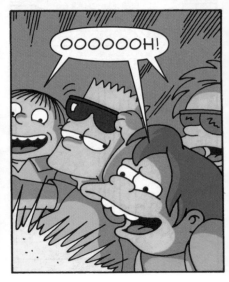

OOOOOOH!

BEHOLD, THE NEWEST IN LUNCHTIME CUISINE! FISH LOGS!
FISH LOGS? VAS IS DAS? I HAF NEVER HEARD OF SUCH A TING!
MMMMM! THEY SMELL SO GOOD.
I WONDER IF THEY TASTE AS GOOD AS THEY SMELL?
CHOMP!
CHEW!
CHEW!
AHHH! SUPOIB, MAN!
YAY!
MEIN SCHOOL-BOUGHT, CHIPPED-BEEF SURPRISE ON A KAISER ROLL CANNOT COMPETE!
NOTHING COMPARES TO A LUNCH MADE AT HOME BY MY MOTHER! :SNIFF: AH, CORN AND CABBAGE SOUFFLE WITH A BIG SLICE OF CREAM PIE FOR DESSERT. EXCELSIOR!
STEP RIGHT UP, FELLOW STUDENTS! ONLY A DOLLAR FOR THE BEST SCHOOL LUNCH AROUND!
SUCH A DEAL! SELL ME ONE, BART!
FISH FROGS?! LET ME SEE.
ME, TOO! MAYBE I'LL KEEP IT DOWN!
NEIN! NEIN! I VAS HERE FIRST!
WHAT SORT OF BRU-HA-HA IS BREWING HERE?
SIMPSON! YOU WOULDN'T HAPPEN TO BE SELLING UNAUTHORIZED LUNCHTIME FOODSTUFFS IN OUR CAFETERIA, WOULD YOU?
NO, SIR, PRINCIPAL SKINNER. I WAS JUST SHOWING THEM MY NEW...EMPTY... LUNCH BOX.
OUR EMPTY LUNCH BOX. PART OF IT'S MINE, PRINCIPAL SKINNER.

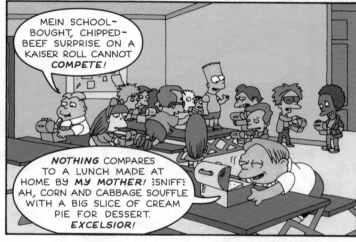

VERY GOOD! CARRY ON.
HMMPH! YOU'D NEVER CATCH **ME** EATING NONFACULTY OR NONMOTHER-APPROVED LUNCHES!
HACK! GOOD LORD, CHOKE!
COUGH!
GEE, MARTIN! WHAT A DUMMY-HEAD! NO ONE HAS EVER **CHOKED** ON A FISH LOG!
HUUGH-HUUGH! BART, I HAVE SEEN THE ERROR OF MY WAYS--***I AM FOREVER IN YOUR DEBT! SOMEDAY, I'LL PAY YOU BACK!***
THINK NOTHING OF IT, MARTIN.
HERE YA GO, MILHOUSE--TEN PERCENT!
FOUR DOLLARS! ***HOORAY!*** I'M RICH!
SOON, BART WAS SELLING FISH LOGS EVERY DAY--AND MAKING ***A LOT*** OF MONEY. BUT I NEVER, EVER FOUND OUT WHAT HE DID WITH THE ***FISH FROGS***.
THANKS FOR THE HELP, RALPH. DON'T WAKE YOUR DAD. I'LL SEE MYSELF OUT.
Police Bribes Pension Fund 0215
Pay to the order of Chief Wiggum $15,000.00
Fifteen thousand dollars and 00/100 dollars
First Springfield National Bank
Fat Tony d'Amico
OW! DADDY, I CAN'T FIND THE RIGHT PORT.
THAT ***PAYOLA CHECK*** HAD FAT TONY'S SIGNATURE. I'LL BET HE CAN SHED SOME LIGHT ON THIS MYSTERY!

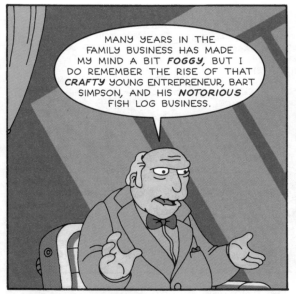

MANY YEARS IN THE FAMILY BUSINESS HAS MADE MY MIND A BIT *FOGGY*, BUT I DO REMEMBER THE RISE OF THAT *CRAFTY* YOUNG ENTREPRENEUR, BART SIMPSON, AND HIS *NOTORIOUS* FISH LOG BUSINESS.

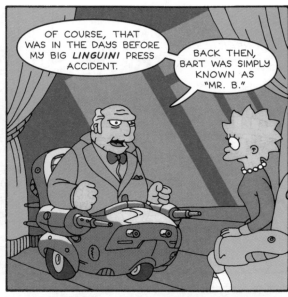

OF COURSE, THAT WAS IN THE DAYS BEFORE MY BIG *LINGUINI* PRESS ACCIDENT.

BACK THEN, BART WAS SIMPLY KNOWN AS "MR. B."

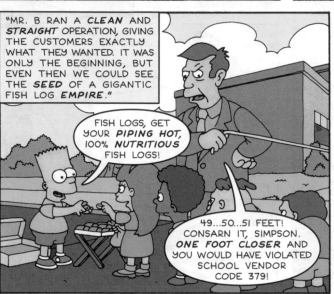

"MR. B RAN A *CLEAN* AND *STRAIGHT* OPERATION, GIVING THE CUSTOMERS EXACTLY WHAT THEY WANTED. IT WAS ONLY THE BEGINNING, BUT EVEN THEN WE COULD SEE THE *SEED* OF A GIGANTIC FISH LOG *EMPIRE*."

FISH LOGS, GET YOUR *PIPING HOT*, 100% *NUTRITIOUS* FISH LOGS!

49...50...51 FEET! CONSARN IT, SIMPSON. *ONE FOOT CLOSER* AND YOU WOULD HAVE VIOLATED SCHOOL VENDOR CODE 379!

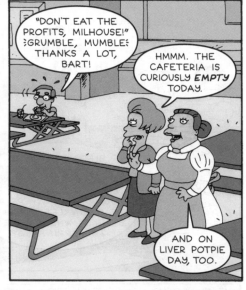

"DON'T EAT THE PROFITS, MILHOUSE!" *GRUMBLE, MUMBLE* THANKS A LOT, BART!

HMMM. THE CAFETERIA IS CURIOUSLY *EMPTY* TODAY.

AND ON LIVER POTPIE DAY, TOO.

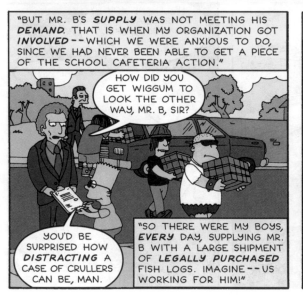

"BUT MR. B'S *SUPPLY* WAS NOT MEETING HIS *DEMAND*. THAT IS WHEN MY ORGANIZATION GOT *INVOLVED* -- WHICH WE WERE ANXIOUS TO DO, SINCE WE HAD NEVER BEEN ABLE TO GET A PIECE OF THE SCHOOL CAFETERIA ACTION."

HOW DID YOU GET WIGGUM TO LOOK THE OTHER WAY, MR. B, SIR?

YOU'D BE SURPRISED HOW *DISTRACTING* A CASE OF CRULLERS CAN BE, MAN.

"SO THERE WERE MY BOYS, *EVERY* DAY, SUPPLYING MR. B WITH A LARGE SHIPMENT OF *LEGALLY PURCHASED* FISH LOGS. IMAGINE -- US WORKING FOR HIM!"

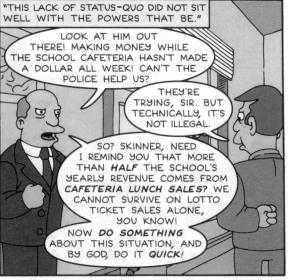

"THIS LACK OF STATUS-QUO DID NOT SIT WELL WITH THE POWERS THAT BE."

LOOK AT HIM OUT THERE! MAKING MONEY WHILE THE SCHOOL CAFETERIA HASN'T MADE A DOLLAR ALL WEEK! CAN'T THE POLICE HELP US?

THEY'RE TRYING, SIR. BUT TECHNICALLY, IT'S NOT ILLEGAL.

SO? SKINNER, NEED I REMIND YOU THAT MORE THAN *HALF* THE SCHOOL'S YEARLY REVENUE COMES FROM *CAFETERIA LUNCH SALES* ALONE? WE CANNOT SURVIVE ON LOTTO TICKET SALES ALONE, YOU KNOW! NOW *DO SOMETHING* ABOUT THIS SITUATION, AND BY GOD, DO IT *QUICK!*

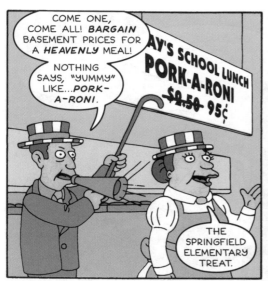

COME ONE, COME ALL! *BARGAIN* BASEMENT PRICES FOR A *HEAVENLY* MEAL!

NOTHING SAYS, "YUMMY" LIKE...PORK-A-RONI.

AY'S SCHOOL LUNCH
PORK-A-RONI
$2.50 95¢

THE SPRINGFIELD ELEMENTARY TREAT.

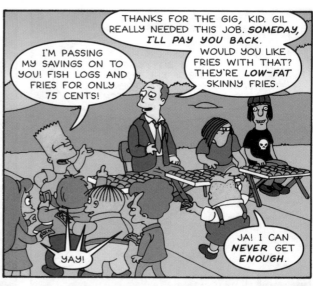

THANKS FOR THE GIG, KID. GIL REALLY NEEDED THIS JOB. *SOMEDAY, I'LL PAY YOU BACK.*

WOULD YOU LIKE FRIES WITH THAT? THEY'RE *LOW-FAT* SKINNY FRIES.

I'M PASSING MY SAVINGS ON TO YOU! FISH LOGS AND FRIES FOR ONLY 75 CENTS!

YAY!

JA! I CAN *NEVER* GET *ENOUGH.*

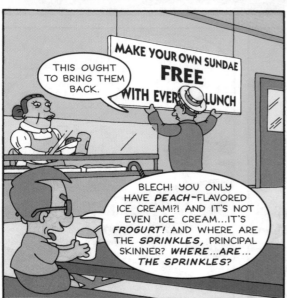

THIS OUGHT TO BRING THEM BACK.

MAKE YOUR OWN SUNDAE
FREE
WITH EVERY LUNCH

BLECH! YOU ONLY HAVE *PEACH*-FLAVORED ICE CREAM!?! AND IT'S NOT EVEN ICE CREAM...IT'S *FROGURT*! AND WHERE ARE THE *SPRINKLES,* PRINCIPAL SKINNER? *WHERE...ARE... THE SPRINKLES?*

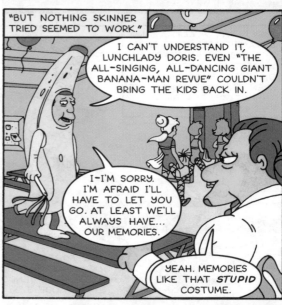

"BUT NOTHING SKINNER TRIED SEEMED TO WORK."

I CAN'T UNDERSTAND IT, LUNCHLADY DORIS. EVEN "THE ALL-SINGING, ALL-DANCING GIANT BANANA-MAN REVUE" COULDN'T BRING THE KIDS BACK IN.

I-I'M SORRY. I'M AFRAID I'LL HAVE TO LET YOU GO. AT LEAST WE'LL ALWAYS HAVE... OUR MEMORIES.

YEAH. MEMORIES LIKE THAT *STUPID* COSTUME.

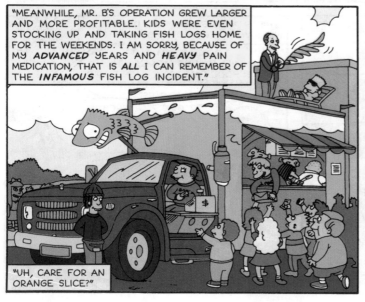

"MEANWHILE, MR. B'S OPERATION GREW LARGER AND MORE PROFITABLE. KIDS WERE EVEN STOCKING UP AND TAKING FISH LOGS HOME FOR THE WEEKENDS. I AM SORRY, BECAUSE OF MY *ADVANCED* YEARS AND *HEAVY* PAIN MEDICATION, THAT IS *ALL* I CAN REMEMBER OF THE *INFAMOUS* FISH LOG INCIDENT."

"UH, CARE FOR AN ORANGE SLICE?"

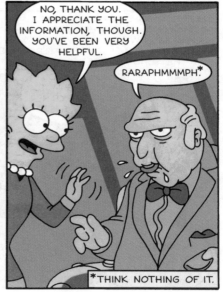

NO, THANK YOU. I APPRECIATE THE INFORMATION, THOUGH. YOU'VE BEEN VERY HELPFUL.

RARAPHMMMPH.*

*THINK NOTHING OF IT.

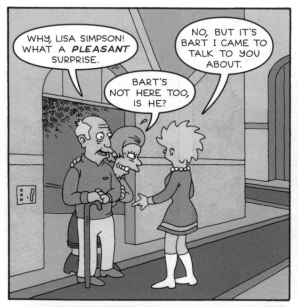

WHY, LISA SIMPSON! WHAT A *PLEASANT* SURPRISE.

BART'S NOT HERE TOO, IS HE?

NO, BUT IT'S BART I CAME TO TALK TO YOU ABOUT.

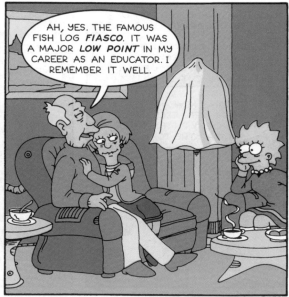

AH, YES. THE FAMOUS FISH LOG *FIASCO*. IT WAS A MAJOR *LOW POINT* IN MY CAREER AS AN EDUCATOR. I REMEMBER IT WELL.

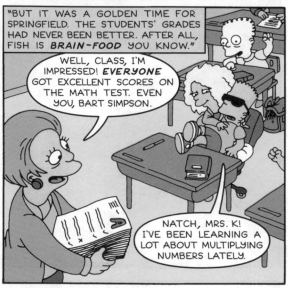

"BUT IT WAS A GOLDEN TIME FOR SPRINGFIELD. THE STUDENTS' GRADES HAD NEVER BEEN BETTER. AFTER ALL, FISH IS *BRAIN-FOOD* YOU KNOW."

WELL, CLASS, I'M IMPRESSED! *EVERYONE* GOT EXCELLENT SCORES ON THE MATH TEST. EVEN YOU, BART SIMPSON.

NATCH, MRS. K! I'VE BEEN LEARNING A LOT ABOUT MULTIPLYING NUMBERS LATELY.

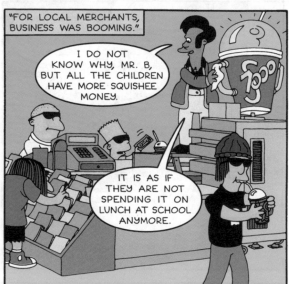

"FOR LOCAL MERCHANTS, BUSINESS WAS BOOMING."

I DO NOT KNOW WHY, MR. B, BUT ALL THE CHILDREN HAVE MORE SQUISHEE MONEY.

IT IS AS IF THEY ARE NOT SPENDING IT ON LUNCH AT SCHOOL ANYMORE.

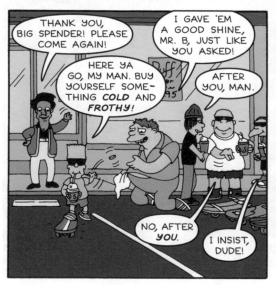

THANK YOU, BIG SPENDER! PLEASE COME AGAIN!

I GAVE 'EM A GOOD SHINE, MR. B, JUST LIKE YOU ASKED!

HERE YA GO, MY MAN. BUY YOURSELF SOMETHING *COLD* AND *FROTHY!*

AFTER YOU, MAN.

NO, AFTER *YOU.*

I INSIST, DUDE!

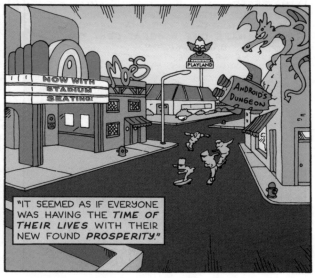

"IT SEEMED AS IF EVERYONE WAS HAVING THE *TIME OF THEIR LIVES* WITH THEIR NEW FOUND *PROSPERITY.*"

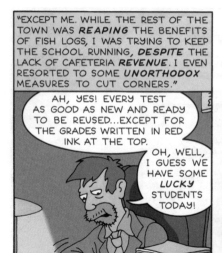

"EXCEPT ME. WHILE THE REST OF THE TOWN WAS *REAPING* THE BENEFITS OF FISH LOGS, I WAS TRYING TO KEEP THE SCHOOL RUNNING, *DESPITE* THE LACK OF CAFETERIA *REVENUE*. I EVEN RESORTED TO SOME *UNORTHODOX* MEASURES TO CUT CORNERS."

AH, YES! EVERY TEST AS GOOD AS NEW AND READY TO BE REUSED...EXCEPT FOR THE GRADES WRITTEN IN RED INK AT THE TOP.

OH, WELL, I GUESS WE HAVE SOME *LUCKY* STUDENTS TODAY!

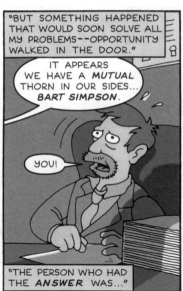

"BUT SOMETHING HAPPENED THAT WOULD SOON SOLVE ALL MY PROBLEMS--OPPORTUNITY WALKED IN THE DOOR."

IT APPEARS WE HAVE A *MUTUAL* THORN IN OUR SIDES... *BART SIMPSON*.

YOU!

"THE PERSON WHO HAD THE *ANSWER* WAS..."

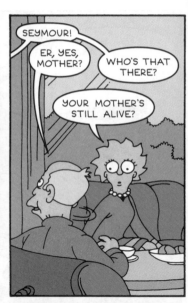

SEYMOUR!

ER, YES, MOTHER?

WHO'S THAT THERE?

YOUR MOTHER'S STILL ALIVE?

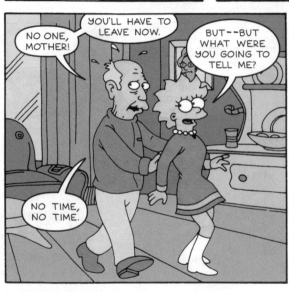

NO ONE, MOTHER!

YOU'LL HAVE TO LEAVE NOW.

BUT--BUT WHAT WERE YOU GOING TO TELL ME?

NO TIME, NO TIME.

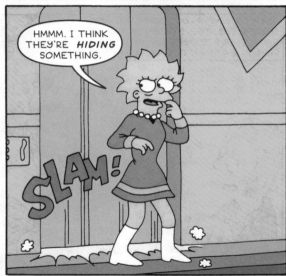

HMMM. I THINK THEY'RE *HIDING* SOMETHING.

SLAM!

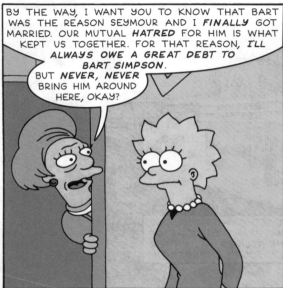

BY THE WAY, I WANT YOU TO KNOW THAT BART WAS THE REASON SEYMOUR AND I *FINALLY* GOT MARRIED. OUR MUTUAL *HATRED* FOR HIM IS WHAT KEPT US TOGETHER. FOR THAT REASON, *I'LL ALWAYS OWE A GREAT DEBT TO BART SIMPSON.*

BUT *NEVER, NEVER* BRING HIM AROUND HERE, OKAY?

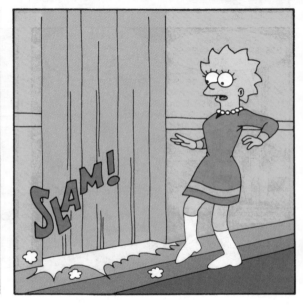

SLAM!

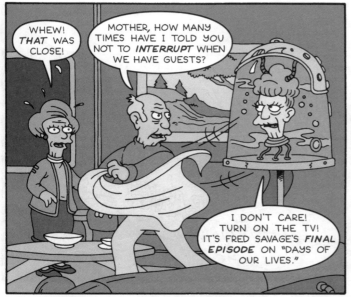

WHEW! *THAT* WAS CLOSE!

MOTHER, HOW MANY TIMES HAVE I TOLD YOU NOT TO *INTERRUPT* WHEN WE HAVE GUESTS?

I DON'T CARE! TURN ON THE TV! IT'S FRED SAVAGE'S *FINAL EPISODE* ON "DAYS OF OUR LIVES."

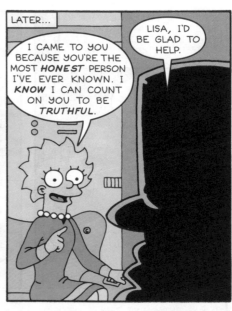

LATER...

I CAME TO YOU BECAUSE YOU'RE THE MOST *HONEST* PERSON I'VE EVER KNOWN. I *KNOW* I CAN COUNT ON YOU TO BE *TRUTHFUL*.

LISA, I'D BE GLAD TO HELP.

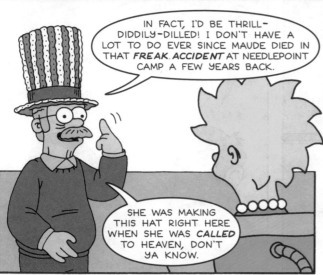

IN FACT, I'D BE THRILL-DIDDILY-DILLED! I DON'T HAVE A LOT TO DO EVER SINCE MAUDE DIED IN THAT *FREAK ACCIDENT* AT NEEDLEPOINT CAMP A FEW YEARS BACK.

SHE WAS MAKING THIS HAT RIGHT HERE WHEN SHE WAS *CALLED* TO HEAVEN, DON'T YA KNOW.

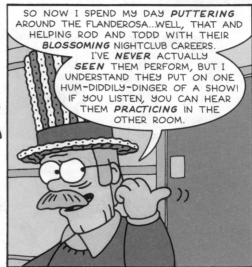

SO NOW I SPEND MY DAY *PUTTERING* AROUND THE FLANDEROSA...WELL, THAT AND HELPING ROD AND TODD WITH THEIR *BLOSSOMING* NIGHTCLUB CAREERS. I'VE *NEVER* ACTUALLY *SEEN* THEM PERFORM, BUT I UNDERSTAND THEY PUT ON ONE HUM-DIDDILY-DINGER OF A SHOW! IF YOU LISTEN, YOU CAN HEAR THEM *PRACTICING* IN THE OTHER ROOM.

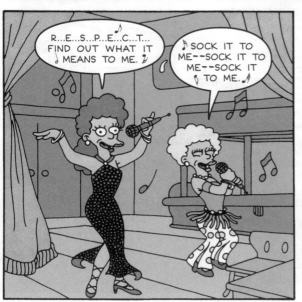

R...E...S...P...E...C...T... FIND OUT WHAT IT MEANS TO ME.

SOCK IT TO ME--SOCK IT TO ME--SOCK IT TO ME.

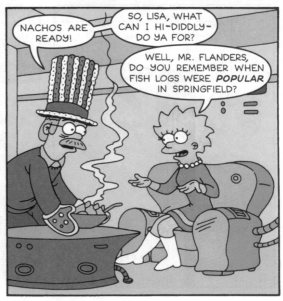

NACHOS ARE READY!

SO, LISA, WHAT CAN I HI-DIDDILY-DO YA FOR?

WELL, MR. FLANDERS, DO YOU REMEMBER WHEN FISH LOGS WERE *POPULAR* IN SPRINGFIELD?

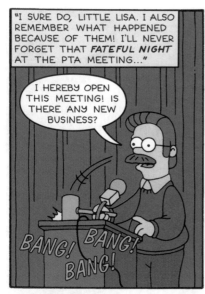

"I SURE DO, LITTLE LISA. I ALSO REMEMBER WHAT HAPPENED BECAUSE OF THEM! I'LL NEVER FORGET THAT *FATEFUL NIGHT* AT THE PTA MEETING…"

I HEREBY OPEN THIS MEETING! IS THERE ANY NEW BUSINESS?

BANG! BANG! BANG!

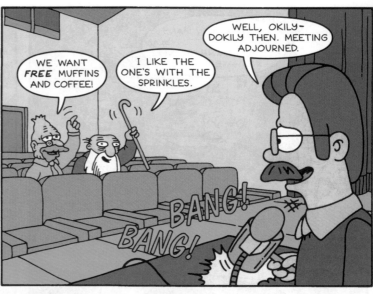

WE WANT *FREE* MUFFINS AND COFFEE!

I LIKE THE ONE'S WITH THE SPRINKLES.

WELL, OKILY-DOKILY THEN. MEETING ADJOURNED.

BANG! BANG! BANG!

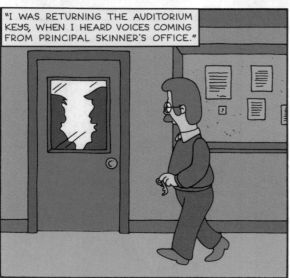

"I WAS RETURNING THE AUDITORIUM KEYS, WHEN I HEARD VOICES COMING FROM PRINCIPAL SKINNER'S OFFICE."

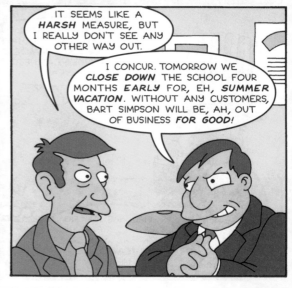

IT SEEMS LIKE A *HARSH* MEASURE, BUT I REALLY DON'T SEE ANY OTHER WAY OUT.

I CONCUR. TOMORROW WE *CLOSE DOWN* THE SCHOOL FOUR MONTHS *EARLY* FOR, EH, *SUMMER VACATION*. WITHOUT ANY CUSTOMERS, BART SIMPSON WILL BE, AH, OUT OF BUSINESS *FOR GOOD!*

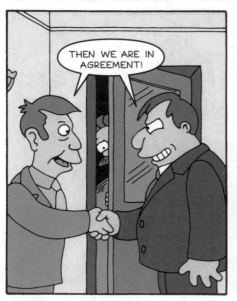

THEN WE ARE IN AGREEMENT!

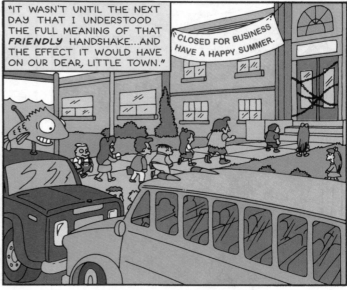

"IT WASN'T UNTIL THE NEXT DAY THAT I UNDERSTOOD THE FULL MEANING OF THAT *FRIENDLY* HANDSHAKE…AND THE EFFECT IT WOULD HAVE ON OUR DEAR, LITTLE TOWN."

CLOSED FOR BUSINESS HAVE A HAPPY SUMMER.

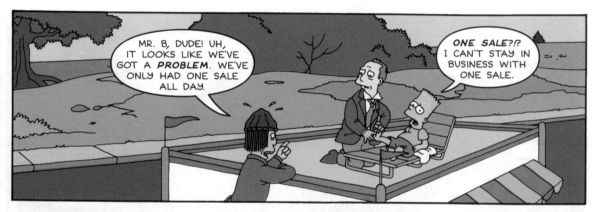

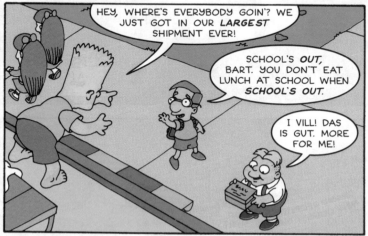

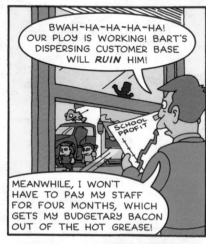

"BUT THE MAYOR AND PRINCIPAL SKINNER DIDN'T FORESEE THE DING-DANG-DILLY OF A PICKLE THEY PUT THE TOWN IN! WE WEREN'T *READY* FOR AN EARLY SCHOOL VACATION. THERE WAS NO SUMMER BLOCKBUSTER AT THE MOVIE HOUSE, NO WATER PARKS OPEN, NO MASSIVE COMIC BOOK CROSSOVER...NO *DISTRACTIONS* AT ALL!

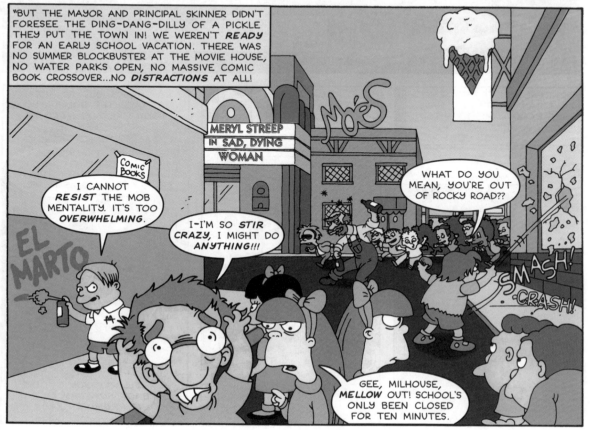

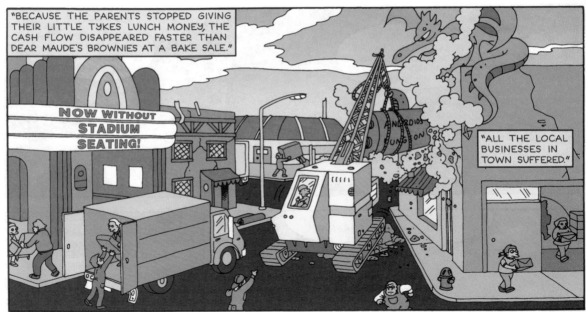

"BECAUSE THE PARENTS STOPPED GIVING THEIR LITTLE TYKES LUNCH MONEY, THE CASH FLOW DISAPPEARED FASTER THAN DEAR MAUDE'S BROWNIES AT A BAKE SALE."

NOW WITHOUT STADIUM SEATING!

"ALL THE LOCAL BUSINESSES IN TOWN SUFFERED."

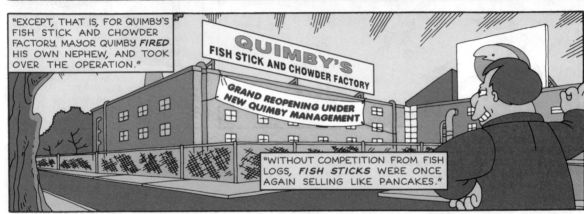

"EXCEPT, THAT IS, FOR QUIMBY'S FISH STICK AND CHOWDER FACTORY. MAYOR QUIMBY *FIRED* HIS OWN NEPHEW, AND TOOK OVER THE OPERATION."

QUIMBY'S
FISH STICK AND CHOWDER FACTORY

GRAND REOPENING UNDER NEW QUIMBY MANAGEMENT

"WITHOUT COMPETITION FROM FISH LOGS, *FISH STICKS* WERE ONCE AGAIN SELLING LIKE PANCAKES."

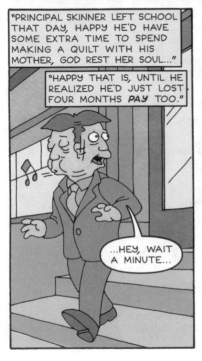

"PRINCIPAL SKINNER LEFT SCHOOL THAT DAY, HAPPY HE'D HAVE SOME EXTRA TIME TO SPEND MAKING A QUILT WITH HIS MOTHER, GOD REST HER SOUL..."

"HAPPY THAT IS, UNTIL HE REALIZED HE'D JUST LOST FOUR MONTHS *PAY* TOO."

...HEY, WAIT A MINUTE...

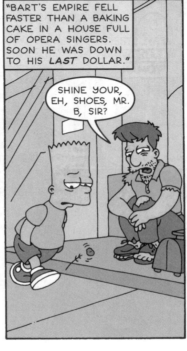

"BART'S EMPIRE FELL FASTER THAN A BAKING CAKE IN A HOUSE FULL OF OPERA SINGERS. SOON HE WAS DOWN TO HIS *LAST* DOLLAR."

SHINE YOUR, EH, SHOES, MR. B, SIR?

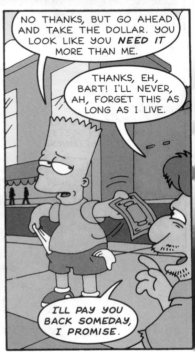

NO THANKS, BUT GO AHEAD AND TAKE THE DOLLAR. YOU LOOK LIKE YOU *NEED IT* MORE THAN ME.

THANKS, EH, BART! I'LL NEVER, AH, FORGET THIS AS LONG AS I LIVE.

ILL PAY YOU BACK SOMEDAY, I PROMISE.

BUT WHAT HAPPENED? WHEN I CAME HOME AFTER TWO WEEKS OF SAXOPHONE CAMP, EVERYTHING WAS NORMAL.
OH, WELL, THE FEDERAL GOVERNMENT DECLARED SPRINGFIELD A DISASTER AREA, AND WE GOT ALL KINDS OF RELIEF MONEY.
THEY REOPENED THE SCHOOL AND LIFE WENT BACK TO NORMAL. EXCEPT OUR TAXES WENT UP.
THAT EXPLAINS THE RISE AND FALL OF BART'S EMPIRE, BUT I'M STILL AT A LOSS. WHO GAVE HIM THE DIGESTIVE TRACT?
IT WASN'T YOU, WAS IT MR. FLANDERS?
HEAVENS, NO! WHY, MY PENSION BARELY PAYS FOR THE BOYS' ESTROGEN TREATMENTS. POOR LITTLE FELLAS HAVE SOME SORT OF HORMONE IMBALANCE.
WE'RE OFF TO THE CLUB, DADDY.
HI, LISA. OOH, NICE OUTFIT!
SO, WHO WAS THE MYSTERIOUS BENEFACTOR? POLICE FUGITIVE FAT TONY? CHOKING MARTIN? OUT OF WORK GIL OR LUNCH LADY DORIS? GRATEFUL, SPITEFUL EDNA SKINNER? LAZY BUM FREDDY QUIMBY? WHO?!
LISA, I'M SO GLAD YOU'RE BACK, THE...
...THE OPERATION WAS A SUCCESS!!
HRRMMMM!
DID YOU FIND OUT WHO THE RICH GUY WAS WHO GOT BART HIS NEW STOMACH? I COULD USE A HOVER-CAR.
SIGH! NO, AND I'M EVEN MORE CONFUSED THAN EVER. BART, CAN YOU TELL ME?
HI, EVERYBODY!
HI, DR. NICK.
GUESS WHAT? THERE'S SOMEBODY HERE YOU MIGHT WANT TO MEET!
THE CANDY STRIPER?
CLOSE! BART, IT'S YOUR MYSTERIOUS BENEFACTOR!
YOU!?!
WHO'S THAT?

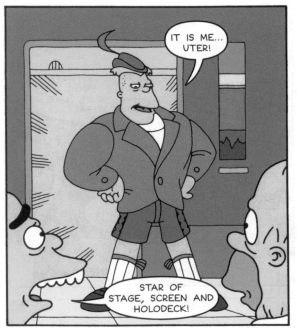

IT IS ME... UTER!

STAR OF STAGE, SCREEN AND HOLODECK!

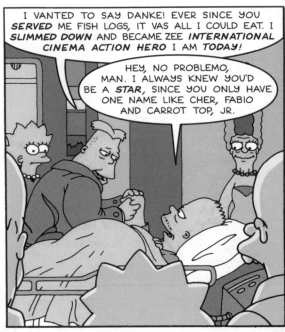

I VANTED TO SAY DANKE! EVER SINCE YOU *SERVED* ME FISH LOGS, IT VAS ALL I COULD EAT. I *SLIMMED DOWN* AND BECAME ZEE *INTERNATIONAL CINEMA ACTION HERO* I AM *TODAY*!

HEY, NO PROBLEMO, MAN. I ALWAYS KNEW YOU'D BE A *STAR*, SINCE YOU ONLY HAVE ONE NAME LIKE CHER, FABIO AND CARROT TOP, JR.

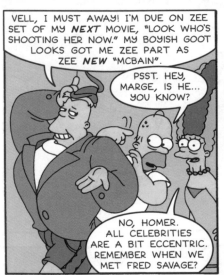

VELL, I MUST AWAY! I'M DUE ON ZEE SET OF MY *NEXT* MOVIE, "LOOK WHO'S SHOOTING HER NOW." MY BOYISH GOOT LOOKS GOT ME ZEE PART AS ZEE *NEW* "MCBAIN".

PSST. HEY, MARGE, IS HE... YOU KNOW?

NO, HOMER. ALL CELEBRITIES ARE A BIT ECCENTRIC. REMEMBER WHEN WE MET FRED SAVAGE?

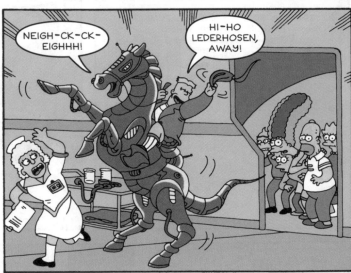

NEIGH-CK-CK-EIGHHH!

HI-HO LEDERHOSEN, AWAY!

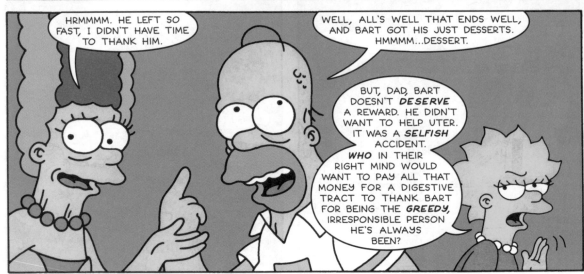

HRMMMM. HE LEFT SO FAST, I DIDN'T HAVE TIME TO THANK HIM.

WELL, ALL'S WELL THAT ENDS WELL, AND BART GOT HIS JUST DESSERTS. HMMMM...DESSERT.

BUT, DAD, BART DOESN'T *DESERVE* A REWARD. HE DIDN'T WANT TO HELP UTER. IT WAS A *SELFISH* ACCIDENT. *WHO* IN THEIR RIGHT MIND WOULD WANT TO PAY ALL THAT MONEY FOR A DIGESTIVE TRACT TO THANK BART FOR BEING THE *GREEDY*, IRRESPONSIBLE PERSON HE'S ALWAYS BEEN?

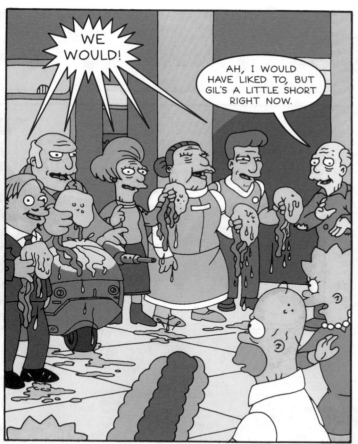

WE WOULD!

AH, I WOULD HAVE LIKED TO, BUT GIL'S A LITTLE SHORT RIGHT NOW.

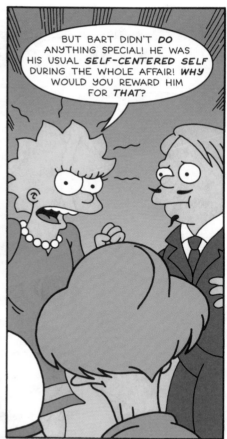

BUT BART DIDN'T *DO* ANYTHING SPECIAL! HE WAS HIS USUAL *SELF-CENTERED SELF* DURING THE WHOLE AFFAIR! *WHY* WOULD YOU REWARD HIM FOR *THAT*?

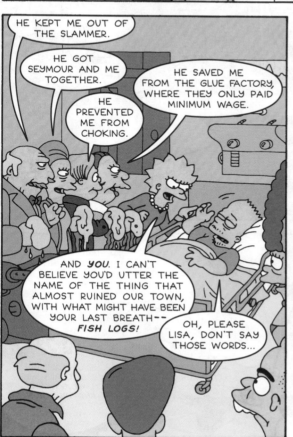

HE KEPT ME OUT OF THE SLAMMER.

HE GOT SEYMOUR AND ME TOGETHER.

HE SAVED ME FROM THE GLUE FACTORY, WHERE THEY ONLY PAID MINIMUM WAGE.

HE PREVENTED ME FROM CHOKING.

AND *YOU*. I CAN'T BELIEVE YOU'D UTTER THE NAME OF THE THING THAT ALMOST RUINED OUR TOWN, WITH WHAT MIGHT HAVE BEEN YOUR LAST BREATH-- *FISH LOGS!*

OH, PLEASE LISA, DON'T SAY THOSE WORDS...

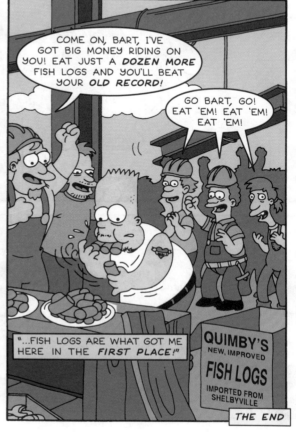

COME ON, BART, I'VE GOT BIG MONEY RIDING ON YOU! EAT JUST A *DOZEN MORE* FISH LOGS AND YOU'LL BEAT YOUR *OLD RECORD!*

GO BART, GO! EAT 'EM! EAT 'EM! EAT 'EM!

"...FISH LOGS ARE WHAT GOT ME HERE IN THE *FIRST PLACE!*"

QUIMBY'S
NEW, IMPROVED
FISH LOGS
IMPORTED FROM SHELBYVILLE

THE END

Where Has All The FLOUR Gone?

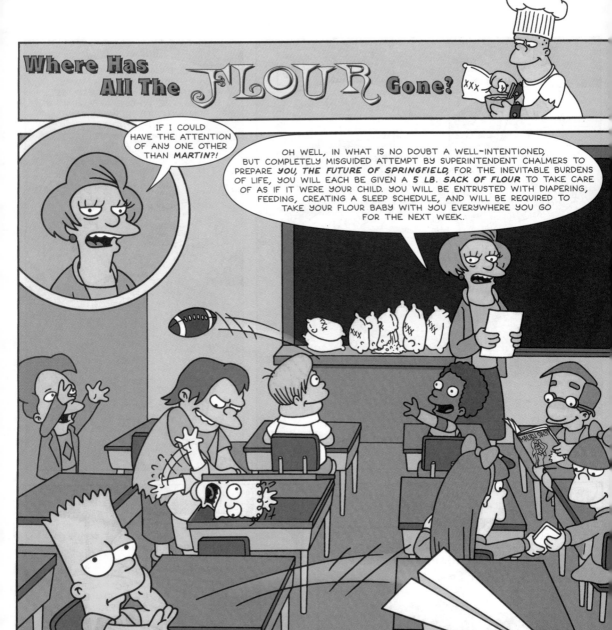

IF I COULD HAVE THE ATTENTION OF ANY ONE OTHER THAN *MARTIN*?!

OH WELL, IN WHAT IS NO DOUBT A WELL-INTENTIONED, BUT COMPLETELY MISGUIDED ATTEMPT BY SUPERINTENDENT CHALMERS TO PREPARE *YOU, THE FUTURE OF SPRINGFIELD*, FOR THE INEVITABLE BURDENS OF LIFE, YOU WILL EACH BE GIVEN A *5 LB. SACK OF FLOUR* TO TAKE CARE OF AS IF IT WERE YOUR CHILD. YOU WILL BE ENTRUSTED WITH DIAPERING, FEEDING, CREATING A SLEEP SCHEDULE, AND WILL BE REQUIRED TO TAKE YOUR FLOUR BABY WITH YOU EVERYWHERE YOU GO FOR THE NEXT WEEK.

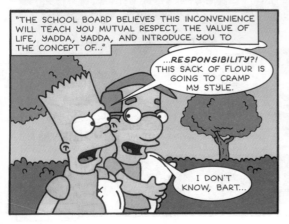

"THE SCHOOL BOARD BELIEVES THIS INCONVENIENCE WILL TEACH YOU MUTUAL RESPECT, THE VALUE OF LIFE, YADDA, YADDA, AND INTRODUCE YOU TO THE CONCEPT OF..."

...*RESPONSIBILITY*?! THIS SACK OF FLOUR IS GOING TO CRAMP MY STYLE.

I DON'T KNOW, BART...

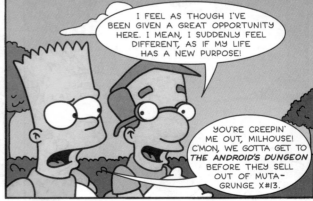

I FEEL AS THOUGH I'VE BEEN GIVEN A GREAT OPPORTUNITY HERE. I MEAN, I SUDDENLY FEEL DIFFERENT, AS IF MY LIFE HAS A NEW PURPOSE!

YOU'RE CREEPIN' ME OUT, MILHOUSE! C'MON, WE GOTTA GET TO *THE ANDROID'S DUNGEON* BEFORE THEY SELL OUT OF MUTA-GRUNGE X#13.

OH BOY! IT'S FINALLY HERE! IT'S THE LAST COPY AND IT'S ALL *MINE!!* AREN'T YOU GOING TO GET ANYTHING, MILHOUSE?

I REALLY SHOULD START SAVING MY MONEY, BART. I'M NOT ALONE IN THE WORLD ANYMORE. THERE'S SOMEONE WHO NEEDS ME NOW, AND I NEED TO THINK OF HIS FUTURE.

10 MINUTES LATER...

DUDE, WHERE IS THE NEWEST ISSUE OF MUTA-GRUNGE X?!

WELL, MY FINE FELONIOUS FELLOWS--IT JUST SO HAPPENS THAT ONE *BART SIMPSON* JUST PURCHASED THE VERY *LAST* COPY.

THE NEXT DAY...

OH, BART SIMPSON, YOU ARE *SO* DEAD!

BART, WHAT ARE YOU *DOING?!* YOU CAN'T TREAT YOUR CHILD LIKE THAT. DON'T FORCE ME TO REPORT YOU TO SOCIAL SERVICES FOR CHILD ABUSE.

A CHILD IS A PROMISE FOR A BETTER TOMORROW. *MY* BABY'S GOING TO *COLLEGE,* AS LONG AS I CAN KEEP IT SAFE FROM BOLL WEEVILS, *EUUGGHH!*

WHUH?

EGADS, MAN! HAVE YOU LOST ALL REASON? MILHOUSE IS RIGHT, IF NOT A LITTLE OVER-ENTHUSIASTIC.

A CHILD'S MIND IS A DELICATE INSTRUMENT-- IT CAN ONLY ACHIEVE NEW LEVELS OF UNDERSTANDING THROUGH STIMULATION AND PARENTAL INTERACTION. NOTED CHILD PSYCHOLOGIST T. BERRY BRAZELTON CALLS THESE SUDDEN MOMENTS OF AWARENESS--*TOUCHPOINTS.* GET INVOLVED WITH YOUR CHILD, BART. PLAY WITH IT.

IT'S SO BEAUTIFUL.

ANYTHING TO SHUT YOU NAMBY-PAMBIES UP.

THIS IS GOING NOWHERE FAST. I'M *PLAYING* WITH A *SACK* OF FLOUR. TOUCH *THIS,* MARTIN!

RIINNGGGG!!!

RIINNGGGG!!!

ALL RIGHT CHILDREN, LUNCHTIME IS OVER! GET BACK TO CLASS. OH, AND SOMEONE FIND GROUNDSKEEPER WILLIE, IT SEEMS WE'VE HAD ANOTHER TRAGIC FLOUR SPILLAGE.

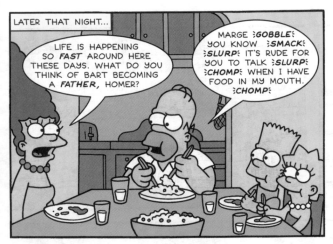

LATER THAT NIGHT...

LIFE IS HAPPENING SO *FAST* AROUND HERE THESE DAYS. WHAT DO YOU THINK OF BART BECOMING A *FATHER*, HOMER?

MARGE :GOBBLE: YOU KNOW :SMACK: :SLURP: IT'S RUDE FOR YOU TO TALK :SLURP: :CHOMP: WHEN I HAVE FOOD IN MY MOUTH. :CHOMP:

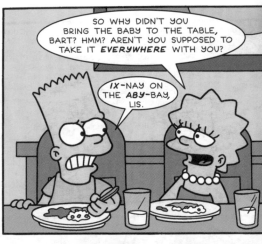

SO WHY DIDN'T YOU BRING THE BABY TO THE TABLE, BART? HMM? AREN'T YOU SUPPOSED TO TAKE IT *EVERYWHERE* WITH YOU?

IX-NAY ON THE *ABY-BAY*, LIS.

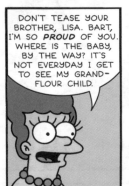

DON'T TEASE YOUR BROTHER, LISA. BART, I'M SO *PROUD* OF YOU. WHERE IS THE BABY, BY THE WAY? IT'S NOT EVERYDAY I GET TO SEE MY GRAND-FLOUR CHILD.

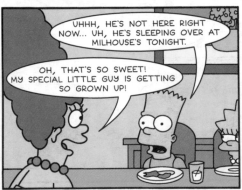

UHHH, HE'S NOT HERE RIGHT NOW... UH, HE'S SLEEPING OVER AT MILHOUSE'S TONIGHT.

OH, THAT'S SO SWEET! MY SPECIAL LITTLE GUY IS GETTING SO GROWN UP!

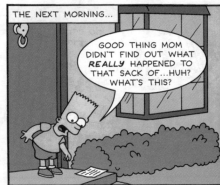

THE NEXT MORNING...

GOOD THING MOM DIDN'T FIND OUT WHAT *REALLY* HAPPENED TO THAT SACK OF...HUH? WHAT'S THIS?

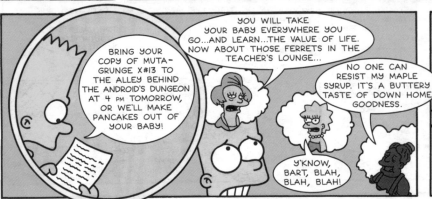

BRING YOUR COPY OF MUTA-GRUNGE X#13 TO THE ALLEY BEHIND THE ANDROID'S DUNGEON AT 4 PM TOMORROW, OR WE'LL MAKE PANCAKES OUT OF YOUR BABY!

YOU WILL TAKE YOUR BABY EVERYWHERE YOU GO...AND LEARN...THE VALUE OF LIFE. NOW ABOUT THOSE FERRETS IN THE TEACHER'S LOUNGE...

NO ONE CAN RESIST MY MAPLE SYRUP. IT'S A BUTTERY TASTE OF DOWN HOME GOODNESS.

Y'KNOW, BART, BLAH, BLAH, BLAH!

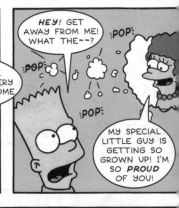

HEY! GET AWAY FROM ME! WHAT THE--? :POP: :POP: :POP:

MY SPECIAL LITTLE GUY IS GETTING SO GROWN UP! I'M SO *PROUD* OF YOU!

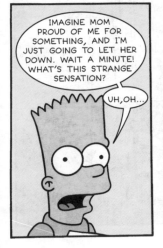

IMAGINE MOM PROUD OF ME FOR SOMETHING, AND I'M JUST GOING TO LET HER DOWN. WAIT A MINUTE! WHAT'S THIS STRANGE SENSATION?

UH,OH...

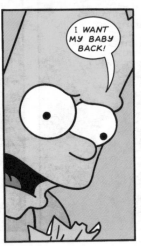

I *WANT* MY BABY BACK!

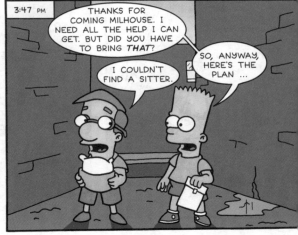

3:47 PM

THANKS FOR COMING MILHOUSE. I NEED ALL THE HELP I CAN GET. BUT DID YOU HAVE TO BRING *THAT*?

I COULDN'T FIND A SITTER.

SO, ANYWAY, HERE'S THE PLAN ...

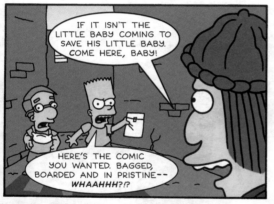

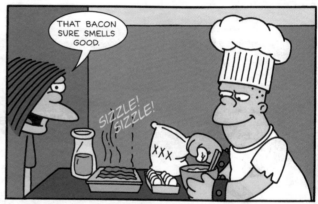

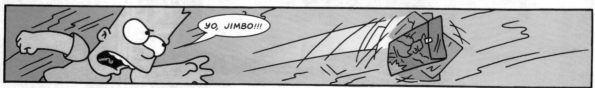

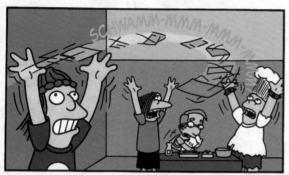

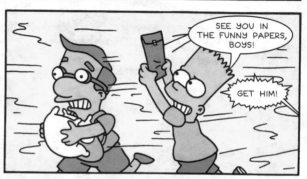

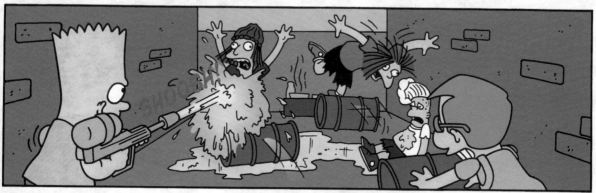

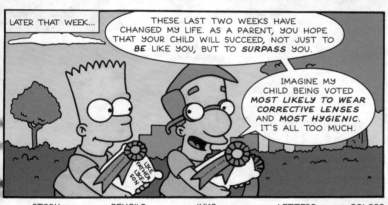

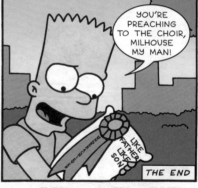

STORY
TERRY DELEGEANE

PENCILS
ERICK TRAN

INKS
STEVE STEERE, JR.

LETTERS
KAREN BATES

COLORS
NATHAN KANE

EDITOR
BILL MORRISON

WEEVIL INSPECTOR
MATT GROENING

SURVIVAL OF THE FATTEST!
SIMPSONS COMICS
#48
US $2.50
CAN $3.50
SIMPSON VS. BURNS
WILL HOMER LOSE HIS LIFE OR JUST HIS APPETITE?
BREAD

TIC TAC D'OH!
SNACKS THAT END WITH "DOODLES"
NAPPING
CHEESE-FOOD PRODUCTS OF THE WORLD
THE COLD SIDE OF THE PILLOW
LARD-BASED FOOD
YOUR BELLY BUTTON
WHAT IS VELVEETA, ALEX?
ABSOLUTELY CORRECT!
$0.00
$47,560.00
$0.00²
Brian
Homer
Albert
SCRIPT MICHAEL LISBE AND NATHAN REGER
PENCILS PHIL ORTIZ
INKS TIM BAVINGTON
LETTERS JEANNINE BLACK
COLORS CHRIS UNGAR
ART SUPERVISION NATHAN KANE
EDITOR BILL MORRISON
FABULOUS PRIZES PROVIDED BY: MATT GROENING

WHUH?
HMM, I DREAMED I WAS WINNING ON JEOPARDY! MUST'VE DOZED OFF DURING THE COMMERCIAL.
WE NOW RETURN TO "ANYTHING FOR DOLLARS," WITH YOUR HOST, CLINT MAJORS!
WIPE WIPE!
BART, GET THAT BABY OUT OF THE WAY. THE SHOW'S BACK ON, AND THE SCREEN IS CLEAN ENOUGH.
WELCOME BACK! AND NOW, IT'S TIME FOR THE "BOBBING FOR DOLLARS" SEGMENT!
"BOBBING FOR DOLLARS." THIS IS MY FAVORITE TIME OF DAY.
I THOUGHT YOUR FAVORITE TIME OF DAY IS WHEN APU THROWS OUT THE EXPIRED YOGURT BEHIND THE KWIK-E-MART.
JELLO-BRAND HOOF DOGS
BUZZ COLA
CALAMARI-O'S
UGARED BUTTER Now In Bite-Size Balls!
BEER
THAT'S A PRETTY GOOD TIME, TOO.

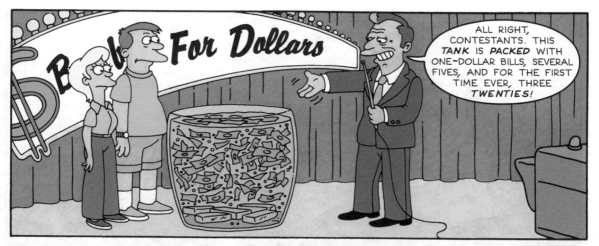

B **b** For Dollars

ALL RIGHT, CONTESTANTS. THIS *TANK* IS *PACKED* WITH ONE-DOLLAR BILLS, SEVERAL FIVES, AND FOR THE FIRST TIME EVER, THREE *TWENTIES!*

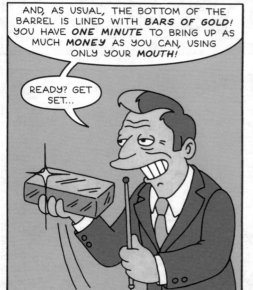

AND, AS USUAL, THE BOTTOM OF THE BARREL IS LINED WITH *BARS OF GOLD!* YOU HAVE *ONE MINUTE* TO BRING UP AS MUCH *MONEY* AS YOU CAN, USING ONLY YOUR *MOUTH!*

READY? GET SET...

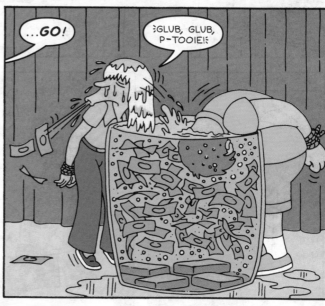

...GO!

¡GLUB, GLUB, P-TOOIE!¡

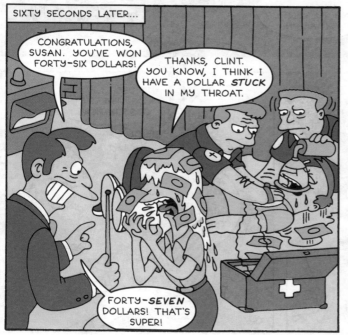

SIXTY SECONDS LATER...

CONGRATULATIONS, SUSAN. YOU'VE WON FORTY-SIX DOLLARS!

THANKS, CLINT. YOU KNOW, I THINK I HAVE A DOLLAR *STUCK* IN MY THROAT.

FORTY-*SEVEN* DOLLARS! THAT'S SUPER!

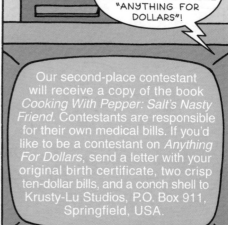

WELL, THAT'S ALL THE TIME WE HAVE TODAY! JOIN US TOMORROW FOR MORE "ANYTHING FOR DOLLARS"!

Our second-place contestant will receive a copy of the book *Cooking With Pepper: Salt's Nasty Friend.* Contestants are responsible for their own medical bills. If you'd like to be a contestant on *Anything For Dollars,* send a letter with your original birth certificate, two crisp ten-dollar bills, and a conch shell to Krusty-Lu Studios, P.O. Box 911, Springfield, USA.

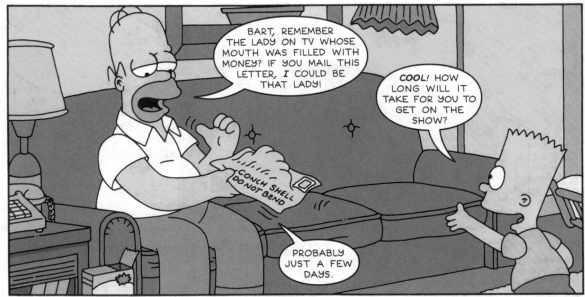

BART, REMEMBER THE LADY ON TV WHOSE MOUTH WAS FILLED WITH MONEY? IF YOU MAIL THIS LETTER, *I* COULD BE THAT LADY!

COOL! HOW LONG WILL IT TAKE FOR YOU TO GET ON THE SHOW?

CONCH SHELL DO NOT BEND

PROBABLY JUST A FEW DAYS.

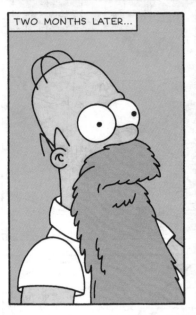

TWO MONTHS LATER...

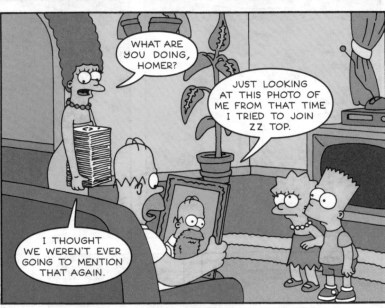

WHAT ARE YOU DOING, HOMER?

JUST LOOKING AT THIS PHOTO OF ME FROM THAT TIME I TRIED TO JOIN ZZ TOP.

I THOUGHT WE WEREN'T EVER GOING TO MENTION THAT AGAIN.

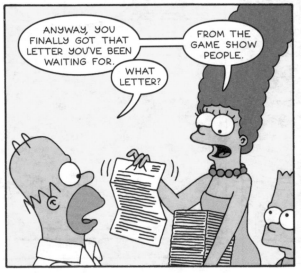

ANYWAY, YOU FINALLY GOT THAT LETTER YOU'VE BEEN WAITING FOR.

FROM THE GAME SHOW PEOPLE.

WHAT LETTER?

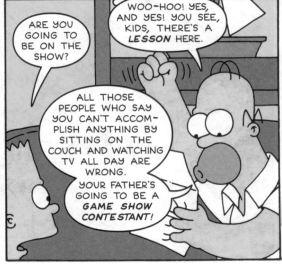

ARE YOU GOING TO BE ON THE SHOW?

WOO-HOO! YES, AND YES! YOU SEE, KIDS, THERE'S A *LESSON* HERE.

ALL THOSE PEOPLE WHO SAY YOU CAN'T ACCOMPLISH ANYTHING BY SITTING ON THE COUCH AND WATCHING TV ALL DAY ARE WRONG.

YOUR FATHER'S GOING TO BE A *GAME SHOW CONTESTANT!*

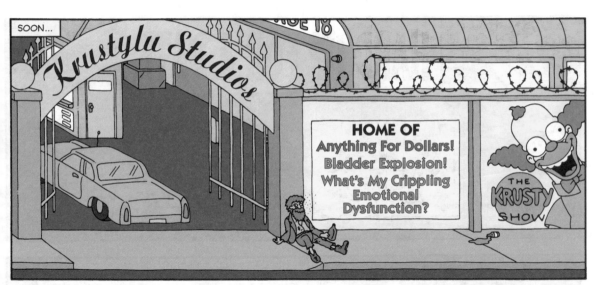

Krustylu Studios

HOME OF
Anything For Dollars!
Bladder Explosion!
What's My Crippling Emotional Dysfunction?

THE KRUSTY SHOW

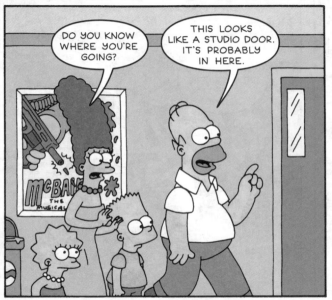

DO YOU KNOW WHERE YOU'RE GOING?

THIS LOOKS LIKE A STUDIO DOOR. IT'S PROBABLY IN HERE.

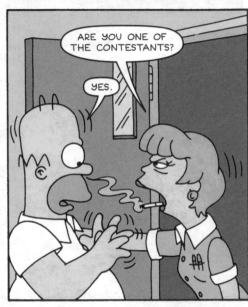

ARE YOU ONE OF THE CONTESTANTS?

YES.

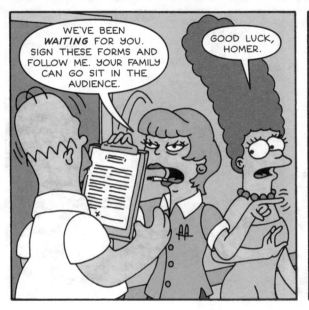

WE'VE BEEN *WAITING* FOR YOU. SIGN THESE FORMS AND FOLLOW ME. YOUR FAMILY CAN GO SIT IN THE AUDIENCE.

GOOD LUCK, HOMER.

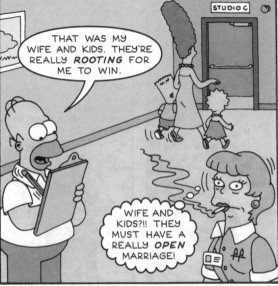

THAT WAS MY WIFE AND KIDS. THEY'RE REALLY *ROOTING* FOR ME TO WIN.

WIFE AND KIDS?!! THEY MUST HAVE A REALLY *OPEN* MARRIAGE!

STUDIO C

HARD UP FOR A DATE

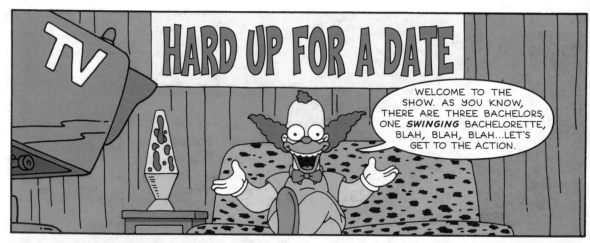

WELCOME TO THE SHOW. AS YOU KNOW, THERE ARE THREE BACHELORS, ONE *SWINGING* BACHELORETTE, BLAH, BLAH, BLAH...LET'S GET TO THE ACTION.

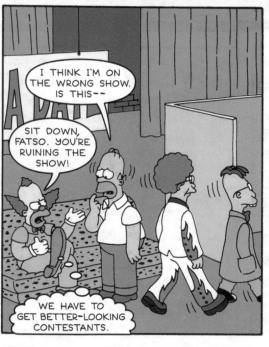

I THINK I'M ON THE WRONG SHOW. IS THIS--

SIT DOWN, FATSO. YOU'RE RUINING THE SHOW!

WE HAVE TO GET BETTER-LOOKING CONTESTANTS.

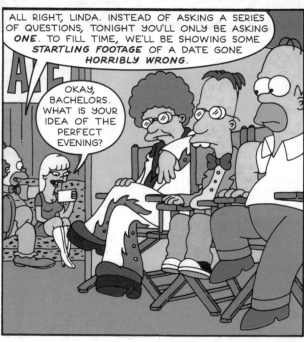

ALL RIGHT, LINDA. INSTEAD OF ASKING A SERIES OF QUESTIONS, TONIGHT YOU'LL ONLY BE ASKING *ONE*. TO FILL TIME, WE'LL BE SHOWING SOME *STARTLING FOOTAGE* OF A DATE GONE *HORRIBLY WRONG*.

OKAY, BACHELORS. WHAT IS YOUR IDEA OF THE PERFECT EVENING?

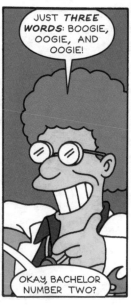

JUST *THREE WORDS*: BOOGIE, OOGIE, AND OOGIE!

OKAY, BACHELOR NUMBER TWO?

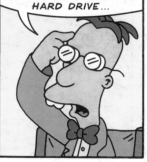

WELL, AS I'VE DONE QUITE SUCCESSFULLY WITH A NUMBER OF WOO, HOY WOMEN, I'D TAKE YOU TO MY PRIVATE *CHAT ROOM* ENNG, WEE AND THEN AFTER WE'VE HAD A CHANCE TO GET TO KNOW EACH OTHER WITH THE SMALL TALK AND THE HARMLESS LYING AND SO FORTH, I'D *DOWNLOAD* YOU ONTO MY *HARD DRIVE*...

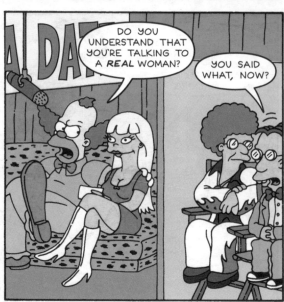

DO YOU UNDERSTAND THAT YOU'RE TALKING TO A *REAL* WOMAN?

YOU SAID WHAT, NOW?

NUMBER THREE?
WELL, IF I WASN'T ON THE WRONG SHOW, I'D TELL YOU HOW NICE YOU WERE, TAKE YOU OUT FOR ICE CREAM, AND THEN WE'D GO BOWLING.
I WANT BACHELOR NUMBER THREE.
HIM? WHY HIM? HE'S DISGUSTING! OH RIGHT, YOU CAN'T SEE HIM!
COOL, WE'RE GONNA HAVE A NEW MOM! AND SHE'S HOT!
IT'S OKAY, MOM. DAD WON'T GO ON THE DATE.
OH, I KNOW THAT, HONEY. YOUR FATHER ONLY HAS EYES FOR ME.
WOO-HOO! WOO-HOO! I WON! AND YOU'RE HOT!
WAIT A MINUTE, HOW OLD ARE YOU?
NINETEEN.
WOO-HOO!
HOMER, YOU KNOW YOU'RE NOT ACTUALLY GOING ON THIS DATE?
PLEASE, MARGE, DON'T EMBARRASS ME IN FRONT OF THE GAME SHOW PEOPLE. LET'S TALK ABOUT THIS AT HOME.

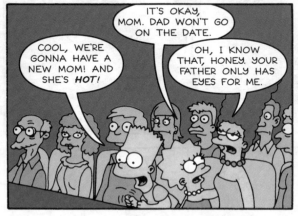

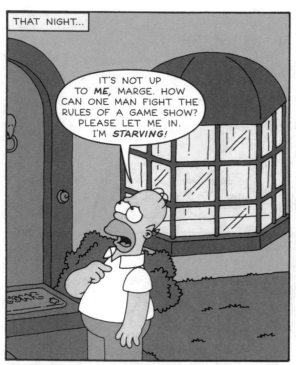

THAT NIGHT...

IT'S NOT UP TO *ME*, MARGE. HOW CAN ONE MAN FIGHT THE RULES OF A GAME SHOW? PLEASE LET ME IN. I'M *STARVING!*

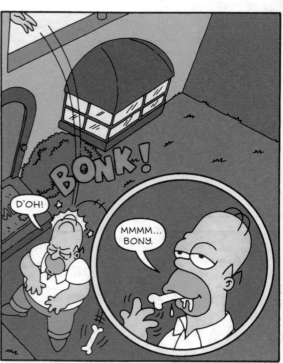

BONK!

D'OH!

MMMM... BONY.

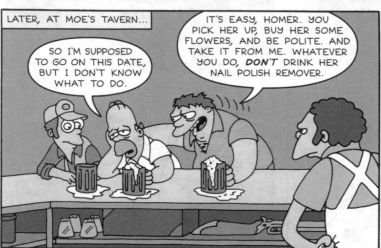

LATER, AT MOE'S TAVERN...

SO I'M SUPPOSED TO GO ON THIS DATE, BUT I DON'T KNOW WHAT TO DO.

IT'S EASY, HOMER. YOU PICK HER UP, BUY HER SOME FLOWERS, AND BE POLITE. AND TAKE IT FROM ME. WHATEVER YOU DO, *DON'T* DRINK HER NAIL POLISH REMOVER.

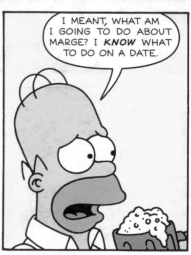

I MEANT, WHAT AM I GOING TO DO ABOUT MARGE? I *KNOW* WHAT TO DO ON A DATE.

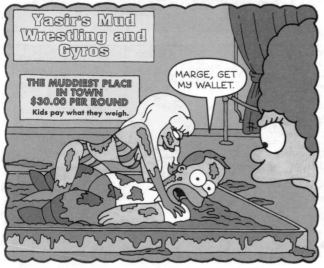

MARGE, GET MY WALLET.

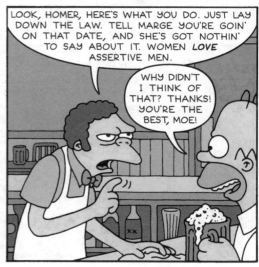

LOOK, HOMER, HERE'S WHAT YOU DO. JUST LAY DOWN THE LAW. TELL MARGE YOU'RE GOIN' ON THAT DATE, AND SHE'S GOT NOTHIN' TO SAY ABOUT IT. WOMEN *LOVE* ASSERTIVE MEN.

WHY DIDN'T I THINK OF THAT? THANKS! YOU'RE THE BEST, MOE!

SOON...

I DON'T CARE *WHAT* MOE SAID. IF YOU WANT TO COME BACK *INSIDE,* YOU HAVE TO GO BACK TO KRUSTY AND *CANCEL* THAT DATE.

COME ON, MARGE! I HAVEN'T BEEN ON A DATE IN TEN YEARS. NOT SINCE WE GOT *MARRIED!*

WELL, I GUESS YOU'LL BE STAYING *OUTSIDE* TONIGHT.

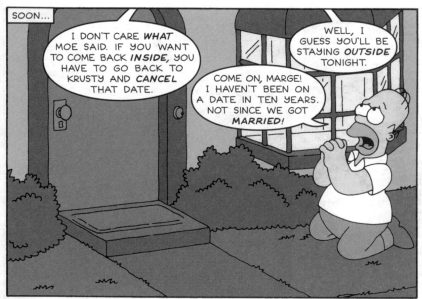

OKAY, FINE. I'LL DO IT.

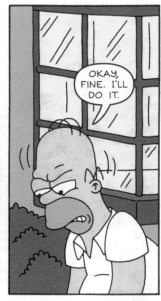

THE NEXT DAY...

KRUSTY, PLEASE, BE REASONABLE. I'M *MARRIED.*

I'M SORRY, I STILL DON'T UNDERSTAND WHAT THE PROBLEM IS. YOU CAN'T GO ON A DATE BECAUSE YOU'RE MARRIED?

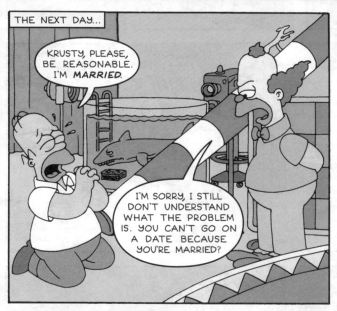

LOOK HERE. YOU SIGNED THIS CONTRACT, AND NOW YOU HAVE TO GO ON THIS DATE. WIFE OR NO WIFE!

MAYBE THERE'S ANOTHER SOLUTION.

CONTRACT

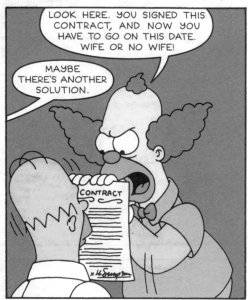

ANOTHER *SOLUTION?* GREAT, I'LL DO *ANYTHING!*

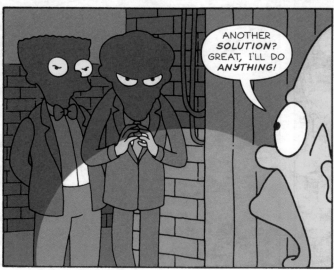

ANYTHING?

:GASP: MY BOSS, MR. BURNS! WHAT ARE *YOU* DOING HERE?

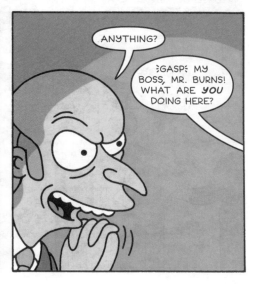

141

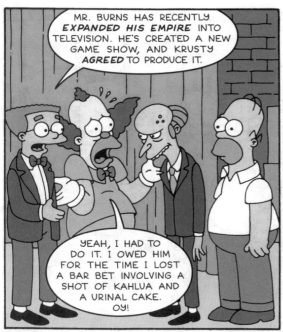

MR. BURNS HAS RECENTLY *EXPANDED HIS EMPIRE* INTO TELEVISION. HE'S CREATED A NEW GAME SHOW, AND KRUSTY *AGREED* TO PRODUCE IT.

YEAH, I HAD TO DO IT. I OWED HIM FOR THE TIME I LOST A BAR BET INVOLVING A SHOT OF KAHLUA AND A URINAL CAKE. OY!

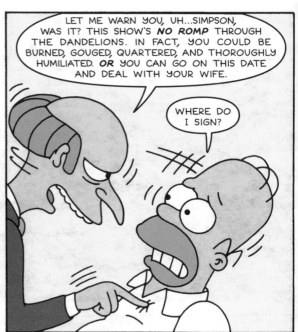

LET ME WARN YOU, UH...SIMPSON, WAS IT? THIS SHOW'S *NO ROMP* THROUGH THE DANDELIONS. IN FACT, YOU COULD BE BURNED, GOUGED, QUARTERED, AND THOROUGHLY HUMILIATED. *OR* YOU CAN GO ON THIS DATE AND DEAL WITH YOUR WIFE.

WHERE DO I SIGN?

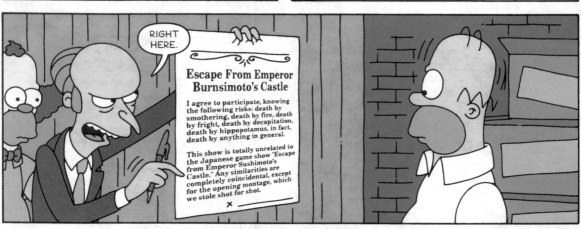

RIGHT HERE.

Escape From Emperor Burnsimoto's Castle

I agree to participate, knowing the following risks: death by smothering, death by fire, death by fright, death by decapitation, death by hippopotamus, in fact, death by anything in general.

This show is totally unrelated to the Japanese game show "Escape from Emperor Sushimoto's Castle." Any similarities are completely coincidental, except for the opening montage, which we stole shot for shot.

✗ _____

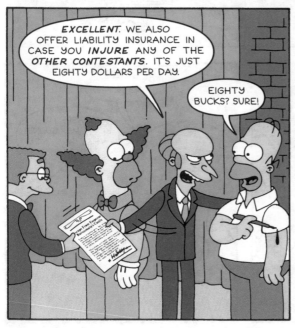

EXCELLENT. WE ALSO OFFER LIABILITY INSURANCE IN CASE YOU *INJURE* ANY OF THE *OTHER CONTESTANTS.* IT'S JUST EIGHTY DOLLARS PER DAY.

EIGHTY BUCKS? SURE!

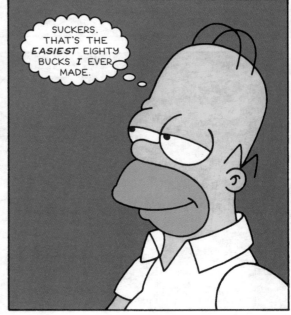

SUCKERS. THAT'S THE *EASIEST* EIGHTY BUCKS *I* EVER MADE.

GAME DAY!

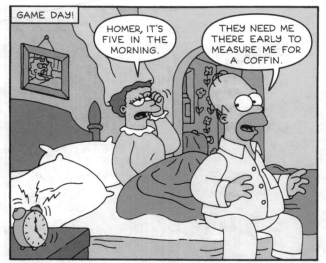

HOMER, IT'S FIVE IN THE MORNING.

THEY NEED ME THERE EARLY TO MEASURE ME FOR A COFFIN.

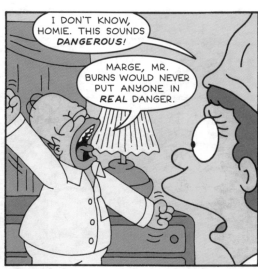

I DON'T KNOW, HOMIE. THIS SOUNDS *DANGEROUS!*

MARGE, MR. BURNS WOULD NEVER PUT ANYONE IN *REAL* DANGER.

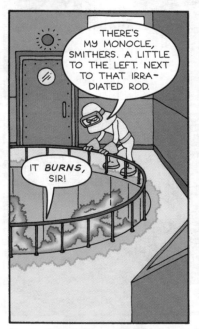

THERE'S MY MONOCLE, SMITHERS. A LITTLE TO THE LEFT. NEXT TO THAT IRRA-DIATED ROD.

IT *BURNS*, SIR!

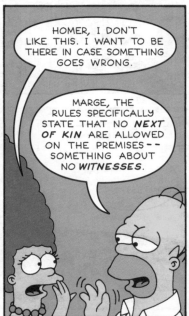

HOMER, I DON'T LIKE THIS. I WANT TO BE THERE IN CASE SOMETHING GOES WRONG.

MARGE, THE RULES SPECIFICALLY STATE THAT NO *NEXT OF KIN* ARE ALLOWED ON THE PREMISES-- SOMETHING ABOUT NO *WITNESSES.*

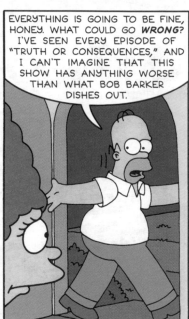

EVERYTHING IS GOING TO BE FINE, HONEY. WHAT COULD GO *WRONG?* I'VE SEEN EVERY EPISODE OF "TRUTH OR CONSEQUENCES," AND I CAN'T IMAGINE THAT THIS SHOW HAS ANYTHING WORSE THAN WHAT BOB BARKER DISHES OUT.

SOON...

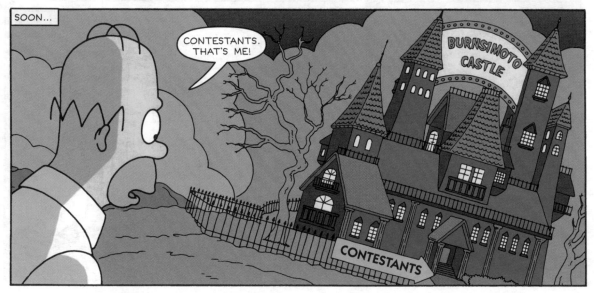

CONTESTANTS. THAT'S ME!

BURNSIMOTO CASTLE

CONTESTANTS

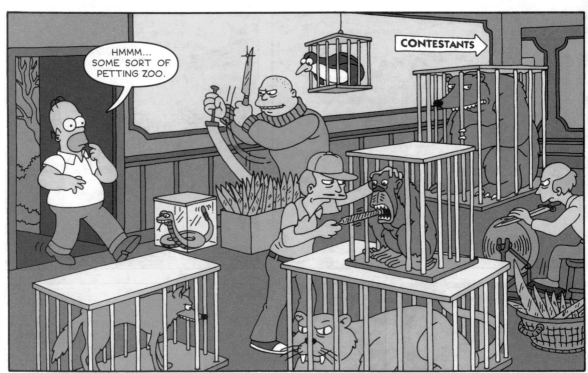

HMMM... SOME SORT OF PETTING ZOO.

CONTESTANTS

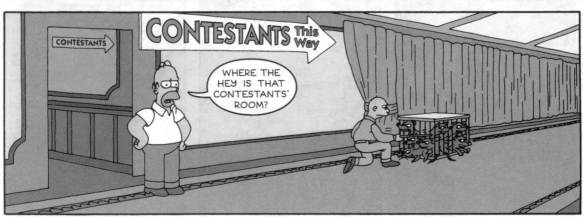

CONTESTANTS

CONTESTANTS This Way

WHERE THE HEY IS THAT CONTESTANTS' ROOM?

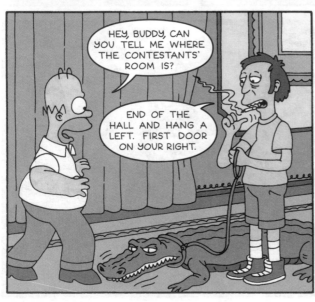

HEY, BUDDY, CAN YOU TELL ME WHERE THE CONTESTANTS' ROOM IS?

END OF THE HALL AND HANG A LEFT. FIRST DOOR ON YOUR RIGHT.

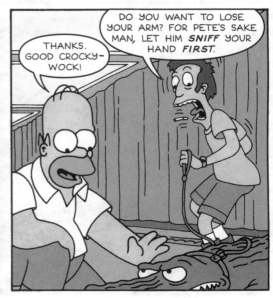

THANKS. GOOD CROCKY-WOCK!

DO YOU WANT TO LOSE YOUR ARM? FOR PETE'S SAKE MAN, LET HIM *SNIFF* YOUR HAND *FIRST*.

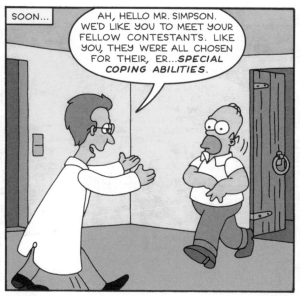

SOON...

AH, HELLO MR. SIMPSON. WE'D LIKE YOU TO MEET YOUR FELLOW CONTESTANTS. LIKE YOU, THEY WERE ALL CHOSEN FOR THEIR, ER...*SPECIAL COPING ABILITIES*.

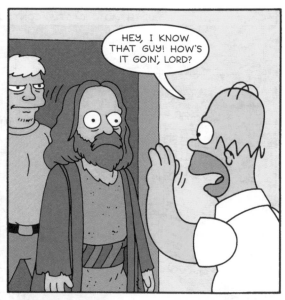

HEY, I KNOW THAT GUY! HOW'S IT GOIN', LORD?

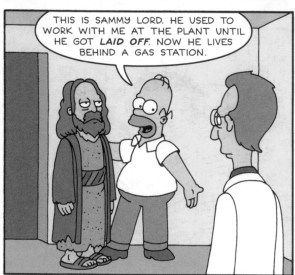

THIS IS SAMMY LORD. HE USED TO WORK WITH ME AT THE PLANT UNTIL HE GOT *LAID OFF*. NOW HE LIVES BEHIND A GAS STATION.

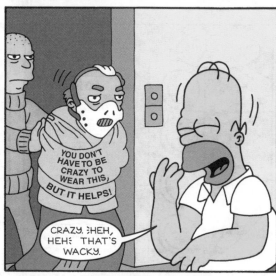

YOU DON'T HAVE TO BE CRAZY TO WEAR THIS, BUT IT HELPS!

CRAZY. HEH, HEH, THAT'S WACKY.

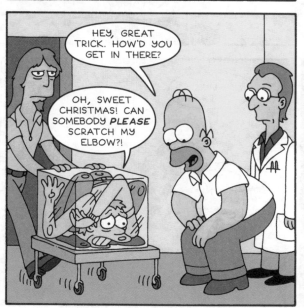

HEY, GREAT TRICK. HOW'D YOU GET IN THERE?

OH, SWEET CHRISTMAS! CAN SOMEBODY *PLEASE* SCRATCH MY ELBOW?!

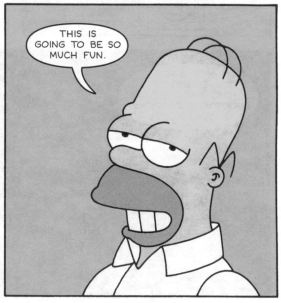

THIS IS GOING TO BE SO MUCH FUN.

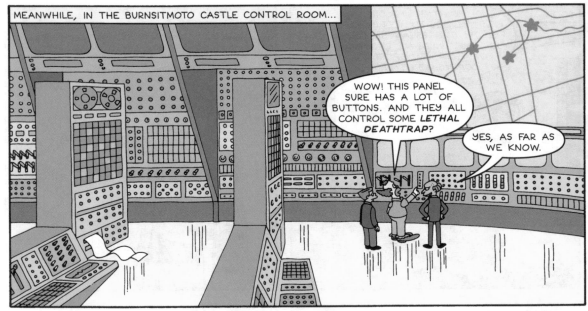

MEANWHILE, IN THE BURNSITMOTO CASTLE CONTROL ROOM...

WOW! THIS PANEL SURE HAS A LOT OF BUTTONS. AND THEY ALL CONTROL SOME *LETHAL DEATHTRAP*?

YES, AS FAR AS WE KNOW.

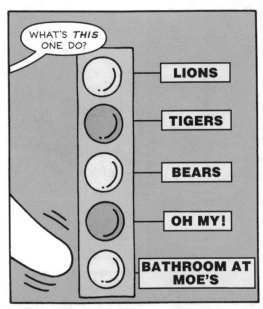

WHAT'S *THIS* ONE DO?

LIONS

TIGERS

BEARS

OH MY!

BATHROOM AT MOE'S

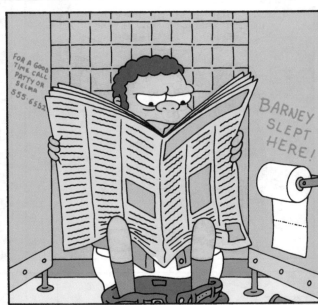

FOR A GOOD TIME CALL PATTY OR SELMA 555-6552

BARNEY SLEPT HERE!

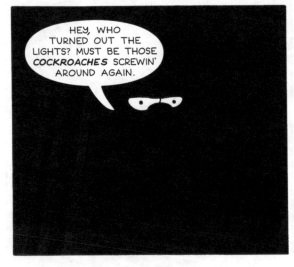

HEY, WHO TURNED OUT THE LIGHTS? MUST BE THOSE *COCKROACHES* SCREWIN' AROUND AGAIN.

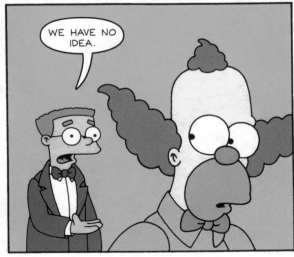

WE HAVE NO IDEA.

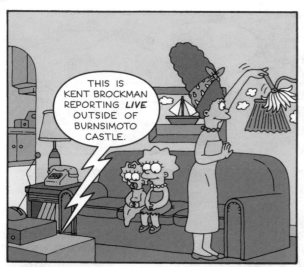

THIS IS KENT BROCKMAN REPORTING *LIVE* OUTSIDE OF BURNSIMOTO CASTLE.

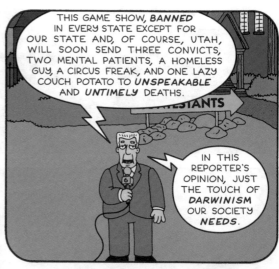

THIS GAME SHOW, *BANNED* IN EVERY STATE EXCEPT FOR OUR STATE AND, OF COURSE, UTAH, WILL SOON SEND THREE CONVICTS, TWO MENTAL PATIENTS, A HOMELESS GUY, A CIRCUS FREAK, AND ONE LAZY COUCH POTATO TO *UNSPEAKABLE* AND *UNTIMELY* DEATHS.

IN THIS REPORTER'S OPINION, JUST THE TOUCH OF *DARWINISM* OUR SOCIETY *NEEDS*.

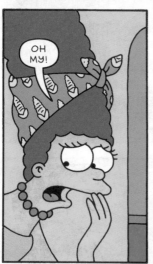

OH MY!

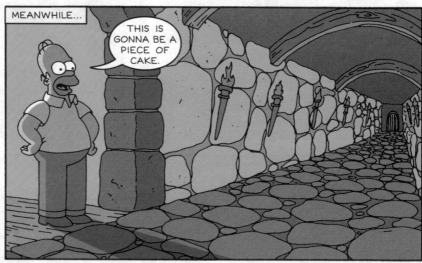

MEANWHILE...

THIS IS GONNA BE A PIECE OF CAKE.

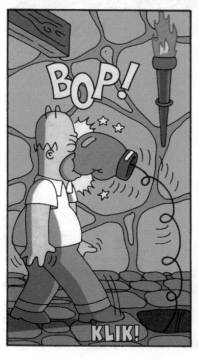

BOP!

KLIK!

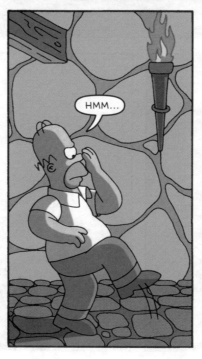

HMM...

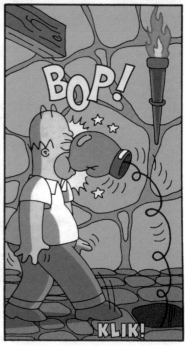

BOP!

KLIK!

MEANWHILE...
COME ON, KIDS. WE'VE GOT TO SAVE YOUR FATHER!
CAN WE PICK UP MILHOUSE ON THE WAY?
NO!
ROW, ROW, ROW YOUR BOAT...
LAKE OF ACID NO FISHING!
OWW! STUPID SULFURIC ACID!
WILD BOAR ROOM
SSSSSSSS
BARNEY? WHAT ARE YOU DOING HERE?
I'LL TELL YOU SOMETHING, HOMER. THESE WILD BOARS CAN REALLY DRINK.
IN THE CONTROL ROOM...
HOW DID HE GET IN THERE?
I MUST HAVE LEFT THE BACK DOOR OPEN AFTER MY SMOKE.
THIS ISN'T DANGER. I'VE SEEN SCARIER THINGS IN LINE AT THE TELEGRAPH OFFICE. I KNOW! TURN OFF THE LIGHTS.
SIR, THE AUDIENCE CAN'T SEE HIM IN THE DARK.
ISN'T THERE A TRAP DOOR UNDER HIM OR SOMETHING?
ACTUALLY, THERE IS.
THEN OPEN IT, YOU BLITHERING TOADY!

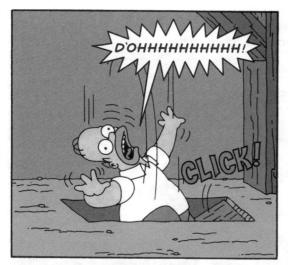

D'OHHHHHHHHHH!

CLICK!

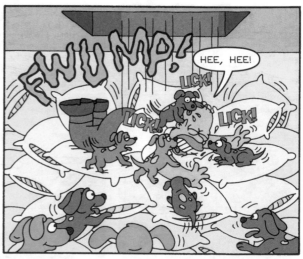

FWUMP!

HEE, HEE!

LICK! LICK! LICK!

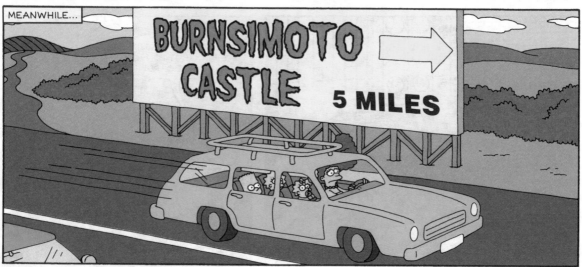

MEANWHILE...

BURNSIMOTO CASTLE 5 MILES

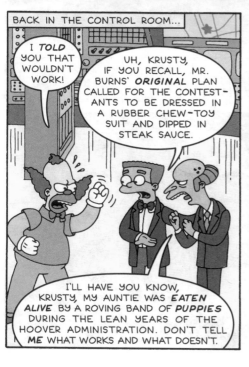

BACK IN THE CONTROL ROOM...

I TOLD YOU THAT WOULDN'T WORK!

UH, KRUSTY, IF YOU RECALL, MR. BURNS' ORIGINAL PLAN CALLED FOR THE CONTESTANTS TO BE DRESSED IN A RUBBER CHEW-TOY SUIT AND DIPPED IN STEAK SAUCE.

I'LL HAVE YOU KNOW, KRUSTY, MY AUNTIE WAS EATEN ALIVE BY A ROVING BAND OF PUPPIES DURING THE LEAN YEARS OF THE HOOVER ADMINISTRATION. DON'T TELL ME WHAT WORKS AND WHAT DOESN'T.

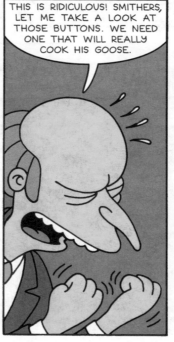

THIS IS RIDICULOUS! SMITHERS, LET ME TAKE A LOOK AT THOSE BUTTONS. WE NEED ONE THAT WILL REALLY COOK HIS GOOSE.

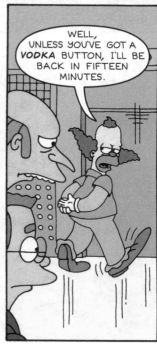

WELL, UNLESS YOU'VE GOT A VODKA BUTTON, I'LL BE BACK IN FIFTEEN MINUTES.

NO, NOT VIOLENT ENOUGH.
POISON DARTS
UMM...TOO NOISY. I WANT TO HEAR HIS SCREAMS OF TERROR.
POISON DARTS
POISON CHAINSAWS
OOH, HOW ABOUT THIS ONE, SMITHERS?
POISON CHAINSAWS
JAMES CAMERON ACADEMY AWARD ACCEPTANCE SPEECH ON A CONTINUOUS LOOP
SIR, PLEASE. HE'S A HUMAN BEING!
ALL RIGHT, JOHNNY COMPASSIONATE, YOU WIN!
UUH, I GIVE UP!
THUNK!
SIR, YOU PRESSED EVERY BUTTON ON THE BOARD!
EXCELLENT! LET THE MASSACRE BEGIN.
...I'M KING OF THE WORLD! I'M KING OF THE...
AWW, SEND BACK THE PUPPIES.
BZZZT
HISSSS
OOK OOK
GRRRR
RAAARRH

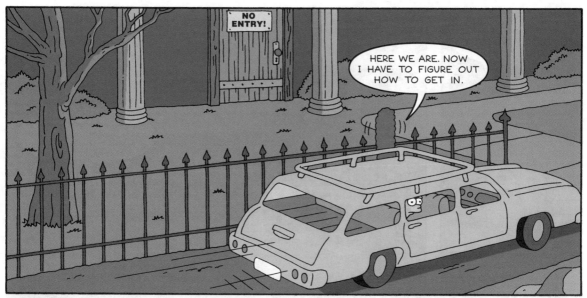

NO ENTRY!

HERE WE ARE. NOW I HAVE TO FIGURE OUT HOW TO GET IN.

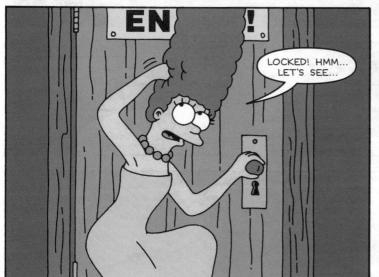

EN !

LOCKED! HMM... LET'S SEE...

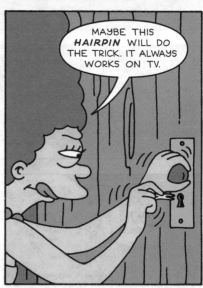

MAYBE THIS *HAIRPIN* WILL DO THE TRICK. IT ALWAYS WORKS ON TV.

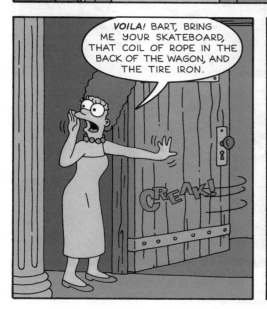

VOILA! BART, BRING ME YOUR SKATEBOARD, THAT COIL OF ROPE IN THE BACK OF THE WAGON, AND THE TIRE IRON.

CREAK!

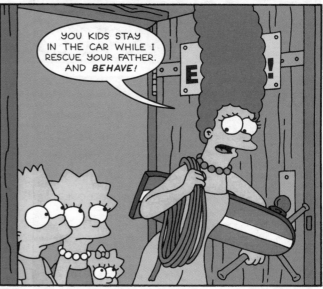

YOU KIDS STAY IN THE CAR WHILE I RESCUE YOUR FATHER. AND *BEHAVE!*

E !

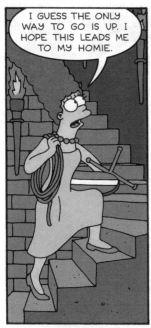

I GUESS THE ONLY WAY TO GO IS UP. I HOPE THIS LEADS ME TO MY HOMIE.

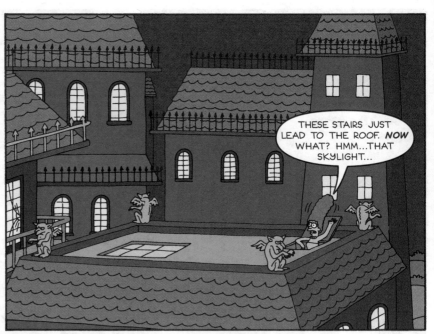

THESE STAIRS JUST LEAD TO THE ROOF. *NOW* WHAT? HMM...THAT SKYLIGHT...

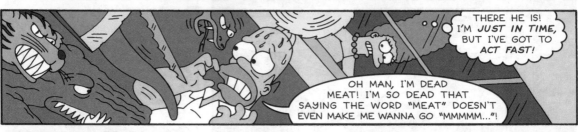

THERE HE IS! I'M *JUST IN TIME*, BUT I'VE GOT TO *ACT FAST!*

OH MAN, I'M DEAD MEAT! I'M SO DEAD THAT SAYING THE WORD "MEAT" DOESN'T EVEN MAKE ME WANNA GO "MMMMM..."!

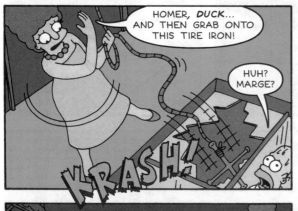

HOMER, *DUCK*... AND THEN GRAB ONTO THIS TIRE IRON!

HUH? MARGE?

KRASH!

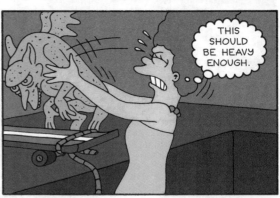

THIS SHOULD BE HEAVY ENOUGH.

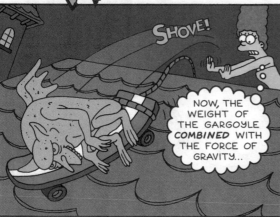

SHOVE!

NOW, THE WEIGHT OF THE GARGOYLE *COMBINED* WITH THE FORCE OF GRAVITY...

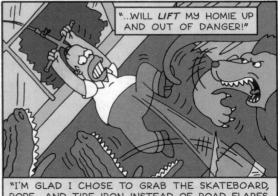

"...WILL *LIFT* MY HOMIE UP AND OUT OF DANGER!"

"I'M GLAD I CHOSE TO GRAB THE SKATEBOARD, ROPE, AND TIRE IRON INSTEAD OF ROAD FLARES, THE DOG'S BLANKET, AND MAGGIE'S TEDDY BEAR!"

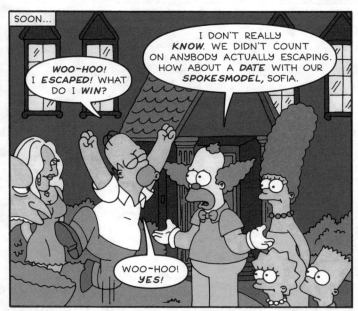

SOON...

WOO-HOO! I *ESCAPED*! WHAT DO I *WIN*?

I DON'T REALLY *KNOW*. WE DIDN'T COUNT ON ANYBODY ACTUALLY ESCAPING. HOW ABOUT A *DATE* WITH OUR *SPOKESMODEL*, SOFIA.

WOO-HOO! *YES*!

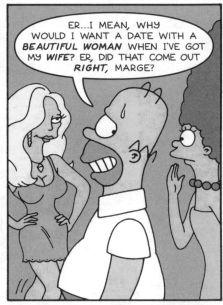

ER...I MEAN, WHY WOULD I WANT A DATE WITH A *BEAUTIFUL WOMAN* WHEN I'VE GOT MY *WIFE*? ER, DID THAT COME OUT *RIGHT*, MARGE?

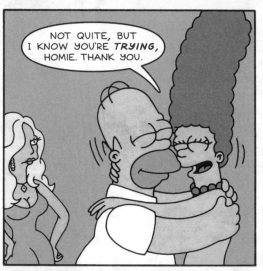

NOT QUITE, BUT I KNOW YOU'RE *TRYING*, HOMIE. THANK YOU.

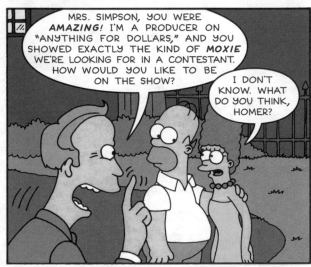

MRS. SIMPSON, YOU WERE *AMAZING*! I'M A PRODUCER ON "ANYTHING FOR DOLLARS," AND YOU SHOWED EXACTLY THE KIND OF *MOXIE* WE'RE LOOKING FOR IN A CONTESTANT. HOW WOULD YOU LIKE TO BE ON THE SHOW?

I DON'T KNOW. WHAT DO YOU THINK, HOMER?

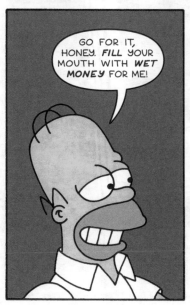

GO FOR IT, HONEY. *FILL* YOUR MOUTH WITH *WET MONEY* FOR ME!

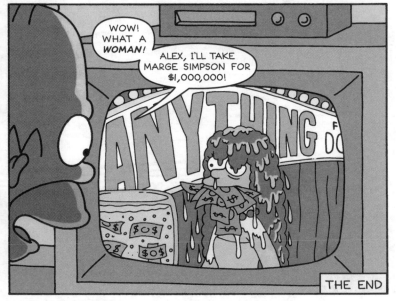

WOW! WHAT A *WOMAN*!

ALEX, I'LL TAKE MARGE SIMPSON FOR $1,000,000!

THE END

153

THE OFFICIAL COCKAMAMIE'S
MAIL-ORDER CULT-ALOG OF COOL POP-CULTURAL
CRAPOLA
COLLECTIBLES!
SPRING 2000
SPRINGFIELD'S MOST INTENTIONALLY IRONIC
NOSTALGIA-FEST!
BAD TASTE IS TIMELESS!!
FACE IT, WE'RE COMPLETELY OFF THE KITSCH-O-METER!!!
LAST BREATH OF "BLEEDING GUMS" MURPHY
SPRINGFIELD BABYLON by KENNETH ANGORA
TSK, TSK...THESE BURSTS OF LETTERING ARE SO TACKY!
ON THE OTHER HAND, I SUPPOSE THEY'RE PERFECTLY APPROPRIATE HERE...
MATT GROENING - SCOTT SHAW!
SPECIAL MILLENNIUM EDITION
(in other words, if an item was made back in the 20th century, it's gotta be worth BIG BUCKS to SOMEBODY!!!)

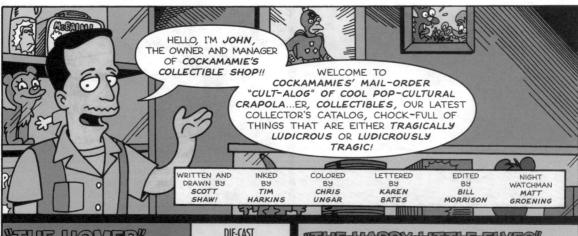

HELLO, I'M *JOHN*, THE OWNER AND MANAGER OF *COCKAMAMIE'S* COLLECTIBLE SHOP!!

WELCOME TO *COCKAMAMIES'* MAIL-ORDER "CULT-ALOG" OF COOL POP-CULTURAL CRAPOLA...ER, *COLLECTIBLES*, OUR LATEST COLLECTOR'S CATALOG, CHOCK-FULL OF THINGS THAT ARE EITHER *TRAGICALLY LUDICROUS* OR *LUDICROUSLY TRAGIC!*

WRITTEN AND DRAWN BY SCOTT SHAW!	INKED BY TIM HARKINS	COLORED BY CHRIS UNGAR	LETTERED BY KAREN BATES	EDITED BY BILL MORRISON	NIGHT WATCHMAN MATT GROENING

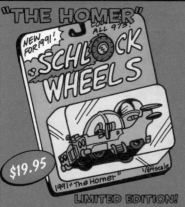

$19.95
LIMITED EDITION!

DIE-CAST "SCHLOCK WHEELS" CAR

Just as the short-lived "Homer" automobile was responsible for the corporate failure of its manufacturer, Powell Motors, this 1/64th scale auto was responsible for the sudden collapse of ITS parent factory!

Mint condition on card.

"THE HAPPY LITTLE ELVES" INSECT HABITARIUM

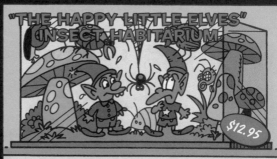

$12.95

What could possibly make the Happy Little Elves even HAPPIER? Their very own INSECT ZOO! (The unfortunate elf-to-bug SIZE RATIO make for a delightfully SICK tableau!) We'll even throw in the insects at no extra charge! Fine condition.

UNCIRCULATED "POOCHIE THE ROCKIN' DOG" ITEMS

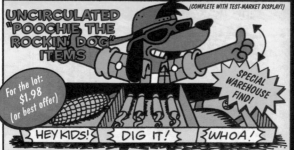

[COMPLETE WITH TEST-MARKET DISPLAY!]

For the lot: $1.98 (or best offer)

SPECIAL WAREHOUSE FIND!

HEY KIDS! DIG IT! WHOA!

As you may recall, Poochie died on the way back to his home planet, (so they say), but fortunately for us, he left these great prototype products in his wake (including OFFICIAL POOCHIE CORNCOB HOLDERS, OFFICIAL POOCHIE FLY-PAPER and THE OFFICIAL POOCHIE PROGRAMMABLE BOOMERANG-WITH-A-BRAIN), all of which went undistributed. Absolutely untouched. Mint condition in display.

DIRK "RADIOACTIVE MAN" RICHTER

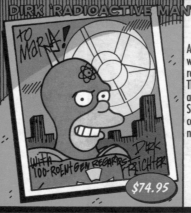

$74.95

Autographed "To MARK, with 1,000-roentgen regards, DIRK RICHTER." This rare item is an absolute MUST for any SERIOUS Radioactive Man collector especially if your name is "MARK"!)

Fine condition.

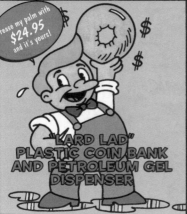

Grease my palm with $24.95 and it's yours!

"LARD LAD" PLASTIC COIN BANK AND PETROLEUM GEL DISPENSER

It's a plastic COIN BANK! (You can "feed" his doughnut!) It's a PETROLEUM GEL DISPENSER! (Just rub his hairdo for a blast of hygenic goo!) It's two totally dissimilar items in one! (Also available in GLAZED, RAINBOW-SPRINKLED and BEEF TALLOW models.)

Slick condition.

"MALIBU STACY'S" HAWAIIAN TIMESHARE CONDO

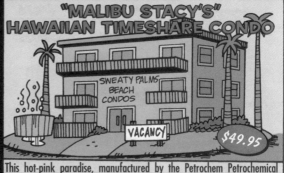

$49.95

This hot-pink paradise, manufactured by the Petrochem Petrochemical Corporation, features a lanai, a hot tub, beach access, a working miniature piña colada blender, and a never-ending sales pitch seminar. (Malibu Stacy NOT included.) Fine condition.

"KRUSTY THE CLOWN" KEYHOLE CAMERA

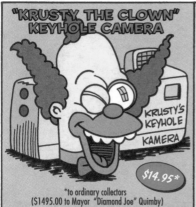

KRUSTY'S KEYHOLE KAMERA

$14.95*

*to ordinary collectors
($1495.00 to Mayor "Diamond Joe" Quimby)

Not many of these have survived over the years, since most of them were destroyed by irate parents and neighbors, especially whenever Mom and Dad were getting frisky! And it includes an undeveloped roll of film! Who knows WHOSE pictures are on that film, possibly even Mayor "Diamond Joe" Quimby, whose nephew Freddie is rumored to be it's original owner!

Very fine condition.

"MCBAIN" EXPLODING FOREIGN EMBASSY PLAYSET

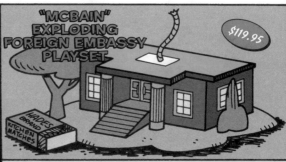

$119.95

Complete in the box, this was concurrently issued to tie in with the feature film, "McBAIN III: A Big Honkin' Line in the Sand," starring Rainier Wolfcastle. Magnesium fuse and box of official "McBain" kitchen matches included! Mint condition (for the time being...)

"ITCHY AND SCRATCHY" LAWN DARTS

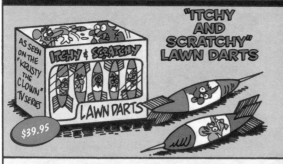

$39.95

These are EXTREMELY RARE items (inexplicably pulled from the toy shelves by some pesky parents' group). Aside from some minor red stains, these are in very fine condition.

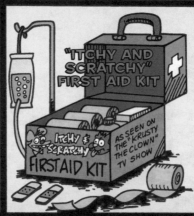

This medical kit comes with antiseptic, bandages, "pretend" painkillers and everything else needed to treat those pesky PUNCTURE WOUNDS!

Very good condition.

$69.95

"ITCHY AND SCRATCHY" HOME TAXIDERMY SET

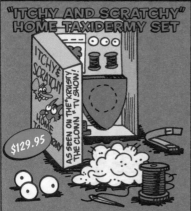

$129.95

This unusual item was marketed in the happenstance that the use of the Itchy and Scratchy First Aid Kit wasn't nearly as effective as originally expected. Complete with plenty of kapok stuffing, spools of high-test sewing thread, and an industrial-strength staple gun.

Mint condition.

"TRUCKASAURUS" MODEL

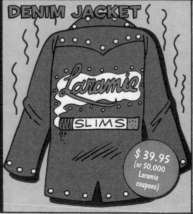

1/24 SCALE

TRUCKASAURUS! MODEL KIT

"RURAL AMERICA'S MOST BELOVED MECHANICAL ARENA MONSTER"

$89.95

(auto insurance not included)

This 1/24th scale model of rural America's favorite scrapheap behemoth is still mint in its box! (Which is probably where you'd be better off keeping it, unless you don't mind seeing Truckasaurus EAT the rest of the vintage model cars in your collection!)

LURLEEN LUMPKIN COUNTRY-WESTERN DEMO RECORDINGS

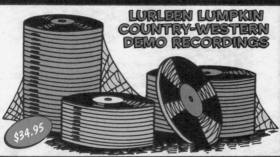

$34.95

Now you can own these one-of-a-kind earliest recordings of Country-Western superstar (once she had those breast implants done) Lurleen Lumpkin! Originally from the collection of Lurleen's first manager, Homer Simpson, these were brought in to Cockamamie's by his jealous wife. Very good condition.

DENIM JACKET

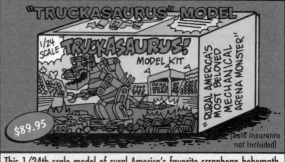

Laramie SLIMS

$ 39.95 (or 50,000 Laramie coupons)

We picked up this item at an estate sale. It was worn only once by its original owner (before she checked into the hospital), a heavy smoker of Laramie Slims cigarettes! The jacket still stinks of cigarettes, otherwise it's in mint condition.

LANCE MURDOCK PLAYSET

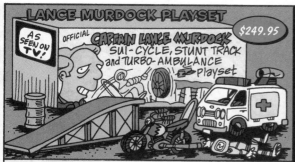

AS SEEN ON TV!

OFFICIAL CAPTAIN LANCE MURDOCK SUI-CYCLE, STUNT TRACK and TURBO-AMBULANCE Playset

$249.95

Who doesn't remember motorcycle daredevil Captain Lance Murdock? (Except, of course, Murdock himself, who's suffered amnesia ever since his last cycle-stunt went so horribly wrong...). This exciting set is in mint condition, except for the Lance Murdock action figure (which is in somewhat poor condition).

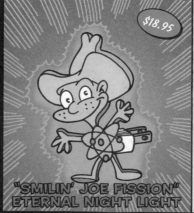

$18.95

"SMILIN' JOE FISSION" ETERNAL NIGHT LIGHT

Molded in the distinctive shape of everyone's favorite nuclear spokes-character, this little beauty will brighten up your collectibles cabinet — no electricity required! (Cockamamie's denies any responsibility for radiation burns or genetic mutations.)

Glowingly bright mint condition.

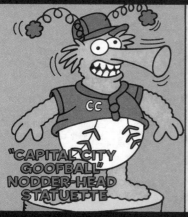

"CAPITAL CITY GOOFBALL" NODDER-HEAD STATUETTE

Personally, the appeal of organized sports completely eludes me but this mint condition mascot's constantly wobbling cranium will provide hours of fun for any and all, baseball fans or not! Why, it's almost HYPNOTIC! You are getting sleepy...sleepy ...you will send me--

$29.95

"FUNZO" ELECTRONIC DOLL

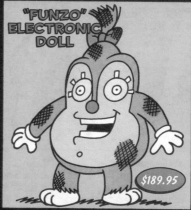

"ALL-RIGHTY!" This is believed to be the last semi-intact interactive "FUNZO" doll to survive its frenzied, but mercifully short craze! Get him before he gets YOU! Slightly fire-damaged, so I can't grade it higher than "good" condition.

$189.95

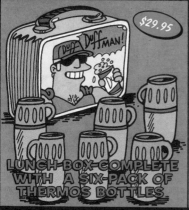

$29.95

LUNCH-BOX-COMPLETE WITH A SIX-PACK OF THERMOS BOTTLES

This brightly lithographed metal lunch box features Duff Man, the overly-familiar beer-swilling superhero used to publicize Duff Beer back in the '70's. (Attention, Barney Gumble — we know you're out there; this box fairly cries out for YOU!)

Very fine condition (at least, to bloodshot, bleary eyes.)

GABBO T-SHIRT

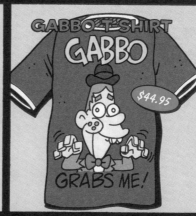

GABBO GRABS ME!

$44.95

"Wooden" it be nice to own this colorful item? Here's a nostalgic reminder of Springfield's brief affair with has-been ventriloquist Arthur Crandall's lovable dummy, "GABBO."

Good condition, with slight splintering.

IMPORTED "MR. SPARKLE" GARDEN HOSE TOY

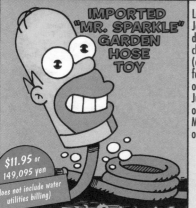

$11.95 or 149,095 yen (does not include water utilities billing)

Look out, straight from Japan, here comes that disrespecter of uncleanliness, Mr. Sparkle (or at least a fairly faithful approximation of the honorable one!) Just hook him up, turn on the faucet and watch Mr. Sparkle "take a bite out of grime!"

Very, very, very, VERY clean condition, mint-plus, even! (Sheesh!)

"KRUSTY THE CLOWN'S SIDESHOW MEL" PLANTER-PAL KIT

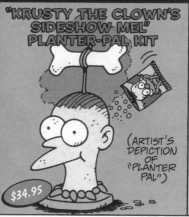

(ARTIST'S DEPICTION OF "PLANTER PAL")

$34.95

Remember that familiar slogan, "Hey, kids, create lots of far-out hairstyles for Sideshow Mel!"? These hydroponic planters haven't been seen since the mid-1980's, when it was discovered that the seeds included in the kits were of the Cannabis sativa variety. Mint condition, in box.

157

"BUZZ COLA" NEON WALL CLOCK

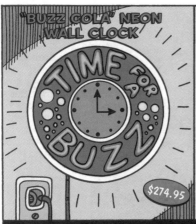

$274.95

Straight out of a 1950's malt shop, this nifty wall clock is trés cool, daddy-O! It DOES run a little fast…like 10 times the normal rate! (And why not? It WAS created to advertise the soda with "all the caffeine and twice the sugar!") Hand movement is a bit shaky (no surprise there), but the clock's overall condition is very fine.

INFLATABLE "CHIPPOS" HIPPOPOTAMUS POOL TOY PREMIUM

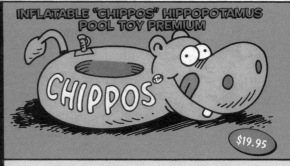

$19.95

Any serious snacker probably remembers these colorful mail-in giveaways, mainly because they tended to leave an orange ring around the pool. Available only in sizes XL through 6XL. Fine condition.

BLEEDING GUMS MURPHY LP BLUES RECORD ALBUMS

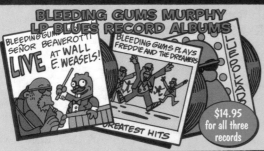

$14.95 for all three records

"Bleeding Gums Murphy And Señor Beaverotti LIVE At Wall E. Weasel's", "Bleeding Gums Plays Freddie And The Dreamers' Greatest Hits" and "Blue Polka-Dots With Bleeding Gums Murphy", are not exactly Bleeding Gums' finest hours, to say the least. However they ARE in excellent near-mint condition. Too bad we can't say the same for Bleeding Gums himself.

VINTAGE HAWAIIAN SHIRTS

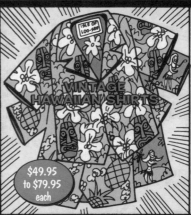

$49.95 to $79.95 each

Aloha oy vey! As a certain someone (Homer Simpson, if you MUST know) once uttered, "There's only two kinds of guys who wear these shirts -- gay guys and big fat party animals!" Well, I don't know anything about big, fat, party animals, but I DO know that these vintage beauties will be the crown jewels of any SENSIBLE man's wardrobe.
Excellent condition.

"CHRISTMAS APE GOES HAWAIIAN" LOBBY CARD SET

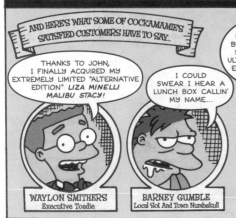

$69.95 for the set of 8 lobby cards.

The "CHRISTMAS APE" films are beloved by Saturday-afternoon matinee-goers of all ages. This 1972 installment featured the hunky heartthrob TROY McCLURE in one of his finest roles as Camp Counselor Leakey.

Fine condition.

"KRUSTY THE CLOWN'S SIDESHOW BOB" CRIME SPREE SCRAPBOOK

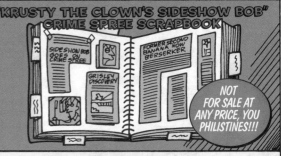

NOT FOR SALE AT ANY PRICE, YOU PHILISTINES!!!

This collection of newspaper and magazine clippings document the multiple rampages of Springfield's favorite attempted SERIAL KILLER and slapstick sidekick, SIDESHOW BOB! Hundreds of hours have gone into the careful cutting, pasting, and annotations that have been--oh, this thing is just SO great, I can't make myself PART with it!

AND HERE'S WHAT SOME OF COCKAMAMIE'S SATISFIED CUSTOMERS HAVE TO SAY...

THANKS TO JOHN, I FINALLY ACQUIRED MY EXTREMELY LIMITED "ALTERNATIVE EDITION" LIZA MINELLI MALIBU STACY!

I COULD SWEAR I HEAR A LUNCH BOX CALLIN' MY NAME...

ALTHOUGH I NORMALLY REJECT THE NOTION OF PATRONIZING A RIVAL'S BUSINESS, THANKS TO COCKAMAMIE'S SERVICES, I FINALLY OBTAINED THE ULTRA-SCARCE FALLOUT BOY LIMITED-EDITION MINI-SERIES WITH MULTIPLE-VARIANT LENTICULAR HOLO-FOIL POP-UP COVERS!

SO THAT'S IT FOR THIS CATALOG! I'M SURE YOU'RE ALREADY REACHING FOR YOUR WALLET! WE'LL ALSO CONSIDER TRADES (AT 100TH OF THE RETAIL VALUE OF YOUR OFFERED-UP COLLECTIBLE.)

AND DON'T FORGET TO VISIT US ON-LINE AT WWW.COCKAMAMIES.COM FOR EXCLUSIVE OFFERS SUCH AS OUR ITCHY AND SCRATCHY CARPAL TUNNEL WRIST BRACES!! SO WHO EVER HEARD OF EBUY?!?

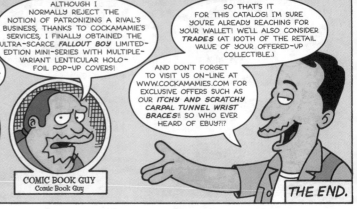

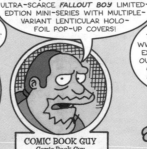

WAYLON SMITHERS
Executive Toadie

BARNEY GUMBLE
Local Sot And Town Numbskull

COMIC BOOK GUY
Comic Book Guy

THE END.